Dreamwork for Dramatic Writing

Consciousness, Literature and the Arts

General Editor

Daniel Meyer-Dinkgräfe

Editorial board

Anna Bonshek
John Danvers
Amy Ione
Michael Mangan
Jade Rosina McCutcheon
Gregory Tague
Arthur Versluis
Christopher Webster
Ralph Yarrow

VOLUME 60

The titles published in this series are listed at *brlll.com/cla*

Dreamwork for Dramatic Writing

Dreamwrighting for Stage and Screen

By

David A. Crespy

BRILL

LEIDEN | BOSTON

Cover illustration by Meg Phillips Crespy.

The Library of Congress Cataloging-in-Publication Data is available online at https://catalog.loc.gov
LC record available at https://lccn.loc.gov/2023026755

Typeface for the Latin, Greek, and Cyrillic scripts: "Brill". See and download: brill.com/brill-typeface.

ISSN 1573-2193
ISBN 978-90-04-53595-4 (hardback)
ISBN 978-90-04-53596-1 (e-book)

Copyright 2024 by Koninklijke Brill NV, Leiden, The Netherlands.
Koninklijke Brill NV incorporates the imprints Brill, Brill Nijhoff, Brill Hotei, Brill Schöningh, Brill Fink, Brill mentis, Vandenhoeck & Ruprecht, Böhlau, V&R unipress and Wageningen Academic.
All rights reserved. No part of this publication may be reproduced, translated, stored in a retrieval system, or transmitted in any form or by any means, electronic, mechanical, photocopying, recording or otherwise, without prior written permission from the publisher. Requests for re-use and/or translations must be addressed to Koninklijke Brill NV via brill.com or copyright.com.

This book is printed on acid-free paper and produced in a sustainable manner.

Contents

Acknowledgements IX

Introduction
Dreamwork for Dramatic Writing 1
1   An Organic Approach to Magic and Theatricality   1
2   How to Use This Book   8

1   **The Dreamwright Workshop**
    Relaxation, The Trance State, and Daydreaming   12
    1   Step 1 – The Warm-Up – Getting into the Flow   17
    2   Step 2 – Devising your Dream Cache – Gathering the Stuff of Your Imagination   22
    3   Step 3 – Writing a Dream – Freeing Your Natural Creativity   29
    4   Step 4 – Dream Dramatic Concept Outline – Germinating the Dramatic Seed   31
    5   Step 5 – Character Dreams – Exploring the World within Your Character   35
    6   Step 6 – Dream Adjacent Writing Exercises – Giving over to the Magic of Dreaming   36

2   **Structure of the Dreamwork, Myth, Ceremony, and Ritual**
    August Strindberg's Dream Play *and Orson Welles* Citizen Kane   53
    1   *A Dream Play*: August Strindberg's Growing Castle of Suffering   53
    2   Orson Welles and the Flashback Dream Structure   63

3   **Ancient Dream Structures: Myths and the Greek Chorus**
    Sophocles' Oedipus the King, *Paula Vogel's* How I Learned to Drive, *Lanford Wilson's* Book of Days, *and Marcel Camus'* Black Orpheus   69
    1   The Ur-Detective Story: Sophocles *Oedipus Rex* and the Importance of Working Backwards   69
    2   *How I Learned to Drive* – Paul Vogel's Contemporizing the Chorus   74
    3   Lanford Wilson's *Book of Days* – The Lyric Chorus   79
    4   Marcel Camus' *Black Orpheus* – The Liminality of Carnival   81

4   **African-American Dream Funhouse – Creating Ritual Liminality**
    Adrienne Kennedy's Funny House of a Negro *and Julie's Dash's*
    Daughters of the Dust   87
    1   Adrienne Kennedy: Syncopated Mimesis of a Many-Faced
        Storyteller   87
    2   Julie Dash and the Structure of the Griot's Song   93

5   **Transfiguration of Gender and Identity – Transformations, Mutability, and Androgyny**
    Jean Genet's The Balcony *and Sally Potter's* Orlando   99
    1   Jean Genet: Criminal Gender Illusionist   99
    2   *Orlando* – Sally Potter – a History of Gender Fluidity   102

6   **The Dreamer's Heart – Thinking Backwards First**
    Character Dreams and Storytelling – McDonagh's The Pillowman
    and Christopher Nolan's: Memento   107
    1   Story Structure in McDonagh's *The Pillowman*   109
    2   Hairpin: The Structure of Christopher Nolan's *Memento*   113

7   **Magic Plot Cards – The Dreamwright as Storyteller**
    Tony Kushner's Angels in America, *Charlie Kaufman's* Eternal Sunshine
    of the Spotless Mind, *Guillermo Arriaga's* 21 Grams   119
    1   Tony Kushner's *Angels in America* – A Reluctant Prophet and a
        Reformed Sinner   126
    2   The Persistence (and Absence) of Memory: Lucid Dreaming in
        Charlie Kaufman's *Eternal Sunshine of the Spotless Mind*   136
    3   Guillermo Arriaga's *21 Grams* – Daily Dreams and Time Jumps   138

8   **The Snap of the Heartstring – Symbolism and Romanticism**
    Chekhov's The Cherry Orchard, *José Rivera's* Cloud Tectonics,
    Marguerite Duras' Hiroshima Mon Amour   143
    1   Snapping of a String – The Essence of Chekhov's Symbolism   145
    2   Exercises in Chekhov's Symbolist Technique   149
    3   José Rivera – *Cloud Tectonics* – Latinx Realism Time Shift   151
    4   Unending Conversations: The Voice-Over Romance of Marguerite
        Duras's *Hiroshima, Mon Amour*   156

CONTENTS

9 Realms of Theatricality – Surrealism and Waking Dreams
   Thornton Wilder's Pullman Car Hiawatha *and David Lynch's*
   Mulholland Drive   160
   1 *Pullman Car Hiawatha*: The Debut of Thornton Wilder's Shaman
      Stage Manager   161
   2 Twisted Noir: The Mobius Detective in David Lynch's *Mulholland
      Drive*   166

10 Inside out – a Feminist Expressionism of Dreaming
   Sarah Ruhl's Eurydice *and Karen Moncrieff's* The Dead Girl   170
   1 Sarah Ruhl's *Eurydice*: Genteel Subversion through Cosmic
      Feminism   170
   2 Karen Moncrieff – *The Dead Girl* – Unpeeling the Onion of
      Grief   177

11 Epic Theatre and The Lucid Dream
   Bertolt Brecht's The Threepenny Opera *and Lucy Alibar's* Beasts
   of the Southern Wild   181
   1 Bertolt Brecht's *The Threepenny Opera* – Verfremdungseffekt and the
      Lucid Dreamer   181
   2 Lucy Alibar – *Beasts of the Southern Wild* – The Lucidity of a
      Child   187

12 Postmodernist Worlds of Slippage
   Pirandello's It Is So! (If You Think So) *and Eleanor Perry's*
   The Swimmer   193
   1 Luigi Pirandello's *It is so! (If You Think So)*: The Conundrum of
      Conflicting Realities   195
   2 Eleanor Perry – *The Swimmer* – Multiverse Pools of Desire   197
   3 Entering the Absurd – Final Clarity of the Insane Vision – Collapse of
      Drama into Performance   202

13 The Absurdist Nightmare and the Dramatic Wet Dream
   Ionesco's The Bald Soprano, *Samuel Beckett's* Play, *and Quentin
   Tarantino's* Pulp Fiction   204
   1 Eugene Ionesco: The Devolving Dramatic Dream of *The Bald
      Soprano*   205
   2 Samuel Beckett's *Play* – Pushing On/Pushing Through – I Can't Go
      on, I'll Go On   211

    3   The Maw of Pop Culture: *Pulp Fiction* and the Structure of Story Threads 213
    4   Pulp Fiction (Scenes in Chronological Order) 214

14 The Breathing of a Play: Music and Ritualized Sacrifice
Edward Albee's Tiny Alice *and Agnès Varda's* Vagabond 220
    1   Edward Albee's *Tiny Alice* – An Uncanny Gothic Chamber Opera 221
    2   Agnes Varda – Oneiric Cinécriture – Writing Your Dreams in Film 225

15 Comedy Shock: Rhythms of Menace and Joy
Harold Pinter's The Birthday Party, *Irene Fornes'* Conduct of Life, *and* Jean-Luc Godard's Weekend 228
    1   Harold Pinter – Playwright of Tension and Release – the Comedy of Unease 228
    2   María Irene Fornés: The Torturer and the Tortured – Conducting Cruel Comedy 232
    3   Jean-Luc Godard's Weekend: The Horrible, Wonderful, Murderous Success of Corinne and Roland 235

Conclusion
The Work of a Dreamwright – Transcending the Possible 240
    1   The Dream Cache 241

Bibliography 243
Index 249

Acknowledgements

I am deeply grateful to the many individuals and organizations that provided me with support, assistance, and inspiration to write *Dreamwork for Dramatic Writing*. Without their guidance and encouragement, it would never have come to pass. To start, I'd like to acknowledge Professor Marvin Carlson, who was my department chair at the City University of New York Graduate Center and served on my dissertation committee. It was at his suggestion that I read the late works of Bert O. States, knowing that I had a profound connection with dreaming and my own dramatic writing. I'm also grateful for my conversations with Bert States, who provided me with great insights into his own research in the phenomenology of dreaming, which were central to my creation of this technique. I'd also like to thank my emeritus colleague at the University of Missouri, Dr. Suzanne Burgoyne, for her ongoing encouragement in my teaching of dreamwork workshops, and her publication of a chapter on this work in her own *Creativity in Theatre Theory and Action in Theatre/Drama Education*. I'm also deeply grateful to my colleagues at Aristotle University, Professors Tatiani Rapatzikou, Zoe Detsi, Tatiana Liani, and my Fulbright host, Giorgos Antoniou, along with the Fulbright Greece organization, and in particular, Nicholas Tourides and Artemis Zenetrou, for their willingness to allow me to teach dreamwork for dramatic writing to their students on both of my Fulbright Scholar residencies there in 2018 and 2023. I was very grateful to my colleagues at the University of Seville, including my Fulbright host Ramón Espejo Romero, Josefa Fernández Martín, and Vicente Chacón Carmona for allowing me to teach this work there as well. I'm very grateful to the staff of Fulbright Spain, including Executive Director, Alberto López San Miguel, Clara Badimón, and Sara Abad for their support of my playwriting efforts throughout my Fulbright residency.

I am deeply grateful to my theatre department chairs Dr. M. Heather Carver and Dr. Miriam Hedges for providing me the Fulbright sabbaticals I needed to complete this work, and to the University of Missouri Research Council, which provided the funding I needed to do my research and teaching in Europe exploring the techniques of dreamwork for dramatic writing with the students there. I would also like to thank the many, many students who studied this technique with me at the MU Department of Theatre and were willing to put up with my somewhat "New Age" approach to teaching playwriting. It was their success that encouraged me to continue this work, and I have been especially impressed by many awards they won through the Kennedy Center American College Theatre Festival, to which I also owe a debt of gratitude, as

KCACTF leaders like Gary Garrison and Gregg Henry gave me the opportunity to teach many workshops under their aegis. I would also like to thank my agent of many years, Mitchell Waters, at Brandt & Hochman Literary Agents, Inc., for his support.

Finally, I am deeply grateful to my wife, Meg Phillips Crespy, who not only designed the beautiful cover for this book, but also has experimented with this technique on her own screenplays, and has become nearly as expert in how it works as I am. She provided me with constant love and encouragement to teach, research, and publish this somewhat unusual work and the courage to bring it to my student and colleagues.

Introduction

Dreamwork for Dramatic Writing

1   An Organic Approach to Magic and Theatricality

This is a book about how to employ a waking dream technique, including dream content, form, and logic, to experiment with non-traditional, non-linear dramatic work for stage and film. In other words, this is a book for dramatists who are looking to experiment with their work; perhaps to take their writing to a very new place. There are many good books on traditional playwriting for beginners, and this book takes a different twist for the more adventurous dramatist. While this may not be the best book for a total novice in the realm of dramatic writing, if you are a different kind of writer to begin with, say, a non-traditionalist poet or fiction writer– this might still be the text for you. It is for both playwrights and screenwriters, and it is specifically geared for writers who work in both fields, with a bit of a lean toward playwrights, as I feel dramatic writing begins with the stage. Fiction writers and poets will also certainly benefit from the exploration of dream content and structure.

But what is the dreamwork anyway? The modern notion of dreamwork is different than the more common idea of dream interpretation or analysis, where a single possible interpretation of a dream, based on the concept of a dream as a vehicle of repressed meaning, is provided to you by an authority who claims to know the meanings of your dreams. Instead, a more flexible of notion of dreamwork suggests that dreams are living creations of a human being in constant flux reacting to the physiology of sleep or trance. Any book by American psychiatrist and dream researcher Allan Hobson will fill you in on the physical nature of dreaming (consider his *Dreaming: A Very Short Introduction*). So, setting aside Freud and Jung (we'll get back to them in a moment) one finds an illimitable creative content to dreams. A dream can mean many things to different people, and more importantly it may mean different things to *you* at different times. I ask that you take a *phenomenological attitude* about dreams – that is, experience the nature of dreaming for the first time, every time. Bracket out all received notions of dreams or dreaming – and *even the notion that dreaming only happens when you sleep* – because of course, everyone daydreams. If you do that, the dreamer within you will take creative control of your experience in the present moment, and your dream will be open to multiple meanings.

As an artist, it is less important to worry about what a dream means, than *how* a dream means, and putting those techniques to work for *you*. Dreamwork for dramatic writing is simply connecting with your creativity through dream awareness and response, and most importantly, experimenting with how dreams work in your *waking* writing technique by using a *dream cache*– a repository of both sleeping and waking dream elements that you will create as part of this process. The bottom-line is: accept that your dreams are an important resource to you, and then use them creatively, rather than worry about *what* they mean.

Most people know of neurologist Sigmund Freud's work with dreams, and that of his student Carl Jung. Both were brilliant thinkers and dream philosophers, and there is much there that speaks to those who are interested in dreams. And most importantly, these two thinkers believed that dreams are *important* – many scientists today do not. If their contribution to dream theory is significant, the most meaningful aspect of their work is that both believed that understanding and connecting with your dreams could provide insight into your life. Freud's notion of the associative process of understanding dreams and what their various elements mean to you through free association is a very useful process – but only if it's *you* who is doing the associating. Again, trust no one else when it comes to the meaning and use of your dreams. Even Freud and Jung – fascinating though they might be as philosophers, thinkers, and explorers in the world of dreams – are not the primary source for the meaning of your dreams – you are.

This volume is a practical handbook for working dramatic "wrighters." And I am using the old definition of wrighting – shaping, bending, crafting human action. Those of us who work in dramatic "wrighting" are creatively sculpting human want, desire, need, to create what playwrights, actors, and directors call *behavior* that become stories for the stage and screen. We don't *write* plays, we *wright* behavior. This book provides a commonsense approach to using the dream trance for playwrights, screenwriters, and teachers of dramatic wrighting/writing, and you don't necessarily have to be able to remember your dreams. There will be nothing mystical or spiritual here – at least not in the doing of the exercises. They do require concentration and focus – not unlike meditation. I've written this book to help you use dreaming as a creative tool to expand your art beyond where it is right now. I'll be using techniques that will seem simple at first (again, like meditation), but you'll discover them to be challenging as you move deeper into your own knowledge of your waking and night dreams, and as you apply them to create plays, screenplays, and television scripts.

INTRODUCTION 3

Why dreams or daydreaming? Because that is where we surprise ourselves. That's where magic and theatricality explode – in the non-reality of dream structure and logic. The goal of this technique is to move your plays from the tedium of reality and cliché into the enchantment of theatre and film magic. That's why we write in this medium, isn't it – to enchant, delight, and captivate? To move our audiences to tears, gasps, or laughter in surprising ways. And ultimately, dreams are fresh inventive stories we tell ourselves (effortlessly, I might add) every night and in our wildest daydreams. In the end, as dramatic writers, we are storytellers who want to tell *new* stories, *fresh* stories, *surprising* stories – and the master storyteller within us is our inner dreamer. Our goal is to move beyond cliché and the tired formulas of stage and film and astonish ourselves and our audiences with new work that they can't get ahead of, second guess, or become bored by because they have seen it all before. And any technique that does that for writers is worth your time and money – because in this age of Peak TV, the new Golden Age of Television, when Netflix, Hulu, and Amazon Prime are consuming massive amounts of content, you need an amazing source of new material – and your dreams and daydreams can provide that source – if you develop the techniques and habits that I will discuss in this book.

There were three sources that originally drew me to use dreams as part of my dramatic writing, two of which are organic to who I am as a writer and an actor. One is the simple organic fact is that I have always remembered my dreams, vividly, and I have often used them in my writing. However, again bear in mind that *you don't need to remember or record your dreams to do this work* – you will be learning to use *daydream technique*, writing within a trance state or within the zone of creativity, using a *dream cache* to get to a place of *flow*. The other source for this work comes from my training as an actor at Rutgers University's Mason Gross School of the Arts, where I studied with William Esper, Kathryn Gately, and Loyd Williamson in the Sanford Meisner technique. I connected deeply with an important part of Meisner's approach to *emotional preparation* – the notion of *the controlled daydream*. It was a revelation to me at the time that a daydream can be crafted to be a creative tool as powerful as real life to create emotional truth. And that as such, it can be used to provide the emotional river of imagination on which the canoe of an actor's sense of truthful doing can soar. It wasn't a huge leap to expand that notion to dramatic writing – and with a careful, nuanced approach to exploring dreamwork, I think it can be helpful to writers who want to organically deepen and enhance the magic and theatricality of their theatrical and film scriptwriting. So, the dreaming we'll mostly do in this book is *daydreaming*, and occasionally using fragments of your night dreams, as well as other material from your waking life. Dreamwork is about reaching an emotional truth that will intensify the meaning, complexity, and nuance of your dramatic writing – and do that in an honest, organic, and surprising way.

There is third reason for my wanting to incorporate dreamwork into playwriting, and that has grown out of my experience with my playwriting students who work from a very limited sense of what is "real" versus what can be "true" in their creative work in drama. One is tied to what is believable, and the other is tied to what is possible. And what is possible is a place I find that is much more likely to produce original, adventurous art, than the realm of the real (which is, incidentally, wholly subjective, and different for everyone). I also find that when reality comes knocking on the door of art, a kind of self-censoring police action occurs – and suddenly playwriting becomes about what you can and cannot do, rather than about what's insanely possible.

And for my students, who live on a steady diet of banal, pedestrian realism fed to them through movies, television, and video games, realism becomes a crutch that limits possibilities – and why would any dramatist want to limit the possibilities of one's art! But exploring non-realistic styles is also something that my students resist, resent, and struggle with – because they're afraid of being weird or phony or not writing something that will have *commercial* value. And this is ironic, because theatre, film, and television are always desperate for new ideas – ideas that are fresh, emotionally powerful, and gripping. So dreamwork provides a portal into that world of imagination – and once that portal is open, the writer will find that it cannot be shut. There is so much material available waiting to be tapped – and it's all organic to that writer. This is not an external technique that is built on gimmicks. It is one that is built on discipline, openness, and concentration – and the change will be discernible almost immediately in your writing. Though the kind of trance-state, controlled daydreaming that we'll do is, at least initially, really hard work –once it links you to your creative zone, your flow– it becomes effortless and provides a new vocabulary for your dramatic writing.

But again, much of my wanting to write about dreamwork for dramatic writing is tied to my personal experience. I have instinctively used the specific, vivid details of my dreams, coupled with profound emotional insights into my own life and creative projects, to "wright" my plays. I find there an intimacy with thought processes, obsessions, fears, phobias, fantasies, and personal mysteries that are powerful, if at times inscrutable. Why do I dream of a yellow taxi falling from the sky outside of the garage of my parents' Philadelphia row house? Why do I awaken, often in tears, after long discussions with my parents in my dreams, knowing, as I do, that they died many years ago? Why do I find myself flying away from a tsunami at the edge of some terrible storming

INTRODUCTION 5

ocean? At some point, however, I stopped asking why, and started just using these strange scenarios to fuel my plays. It was at that moment when I stopped trying to interpret my dreams, and just let them wash over my wrighting, that my own playwriting grew.

As I have noted, I am deeply resistant to the idea that some guru can tell me what my dreams mean – or how to work with them – so my approach is a phenomenological one – meaning that you should always approach your own dreams from your subjective immediate perception of them, as if experiencing them for the first time. That said, if a theorist has influenced my thinking on dreams, it is theatre and performance phenomenologist, Bert O. States, who shared my doubts that anyone, but the dreamer, can interpret that dreamer's experience. States' ideas provided the third major source for the techniques I will discuss in these further chapters.

In three books, *The Rhetoric of Dreams, Dreaming and Storytelling,* and *Seeing In The Dark,* States uses phenomenology, psychological analysis, and neurological case studies to build a detailed model of how dreaming and fiction share certain similar qualities and how writers bring these aspects of dreaming to their writing.[1] States challenges the traditional Freudian interpretation of dreams (as symbolic of various repressions or the manifestation of wish fulfillment) and examines in detail the phenomenon of dreaming itself and *how* dreams work rather than *what* they mean. His research offers a new way to look at drama, particularly non-realistic drama, which he believes, like other forms of fiction, has its roots in the ur-fiction of dreams. Specifically, States suggests that dreams offer a special means for the writer to explore nuances of reality:

> Dreams ... offer something like a complementing definition of the world, one (among other things) that rescues the "real" world from certain limitations of linear and spatial probability.[2]

Taking a phenomenological approach to the dream-like images, action, and characterization means we simply subjectively respond to these phenomena allowing ourselves any interpretation that feels correct – rather than relying upon a preordained system of symbols or archetypes. A phenomenological response to a work of art is, in essence, creating our own work of art. More

---

1   For a thorough exploration of State's work in dreaming and fiction see Bert O. States, *Dreaming and Storytelling* (Ithaca, NY: Cornell University Press), 1993; Bert O. States, *The Rhetoric of Dreams* (Ithaca, NY: Cornell University Press), 1988; Bert O. States, *Seeing In the Dark* (New Haven, CT: Yale University Press), 1997.
2   States, *Dreaming and Storytelling,* 46.

importantly, responding to the experienced reality of the dream, and even moving into the associative trance state of a dream triggers a creative response, moving us closer to the "zone" where we can enter a realm of flow.

What dream plays (and dreams) do is "make strange" or "rescue meaning from" the day-to-day reality of the reader/audience and tease out a new understanding of that reality. This formalist technique is not unlike the nature of art itself, as described by Victor Shklovsky in his famous essay, "Art as Technique," and further elucidated by Brecht; it is a kind of revisioning of reality.[3] States himself considers art, "a species of phenomenology" in a "loose sense.",[4,5] The phenomenon of dreaming in drama has a metadramatic effect, commenting on traditional dramatic structure by subverting it, providing an alternative method of organizing dramatic action versus the Aristotelian crisis/conflict model of playwriting amplified by Archer, Brunetiere, Freytag and others.[6] It relies on the strong emotional shorthand of dreaming itself. What seems bizarre to us in nonrealistic plays still makes a kind of sense despite its strangeness because we are "taught" how to understand non-linear leaps of logic through similar means of understanding in our own dreams.

Dramatists like Eugène Ionesco and Adrienne Kennedy use dream structure the way that Scottish Travelers tell dream stories – as a kind of focusing strategy. Donald Braid, a folklorist and documentarian of Traveler culture describes how the bizarre or uncanny works in the Traveler's dream stories:

> [T]he confusion engendered in dream story performance motivates an ongoing interpretive struggle to make sense out of what happened in the narrated event. As listeners struggle to disentangle the incoherent dimension of the story, their attention will engage other, more coherent messages encoded in the performance ... This engagement increases entertainment potential by drawing individuals into the narrative ... [and] ensures that listeners will explore the narrative sufficiently to understand and remember the key meanings suggested by the narrator through the formal features of his or her performance.[7]

---

3   Bertolt Brecht, *Brecht On Theatre; The Development Of An Aesthetic*, John Willett ed. and trans. (New York, Hill and Wang, 1964).
4   Victor Shklovsky, "Art as Technique," in *Russian Formalist Criticism; Four Essays*, trans. Lee T. Lemon and Marion J. Reis (Lincoln, University of Nebraska Press, 1965).
5   Bert States, *Seeing In the Dark* (New Haven, CT: Yale University Press, 1997), xi.
6   Richard Hornby, *Drama, Metadrama, And Perception* (London: Associated University Presses, 1986), 103.
7   Donald Braid, "'Did It Happen or did it not?': Dream Stories, Worldview, and Narrative Knowing," *Text and Performance Quarterly* (October 1998): 329.

INTRODUCTION 7

In these dream stories there is a "narrative knot" where the stories don't seem to make sense; the listener wonders, "did it happen or did it not?" Is the story nothing but a dream? This slippage of meaning in world of the dream play makes the narrative a bit challenging to understand, thereby requiring more of the listener's attention. We work harder to make sense of nonrealistic drama and its nonlinear technique because our dreams have taught us that important meanings may slip through bizarre knots of narrative. So as viewers, we tend to look closer at these moments, are surprised by them, since they undermine and subvert reality in rather fascinating, unpredictable ways. Since as writers, we're always looking, and often desperate for exactly these kind of elements in our next great dramatic work, fundamentally we have a very practical reason to use dreams to develop our dramatic writing.

And for the screenwriter who is coming to this book, it's important to note the very close link between dreaming and films – if anything, filmmaking is an even better way to get at dreams. Writer/directors like Ingmar Bergman, Stanley Kubrick, David Cronenberg are among many in the film industry who directly create from their dreams. Cronenberg was quoted in an article about his film, *The Method*, touching on Freud, noting that:

> I've always thought movies functioned on the level of dream logic. Even a movie that purports to be a documentary or a very factual account – about, say, the gritty streets of Boston – it's still a dream. You're not in Boston, and even if you are, you're not on the streets, you're in a theater.[8]

Ingmar Bergman drew extensively from his dreams to create his films and noted that "dreams are a sort of creative process," that come from the same "factory" as his films. He notes that he uses reality the "same way dreams do," in that while some dreams may seem very realistic, there is something there that disturbs you. His creative process was ignited by his dreams as a child, so much so that he would mix up "what was reality and what was in my dreams."[9] It is fascinating to note, incidentally, how many extraordinary, cutting-edge dramatists and screenwriters have used their dreams. In fact, our greatest writers have all confessed the importance of dreaming in their lives.

---

8 Rossiter Drake, "David Cronenberg takes on dreams, Freud in compelling 'Method'," December 12, 2011, *San Francisco Examiner* Online Edition. http://www.sfexaminer.com/entertainment/movies/2011/12/david-cronenberg-takes-dreams-freud-compelling-method#ixzz22nPq2Yh1.

9 Raphael Shargel, Ingmar Bergman: Interviews, Univ. Press of Mississippi, Jul 1, 2007, 106–7.

The next step, then, is to start to understand how to systematically connect with the substance of your dreams. This is not an easy task, not only because our bodies and minds are designed by evolution to forget our dreams, but our understanding of our dreams is always already tainted by what we have been told about them. And the physical and mental barriers to getting at your dreams are just as powerful. *It is normal not to be able to remember your dreams.* Powerful chemicals within us separate our waking from our dreaming selves – and those same systems paralyze us while we're dreaming at night so that we do no harm while we're in that vulnerable state – otherwise we would rise and enact the goings-on of our dreams, which would be perilous to ourselves, our roommates, and spouses, not to mention our family pets! However, *you don't need to remember your dreams to do this technique,* instead you'll be training yourself to use your natural organic dream narrative engine to open the faucet to surprising new plots, characters, and dramatic ideas.

What follows then is a series of exercises and ideas to help you begin to throw off the concerns and cares of this world and enter the world of your dreams *in your waking dramatic writing technique*. Remember, that even if you cannot remember your dreams, you can do this work. To do so, however, you will have to let go of some preconceived notions about playwriting and fitting your play within the cookie-cutter crafting that so many playwriting texts seem to parrot. Instead allow yourself to be open to the fluid, transformational, and natural metaverse of your dreamworld. Much of this book is about setting up structures, games, and exercises to free yourself to explore new realms of dramatic expression to surprise yourself. Allow the power of suggestion, daydreaming, and a free-flowing stream of consciousness to guide a kind of surrealist automatic writing that will effortlessly move your mind to your pen or keyboard. Don't question the strangeness of the image, sound, smell, taste, or touch of what comes – and whatever fragments you can find, consider them gifts from your subconscious. The world of your dreams waits before, verdant, fertile, and full of surprises. Let's take the first step – which is to relax!

2 How to Use This Book

This book is designed to work for both a traditional college-level course in dramatic writing developing over a course of about 15 weeks and for the professional writer dipping into this text for techniques and ideas. The goal can be to finish an evening-length script or screenplay, along with several shorter scripts, or to add non-linear aspects to an already existing script. The reader can move chapter to chapter following the logical progression of the book or can jump to chapters that might serve a specific writing task, focusing on character for example, or structure, or specific techniques in expressionism or absurdism. The first chapter is my dreamwork for dramatic writing workshop which I have taught around the US and internationally, and it is designed to take about 2–3 hours per day over the course of about two to three days. The workshop takes you through a set of writing prompts built on dreamwork and moves from gathering the elements of your dreams and daydreams, into constructing a dream, and then onto creating an idea for play or screenplay. The first chapter continues with some further exercises in using dreams to explore your characters, and other dream-exercises to stimulate your writing.

In the following chapters, we'll be looking at many different styles that grow out of dreamwork – all of which suggest many different non-traditional approaches that are all linked to dream logic and structure. Once you let go of traditional approaches to dramatic writing, you are open to a gazillion other ways to structure a play – however, that in itself can be overwhelming, so I've tried to offer you an organized approach to many different examples of non-linear plays and screenplays. Some of these realms are suggested by the -isms; symbolism, magical realism, lyric naturalism, expressionism, Dadaism, epic theatre and metadrama, absurdism, and post-modernism, etc., but it should be noted all these scripts built on structures of non-realistic, non-linear technique follow associative logic, because that is how dreams are formed. Since I am an academic and a scholar, I like to draw upon some of the knowledge in the field of non-linear playwriting, dramatic literature, theatre and film history, and the work of specific non-traditional playwrights and screenwriters. Therefore, each chapter after the initial dreamwork workshop will focus on at least one playwright and one screenwriter, and often more. I will touch upon the *essence* of their non-realistic, non-linear technique as revealed in specific plays and screenplays – most of which are classics in the field, and highly recommended for your professional reading list. The goal isn't for you to simply imitate their work – it is to distill each style into specific dramatic writing technique *essences* suggested by these rather brilliant plays and screenplays. Each essence suggests an exercise that will take your writing to a new place – and while I think these exercises certainly touch upon the traditional Aristotelian dramatic elements of plot, character, thought, language, spectacle, and music, they also suggest a whole new palette of techniques that will allow you to constantly surprise yourself. Feel free to jump in and experiment with the exercises in the various chapters following your writerly bliss – but I would encourage that you explore Chapter one, the initial dreamwork workshop, first.

Bear in mind that you are certainly not expected to read every single play or screenplay I describe in this book – these are only suggestions. Feel free to read the plays as you see fit, and take, as Edward Albee was wont to say about his own self-education (since he failed out of every college he attended), a Gandhian approach to your learning process. The same thing is true of the various exercises that are included in each chapter. You can follow through on each step of the exercise, or you can simply use those aspects of the exercises you find useful. *I don't believe in police work when it comes to making art.* Feel free to stitch together techniques or aspects of the exercises as you find useful – my students certain have. The structure of exercises, which have the feel of games, have led to my students writing wonderful dramatic work simply using it as a kind of skeleton with which to build their dramatic works.

Bear in mind that if you are an instructor of a course in dramatic writing you should feel comfortable doing the same. You don't have to assign every play or screenplay in this book and/or assign every exercise. Some will be more useful to your own work as an instructor of dramatic writing, and others will be less helpful. And bear in mind that these exercises can also work well within the context of traditional drama, providing gateways to theatricality and magic even in otherwise very conventional dramatic writing. Sometimes a little bit of weirdness in a script can go a long way! Use this text, the plays I have suggested, and the exercises I have created in whatever manner best suits your needs – and again, don't feel compelled to follow these techniques slavishly. Consider using them as a bit of a "spice" to season and perk-up otherwise conventional dramatic work for the stage or screen.

However, if you are using this book to complete a new dramatic work, in every other chapter there will be specific projects to complete as you move toward your stage or screenplay. Overall, I will include the following steps in this book: a *basic dramatic concept outline* to work out the initial idea for your dramatic work – whether it is a play, a teleplay, or screenplay. Then you should move into *character study* as your first step into the writing of the script to understand the characters well enough to pull together material into a basic story. After you have explored your characters thoroughly, you are ready to work with *plot cards* – index cards – to stay flexible as you are writing to develop a basic *plot outline*. The *plot outline* is the bare bones of the story which you will flesh out into your *plot/film treatment* – this is a lively prose description of the best production of the script – whether on a Broadway stage or the back lot of a film studio. And then you can get to the work of the *first draft* of the dramatic work, which is a draft you feel is strong enough to be read out loud in a workshop setting. So here are those basic steps in a list:

Dramatic Project Checklist
– *Basic Dramatic Concept Outline* – to work out the initial idea for your dramatic work.

- *Character Study* – to understand the characters well enough to pull together material into a basic story.
- *Plot Cards* – index cards – to develop a basic *plot outline,* even as you stay flexible with it as it develops.
- *Plot Outline* – is the bare bones of the story which you will flesh out into your *plot/film treatment.*
- *Plot/Film Treatment* – the lively prose description of the best production of the script for stage or screen.
- *First Draft* – *the initial draft of the script written well enough to be read out loud in workshop setting.*

This book on dramatic writing is unique in that I will explore the stage and film interchangeably – because I feel that dramatic writing is dramatic writing. Some say that you go to *see* a film, and you *hear* a play – film being driven by stunning visual imagery, and the theatre being a place of gorgeous language. But these days all dramatic writers need a bit of both in their thinking and training, and in this new millennium writers are working in both fields, sometimes simultaneously, along with a small mountain of television writing. I feel that stage writers could easily get by with less dialogue and more visuals, and film-writers could use much deeper characterization, theatricality, and story, so the two fields feed into each other, and audiences are accepting much more adventurous work in both fields, driven by their hunger for dramatic work that keeps them guessing and thinking on their feet. Remember that if your audience can guess what happens next, if they get ahead of your story, they will flip that channel on the remote, and you are dead in the water as a dramatist. Dreamwork can stop that problem.

So now we'll move onto the first workshop, the dreamwork workshop which is key to this entire experience – and you'll be adding to your dream cache or dream journal throughout this course. Since this is not a book about how to collect your dreams or dream reportage, but, in fact, a book on dreamwrighting, using the form, structure, and technique of dreams to get to a creative state of flow, I will be brief about how to gather dream material. There are entire books on the subject, and one I highly recommend Patricia Garfield's *Creative Dreaming* (Atria, 1995), as Garfield was a pioneer in this field. However, I will offer some practical simple suggestions in this book on dream collection based upon my own experience, along with a sample of my dreams. Developing the ability to remember your dreams and record fragments of those dreams is a kind of conditioning. Bear in mind that it is normal to *not* remember your dreams. But you can train yourself to do so – and it is a muscle you need to exercise in order to use it effectively. The goal is to never let go of your dreams, because in reality, your dreams never let go of you!

CHAPTER 1

The Dreamwright Workshop

Relaxation, The Trance State, and Daydreaming

Dreams are the residue of our daily lives. As Ira Progroff writes in his book *At A Journal Workshop*, "dreams reflect the tensions and anxieties that are bound to arise in a person's life out of the conflict between immediate desires and requirements of the long-range goals of his life." Bert States explains dreams as involuntary fiction and fiction as voluntary dreaming. It is important that you learn to record your dreams on a regular basis in a dream journal. At first, don't worry about making this a daily journal – try it first as a spontaneous journal. And here's a somewhat weird suggestion: *Ask* your dreams to help you write! Asking your subconscious self for dream assistance seems odd, but if you can do that, just before you climb into bed, in a peaceful moment of meditation and prayer, you will open something inside of yourself. I call this *The Ask*. Say it out loud or in your mind, "Please, dreams, can you help me write my play?" And be patient, remember that you can do all the work in this book *without* remembering actual dreams.

Practice *The Ask* before you go to bed, and in the morning, without an alarm, as you wake up, try remembering your dream. It will take practice. Ask for help the night before, and in the morning – be receptive. In the morning, try to remember your dream, or even in the middle of night, if your dream wakes you, keeping your eyes closed and shifting body position as you move back mentally in the dream, try to find bits and pieces of the dream – go back as far as you can go into the dream. Trust what comes. Write whatever you can remember from your dreams down on your bedside notepad or vocally record them on your cellphone immediately. Get this material down any way you can – I sometimes take down my dreams on my note app on my iPhone. Allow yourself to slowly develop this habit: Ask your dreams for help the night before and as you wake up from a dream in the morning or night, try to remember the dream and record it.

As part of your journal-keeping regimen, it's useful to keep a daily or near daily dream cache (we'll start one in this chapter), and to come back to it when you are writing and in a creative state. It is important to keep your dream cache close at hand, using a notepad or your cellphone to record the dream *as soon as you've have had it*. Record the dreams without interpretation, merely observing the details and trying to maintain as neutral and objective as possible. In the workshop below, I will remind you of this basic process on recording your dreams which should work, even for people who have difficulty remembering their dreams.

In addition to your daily dreams, record your recurring dreams or recurring dream elements. Which elements seem to occur again and again over the years? Do you have special abilities in your dreams? Do you see the same people? The same places? Do you have "typical" scenarios? To this oneiric mix add the dreams you remember from your childhood or during special events in your life. Note bizarre moments of strange image juxtapositions, impossible actions or activities, unusual emotional connections, and oddly familiar characters. The bizarre in our dreams becomes a clue for what is unsettling us, what is making us think. The strangest aspects are often keys to our creative zone. Remember that dreams are an evolutionary means to our survival as mammals – there is no such thing as an unimportant dream or daydream – so write them all down. The uncanny, the mysterious, the disturbing, or profoundly pleasurable aspects of our dreams provide an emotional landscape we can draw upon as artist. If we stay away from trying to interpret our dreams, and simply respond to them honestly, subjectively, and with thick description, you will find your dreams becoming useful to you.

As you gather your daily dreams, try inventing a "classic" or "waking" dream for yourself: allow the recurring images and emotions to pass through you, focusing on your five senses. *As you create the dream, remember that you have no other reality than the reality of the dream.* Don't judge this dream scenario, just let it occur and write it down without censoring it. This will be new aspect of exploring dreams for you, daydreaming to create an imagined dream is another way to hone your dreamwork skills. It will help you stretch new muscles in your creative technique. Allow the bizarre, uncanny, and illogical elements to predominate – don't worry about making logical sense, allow the associative logic of dreams to make the sense for you. Forget about the notion that "this causes this, which causes this, which causes this, etc." – that is linear thinking. Instead think: "this makes me think of this, then that makes me think of this, etc." Don't worry about making sense, worry about working from your honest emotional response from one unanticipated moment to the next unanticipated moment.

Once you've gotten skilled at creating "classic" or "waking" dreams, start focusing on developing the dreams of your characters. Contemplate the precipitating events of your characters' lives, the conflict that they must now confront, and mingle these play elements with their more general aspirations and life goals. What are their most important concerns? What are their obsessions? How do these goals, concerns, obsessions affect their dream scenarios? I'll help you detail and organize this process below.

Building your Dream Cache: Keeping a Dream Journal

Again, it is *totally normal* to forget your dreams, your body is designed to do just that. It takes time patience, and practice to learn how to record your dreams, and to succeed using this book, *you do not have to actually remember* your dreams – you just need to allow yourself to create a *dream cache*, a repository of dream-like elements to allow you to get into state of daydreaming, trance or better yet, a state of *flow* – this is a term invented by Mihály Csíkszentmihályi, a Hungarian-American psychologist, to describe a state highly conducive to productivity – which we examine in detail later in this chapter. However, here are some very practical ideas about how practice recording your dreams:

1. Decide, first of all, that your dreams are *important* to you, and remind yourself of this daily, and especially before you go to bed at night. Say it to yourself: *my dreams are important to me.*
2. *Ask* your dreams to help you write your play before you go to bed. Allow this *Ask* to be a peaceful ritual, a meditation or prayer before you sleep. This *Ask* should never require a yes or no answer, so keep the question open and broad, so your dream has space to answer. Try the *Ask* several times during your day – so that it remains with you as you move through your daily tasks.
3. Be open to whatever your dream offers, even if it is silly, short, or simple strange. Sometimes you can only remember a few words. But the next day, when you look at those few words, you may be able to recall the entire dream. Dream words are often a talisman into an entire realm.
4. If you can, allow yourself to wake without an alarm clock; you need to feel peaceful and open. Ponder upon the dream you just had. To do so, right after you sense you are awake, keep your eyes closed. Beginning with the last part of the dream you can remember, just before you woke up, work your way back to the beginning or as far as you can. Just stay still, eyes closed, relax into the sensual memories of the dream. With your eyes still closed, shift your position, and try to go back further in the dream. Keep doing this until you've gone as far back into the dream as you can.
5. Before you go to sleep, plan to record your dreams. Keep a pad and pen convenient to your bedside, or make sure your cellphone voice recorder is ready to record.
6. If you decide that you will seek guidance from your dreams for a specific dramatic writing project; consider choosing a moment when you are *buried* in that writing and have hit a specific snag or blockage. Concentrate on that blockage in your *Ask*.

7. Dream recall is best right after a vivid dream. If you can, train yourself to wake up after each vivid episode and write it down, or record it with a voice recorder *with your eyes closed.*
8. As you become accustomed to feeling your dreams are important enough to remember, your ability to remember them will improve. Trust this – most people can't remember their dreams. It takes practice.
9. Of course, share your dreams with a friend, but also write them down or record them on your phone vocally. *Avoid asking other people what they think your dreams mean* – keep the focus on what *you* think they mean.
10. Organize your dream recordings in some manner – by the date you received them, by the subject matter, emotional landscape, and even better, give each dream a unique title.
11. Consider using a personal language of your own to describe your dream to yourself, but don't interpret your dream, instead describe how it makes you feel, what emotions you associate with the images in the dream, the connections you have with each sensory aspect of the dream.
12. Write down *anything* you can remember from your dream. Don't worry if it's fragmentary, or if it is totally strange, ridiculous, or mysterious. It can be a smell, a sound, a texture, a feeling, a taste left in your mouth, or an image that has been seared into your mind. What is key is to your emotional response to it – how did it make you feel?
13. Allow yourself to freely associate with this dream material, even as you record it – anything that pops up might be useful – are there other dreams that you have had recently that are similar. Allow yourself to go back to your dream log to compare.
14. Do you want to draw something or sing? Is there another artistic response you have to your dream? Do you find yourself wanting to make something physical that is somehow tied to the dream – do it right away, in the moment.
15. Pay attention to your feelings and emotional experience of the dream, and to the emotions that grow out of the remembering of the dream. Did it stimulate laughter, tears, sexual tension, fear, joy, anger, or did it cause you to have a physical sensation – something warm and pleasurable or a chill, or a sense of claustrophobia? Did these feelings suddenly shift upon awakening or recall of the dream? Write all that down as part of the dream.
16. Consider now what is happening in your daily life – could you remember any of that from your dream? Were there similar emotional experiences to your waking life?

17. Did you sense you had a "dream lesson"? Or was something shared with you as a kind of wisdom gift? Write that down as well – what you have learned in a dream is often precious, especially to the projects at hand.

A Dream Example

Here is a sample of a dream I had while developing this book on my Fulbright to Spain and Greece in 2022–2023 – I had the dream while I was in Madrid. It was filled with motion – moving from scene to scene in a way that was exciting, but also a bit frightening. I gave it a date, a title, and described it simply but actively, allowing room for my emotional response.

A Dream, 8/27/22, Madrid, Spain, Titled: *The Bearded Man*

In this dream a bearded man took me on a mind-bending meditation which culminated in a strange incoherent news session with alternative journalists documenting the guru's words. I felt happy, enjoying myself.

I was reminded of the hallucinogenic properties of a packet of brown water in a shrink-wrapped package that when heated and ingested became a tool for alien visions. This made me a bit nervous.

I was documenting the 1960s and many playwrights were there. I saw the bearded man again, who invited me to participate. We joined into an ensemble body performance improvisation where I moved in slow motion and could bend and float and levitate with other bodies in space in a very pleasant relaxing creative way.

After this we were a crowd, oddly in my car, with all these foods I had made including pickled items and complex pate sandwiches which everyone had to try. I felt a bit anxious initially about eating the food but then I now *was* the bearded man.

I invited people to experience the food and invited them to swim with me at the Jersey shore in Asbury Park which was a kind of hipster magical place which is where the dream ended. Very cool, a kind of tribal experience.

What did I do with the dream? I allowed it to affect me, and used the motion of the dream, its uncanny and sometimes unsettling flow from scene to scene, to influence my play *Las Semillias de la Expulsión* which is the first play of cycle of six plays *Mi Corazón Español Vive Ahora En Grecia*, about Spanish roots of the Sephardic Jew Community of Thessaloniki, of which I am a descendent. In my play, the character of Bolisa had this same uncanny and even dangerous feeling as she follows her Nona into the court of Ferdinand and Isabella in 15th Century Spain, and then finds herself transformed into Queen Isabella herself.

From this simple example above, I suggest the following as you respond to your dreams: Accept all this strangeness with mindfulness, allow yourself to listen to what is there in the moment, without judgement or the need to interpret. Notice that I only used sensations from the dream, not necessarily the whole dream, to affect my writing. Use what works – what feels most immediately stimulating. Allow yourself compassion, every time you write a character, you walk in someone else's shoes and your dream will always allow you to do that, effortlessly, with the emotional and sensual simplicity and candor that will sometimes surprise you. The next step in this book is to move into the dreamwrighting workshop – and it is here that you must let go of the steering wheel and trust the narrative engine of your dreams to take you on a voyage to unknown places.

1   Step 1 – The Warm-Up – Getting into the Flow

The first step to dreamwork is to learn how to relax – and to use relaxation to build what I like to call the active trance state of daydreaming. Now you might get a bit nervous about the idea of putting yourself into a trance, but the reality is that you do this all the time when you daydream. When you daydream, you allow your imagination to engage with your emotions and flow with it, effortlessly, until you are there, in your daydream, reacting emotionally as if it were real. This is very similar to the daydreaming work actors do using the Sanford Meisner technique of emotional preparation. The active trance state of daydreaming is also another way of thinking about Mihály Csíkszentmihályi's notion of *Flow* or being in the Zone. In the various books written by Csíkszentmihályi (most famously his book, *Flow: The Psychology of Optimal Experience*), the famous Hungarian psychologist looks at how to get at a highly focused mental state to boost creativity and happiness.

According to Csíkszentmihályi, there are specifically nine components to achieving flow, which include: "challenge-skill balance, merging of action and awareness, clarity of goals, immediate and unambiguous feedback, concentration on the task at hand, paradox of control, transformation of time, loss of self-consciousness, and autotelic experience."[1] These elements have always seemed a bit intellectual to me, as a former actor, and so when I approach the notion of flow, I have preferred to focus on major elements – the loss of self-consciousness and the "autotelic experience" (autotelic means to do something for the pure joy of doing it, not for the possibility of external reward). So, if we work toward the active trance state of daydreaming and allow ourselves to indulge in the sheer pleasure of that, the dreamwork – and the writing will come. To get to this state we will work both physically and mentally to relax and become receptive to our own dream material. Because of the psychophysical nature of writing, we'll start with a basic writer's physical warm-up.

Basic Writer's Physical Warm-Up

To arrive to a state of flow, we will work both physically and mentally to relax and become receptive to our own dream material. I suggest that like actors who before they perform, awaken, and engage their muscles and voice, writers should do the same. A warm-up is just that – no more than 20 minutes, and don't push too hard. Wear loose clothing and give yourself space to stretch out. Be gentle with your body and your voice. Check your alignment – work toward "easing up" as if being lifted by the hairs at the base of your skull. This is at the heart of Alexander Technique, which is a way of learning how you can get rid of harmful tension in your body and learning to move mindfully through life.

My suggestion is, if you are at home, start with a basic yoga stretch, such as the Sun Salutation, which provides a full body stretch, accompanied by breathing technique that will help calm your mind. Next focus on loosening your shoulders. Writers hold so much tension in their shoulders, especially after long periods of writing. The following warm-up will help you release that tension so that you'll be open to creative flow, but feel free to use whatever works for you. I have taught this warm-up for many years, and it seems to be very effective – not just at the beginning of the process, but all along the way of the workshop. Taking breaks from this work is important – and the physical warm-up and the breathing work will help refresh you as you dreamwright.

---

1 Fullagar, Clive J.; Kelloway, E. Kevin (2009). "Flow at work: an experience sampling approach." *Journal of* Occupational *and Organizational Psychology* 82 (3): 595–615.

Shoulder Warm-Up

a. Reach your arms up, gently stretch your arms toward the sky; reach with the right arm and then with the left, stretching your fingers, and involve your shoulders in these stretches, but be gentle, like a cat stretching after a nice nap.
b. Circle your arms down reaching out as you go, until your arms are at your sides, drawing a semi-circle with your fingers.
c. Reach your arms down, feeling your fingers becoming rooted into the floor. Keep reaching down, and let your shoulders sink with them, feeling a bit of tension and then ... release.
d. Feel your shoulders floating up to your ears, "Frankenstein" shoulders, tensing them, then ... release and allow them to drop.
e. Roll your shoulders back, back, back ...
f. Roll your shoulders forward, forward, forward, and then ... release.

Continuing with the warm-up, another problem area for writers and anyone who sits at a keyboard for long periods of time is tension in the neck. Try this series of exercises, right after you roll your shoulders, to help get some of the knots out of your neck muscles.

Neck Warm-Up

a. Release your head forward gently, roll it to the right side, nod yes, yes, yes, and allow the weight of your head to give the left side of your neck a nice stretch. You can also place your right hand on your opposite, left shoulder to get an additional stretch.
g. Let your head roll back, open your mouth, allow a nice roll of your neck, and now roll your head to the left side.
h. Allow the weight of your head to give the right side of your neck a nice stretch, and nod yes, yes, yes, while putting your left hand on your opposite, right shoulder to get an additional gentle stretch. Then let your head roll forward and feel like you have a heavy head.
i. Now you will move into your back warm-up, allowing your head to remain dropped forward, feeling released, but heavy.

Back Warm-Up

j. Standing with your feet parallel, shoulder's width apart, let your head drop forward, and allow the weight of your head to roll you down – vertebra by vertebra and breathe out as you do so. Keep your knees slightly bent as you do so.
k. At the bottom, clasp your hands behind your head and let the weight of your hands give you a nice extra stretch in the back of your spine.
l. Drop your hands, shake out your shoulders, your arms, your fingers, your head and neck; gently sway and shake it all out.
m. Roll back up, from your lowest vertebra, building yourself back up, vertebra by vertebra.
n. At the top, reach up as if you are reaching for a beach ball, stretch, let your chest arc up a bit.
o. Now drop your hands behind the nape of your neck, cupping the back of your head and gently lift. You should gently feel your skull lifting out of your spine.
p. Drop your hands down by your sides and bring your arms and chest down – with a sigh out, "Ahhhhhhhhhh." Come to what would be called "the mountain pose" in yoga; arms relaxed and opened out at your sides. Feel your spine lengthened, chest relaxed, head floating, neck released.

Breath Work

After you've completed your physical stretching, I suggest you consider this breathwork – again, first find yourself "easing up" (this is a term tied to Alexander Technique) through the top of your head, even assisting the lift with both hands at the nape of your neck. Your goal here is to find and deepen your breathing – like meditating, with the focus on continuing to relax and open your mind.

a. Three Deep Breaths – Breath in through your nostrils, feel your belly expand, hold it a moment and sigh out completely, on a count of four. Sense release as you do so. Do this at least three times, until you feel that release kick in.
b. Begin with Yawn Sigh – "Ahhhhhhh" – Relax your shoulders and chest. Reach up, yawn and allow your voice to reach the highest note of your vocal range, and slide down to your lowest range. Drop from your waist as you do so. Do this three times at least, until you're aware of full range of sound.

c. Focused Breath: Breathe out with a glottal squeeze – like how one creates a "crowd" sound at a sporting event – "The crowd goes wild! Hahhhhhhhhhhh" – work at exploring how long you can create this sound before you need another breath. Keep your neck and throat relaxed as you do so. Do this at least three times. This is a focused breath, and you should feel as if you are slowly breathing life into one of the characters of your play.

Relaxation Exercise

This relaxation exercise is about learning to use your own imagination to explore the nuances of daydreaming – and to learn how to relax yourself and find a way into your mind's eye that is freeing, gentle, and evocative.

a. Lay flat on a yoga mat or towel. Hands are flat on the ground; both legs are also flat, uncrossed, relaxed. Close your eyes and imagine the following:
   i. You are on a beach, it is a perfect day – warm and lovely, the sound of the surf takes you, you are laying on the fine soft sand – it is warm and engulfing. The sky is blue, the sun is warm, the surf suggests sleep, the surrounding sand is so soft.
   ii. By the magic of the sun, the sand, the surf, the sky, the sound of the breeze in the palms, you find yourself becoming a part of the beach itself, and you are a sand sculpture of yourself.
   iii. You feel the coming of the tide, and as the surf rolls in, it nibbles at your toes, and they mix with the eddying tide, as it swirls and shifts around you, you feel sand particles of you slipping away, and with it all your tension.
      - First your toes slip away
      - Then your ankles
      - Then your shins
      - Then your legs
      - Then your waist
      - Then your hands and arms
      - Then your chest
      - Then your neck
      - Then your head and face
   iv. And this continues until you are totally relaxed and just a part of the sand, the surf and the sky.
   v. Stay in the sand, stay at the beach, stay present and yet totally relaxed.

vi. And as you find yourself drifting, drifting, drifting, you find your mind will become free, able to do anything you want it to do. You are waiting and present, and relaxed and ready to be filled with the magic of the story you will tell yourself.

Now that you have explored a basic physical warm-up, take a moment to enjoy the freedom of a released body – this is a good moment to meditate, focus on your breath, perhaps the rise and contraction of your belly as you breathe in and out. You have allowed yourself to explore relaxation, release, and the rich flow of emotions as you daydreamed. Give yourself a good five to ten minutes to let your mind settle, focusing on your breathing. Then find your writing table or desk, and bring yourself to the same aligned, upright position. If you are typing on a computer, then try to relax your shoulders; if you are writing with a pen on paper, then be relaxed with your grip, and again let your shoulders release. Close your eyes a moment and again focus on the breath. Open them, and then let's take the next step.

2 Step 2 – Devising your Dream Cache – Gathering the Stuff of Your Imagination

Creating a *dream cache* is central to how this book works – and it's important to understand what it is, and what it isn't. It does not necessarily have to contain actual material from your nightly dreams – that is very helpful, and can be deeply insightful, but again, most people cannot remember their dreams. A dream cache is simply a receptable for what I call *dream elements*, fleeting images, thoughts, desires, feelings that come in a moment of release, of daydreaming, of trance, or best of all, *flow*. It is a vessel for all your random, uncensored, unselfconscious thoughts – the ideas that come at those moments when you feel most relaxed and free, and yet mindful, aware, and alive. Some of these *may* be from your dreams, but they may also just be *what you think are from your dreams* and that is enough for now.

Your dream cache is just a paper lunch sack – at first – but as this process continues, we'll be using it to build a plot for a new play, a new character, a plot twist, or a dream itself – each of these elements will have at its core a dream logic base. And bear in mind that this exercise should feel child-like, like the first day of kindergarten – a playground, a playhouse, something fun is going to happen. For this first part, set a timer of about 45 minutes to an hour – but if you need more time, take it. Just give yourself some breaks to stretch, breathe, and meditate – every fifteen minutes or so.

- Gather a paper lunch sack, ideally white (I get mine from Walmart!), some colorful markers, and some multicolored construction paper – I did say that we're going to feel like we're starting kindergarten together!
- Play some gentle music, white noise, anything that relaxes you – it might be new age, jazz, chants, electronic, but it should be quiet and very gentle.
- Take a moment now to draw some images and language on your dream-bag – something evocative. Don't rush. The images could be patterns, symbols, animals, plants, faces, and consider adding poetry, symbolic language, perhaps even runes of your own invention – they represent something you're feeling right now, while suggesting you are open to receiving visions. Let these drawings be the magic that starts your experience today. The cache should feel peaceful, restful, welcoming: something you would like by your bedside tonight, and something help you welcome your day. You can use this dream-bag as a beginning for a new play, to work on a current play, or even to work on a specific character. Make a request of your dream cache right now – what do you want it to tell you?
- Look at your construction paper. Using strips of paper, you'll write down the answers to the following prompts and place them in your dream bag. Your response are your *dream elements*. As you move through the prompts, make sure you tear off *each* dream element onto a *separate* piece of paper – so that you have a wealth of material to draw upon later. Have plenty of strips available, or tear as you go. You will need a lot of construction paper.
- During this process, you should take a moment to stretch, breathe, and relax. While it's best to do this work in a single time frame, you can certainly take longer to create your cache. Just be aware of where you are and how you feel in the present moment – as your environment constantly changes, and your physical body will respond to this writing.
- Now open your bag; prepare to write, tear off what you have written into a strip, and then you'll put that into your dream cache – let's try the first prompts:

Initial Dream Prompts

1. What *dream* did you have *last night*? Write down anything you can remember … a fragment of the dream story, a person in your dream, an object, a color, anything.

2. Do you remember a *childhood dream*? Write down anything you can remember – a fragment of the dream story, a person in your dream, an object, a color, anything.
3. Do you remember a *recurring dream* or *recurring dream element*? Write down anything you can remember – a fragment of the dream story, a person in your dream, an object, a color, anything.

Dramatic Element Prompts

Each one of these next prompts ties into specific elements of a drama for the stage or screen; allow yourself to answer each one, writing down multiple responses, but tearing each one off separately.

Desires

Dramatic scripts are engines of desire – people wanting and needing desperately – and then acting on those needs. These are *big* needs – desperate love, absolute power, grinding revenge. The thrum of unreasonable, passionate desire pulses through every moment in a play, through each character, driving them to do amazing and terrifying things. What desperate *desires* come to mind right now? *Desperate* is the operative word here – even if that desperation comes from a sense of the unreal, of madness, or paralyzing uncertainty. Still your character reaches powerfully for what they *want*. What *needs* obsess you at this moment? Write down as many *desires or needs* as you can – and tie your heart to those yearnings, as it always helps if you empathize deeply with what your characters desperately want *right now*.

Problems/Obstacles

Dramatic action is built on conflict. Characters have crucial, real needs – they pursue them, and the act of reaching for what they want causes an immediate reaction from the Universe, which pushes back – sometimes in a crushing manner. Still your characters reach, and desperately desire for things that seem to be utterly *impossible*. Consider problems or obstacles that feel *real, immediate, and concrete* even if perhaps are mysterious, strange, uncanny. What insurmountable *problems/obstacles* come to your mind right now? Write down as many *problems/obstacles* as you can – the more maddening and frustrating the better.

Feelings

Our emotional life is what makes us fundamentally human. We are driven by our emotions – our fear, our joy, our anger, our kindness. Characters are quite often overwhelmed by their emotions, which fuel their desires, and set them on a path toward destiny. What *emotions* are *you* feeling right now? Happy, sad, blissful, anxiety-ridden, angry, confused? Don't worry if these emotions are reckless, wild, unruly, connect to them deeply and then release them into your dream cache. Write down as many *emotions* stirring within you as you can right now. It is always good to dip deeply into our emotional life and acknowledge and honor that which is within– as a gift of passion to your characters, and to breathe life into them.

Questions

Every dramatic script raises immense questions about our humanity – questions that are perhaps unanswerable but must be raised to begin the task of coming to terms with the complexity of the world. We often think of the *major dramatic question* driving the action of a play or film script. Dramatic action moves forward much like the structure of legal court –principles and ideas drive our desire for justice, coming from profound differences in response to fundamental questions. What fundamental *questions* come to mind right now? What questions inflame you? These are not little questions – they're huge moral questions. Write down as many major *questions* as you can – tear off each question on a separate strip of paper.

People

There is no drama without character – and the characters we write about are often variations on ourselves and the people we love. Modern drama began when writers focused on character rather than plot. Who are the people you see in your mind right now? Write a slip of paper for each *person* as you see them. Write down a name, a hair color, what they might be wearing, a bit of personality. Jot it in for now; you'll come up with details later. Use all five senses to describe them – so that you can really pin them down but do it *quickly*. Write down characters who are *real*, or *totally fictional*, or even *historical* figures you find fascinating. Let them appear to you. Write as many as you can. Who intrigues you right now?

Events

Events shape the structure of drama – life events such as weddings, funerals, births, deaths, the coming and passing of loved ones, all shape how we experience our lives. We are tied to seasonal events, family events, rituals that mark the divisions of our youth, adulthood, and old age. What events haunt you right now? Write a slip of paper for each *event* as it comes to you. It doesn't matter if they're real, fictional, or even historical. Write as many as you can.

Places

The setting for a film or play has a profound effect on the mood, style, and emotion of its dramatic action and can even become a character itself within the drama. Places affect us sensually – we remember the smells of our favorite rooms, the sight of the landscape where we were raised, the sounds we would hear in the morning and evening, the textures and surfaces we could touch and feel. What places can you see right now and what season is it? What is the time of day, and what kind of light brings them to life in your mind? What emotions come to you as you think of them? Write a slip of paper for each *place* as it comes to you. Consider *real* places in your life, but also create *fictional* or *historical* places and tab them in with brief *physical* descriptions – what can you see, hear, taste, feel, and smell? Write as many as you can. Imagine you can fly to each place in your imagination as you quickly write them down as accurately as you can.

Animals

Animals are profound symbols in plays. Chekhov named his play about a struggling, lost, and totally unrealistic young actress *The Seagull*. In another play about a boorish individual, Chekhov named the play *The Bear*. In stories or plays, animals become avatars for the characters. What animals come to you right now? Allow yourself an emotional response to the animal. We often react spontaneously and quickly to animals around us. Write a slip of paper for each *animal* as it appears to you. Maybe it's one you *fear*, one that is a *mystery* to you, or one you *loved* as a child. Consider pets, monsters, and all manner of animals – birds, insects, mammals, sea creatures, and imagine yourself, your family, and your characters as animals. What kinds of creatures might they be? Real? Symbolic? An animal from legends or history? A cryptid? A fantasy creature? Write as many as you can and give them a brief physical description.

Plants

Shakespeare's plays are filled with flowers, plants, and herbs. Consider the wildflowers and herbs in *Midsummer Night's Dream* or Orphelia's floral madness in *Hamlet*. The flora of a story or play become profoundly important as part of the setting, character, even plotting of a drama. What plants can you see right now? Flowers, trees, shrubs, fruit, herbs? Write a slip of paper for each *plant* as it comes to you. And bear in mind that the smell, taste, color, texture, and aural sensations of plant life has a huge emotional and symbolic quality in our daily life. A bright bouquet of roses immediately suggests one thing, depending upon the color; the pungent funk of wisteria in Springtime brings another feeling, a huge looming oak tree in the distance, presiding over an open pasture suggests a certain point in our lives; and lush ferns in deep wood evoke yet another emotion. Write down as many plants, flowers, trees, grasses, as you can, and tab each in with a sensual detail.

Objects

Well-made plays in the nineteenth century often revolved around a single meaningful prop. Eugène Scribe wrote an entire play on a single prop titled *The Glass of Water*, and another *A Scrap of Paper* was written by Victorien Sardou that was one of the great comedies of its time. But these techniques were not relegated only to the 19th Century melodrama; using that same glass of water, Harold Pinter wrote an incredibly threatening scene in his *The Homecoming*, verging on a kind menacing hilarity. Objects have enormous power – in mysteries quite often they're the weapon of choice for a murderer, or in great films, such as *The Lord of the Rings* and the endlessly entertaining *Harry Potter* movies, simple objects become magical symbols for something much more profound. What objects can you see right now? Consider ordinary objects as well as the sublime. What is in your hand right? Write a slip of paper for each *object* as it comes to you, and give each a tangible, specific description using all five senses.

Writer's Challenge: If you're working in a group, take a moment to look at each person in your writers' circle. Allow open thoughts to come to you in your physical and spiritual moment of connection with that other writer – consider their mood, personality, appearance, and your relationship to them. Write down three dream elements for that other participant, and if you can, write three elements for every other writer in the room. Share these elements either directly or anonymously with that writer. Be kind, gentle, helpful, and giving – offer them something tied directly to the present moment, your revelation of who they are and the possibilities that await them through an understanding of their dreams.

The Next Step – Creating with Dream Elements

Now that we've gathered all this information, we are ready to start working with your dream elements to create a dream, a dramatic idea for a play or screenplay, and to explore the characters in the story. In each case you'll want to allow the ideas to flow in two different ways – 1) you can simply pull things out of your dream cache and work with each in the strict order it comes out of your cache; or 2) you can pull several dream elements out and work with whichever one works best in the scenario you are creating. If it doesn't work, toss it aside and keep picking. One way follows *chance art* with no mediation from you; the other way allows that same chance art to happen but works with a slightly more considered approach. *Chance art* comes to us directly from the Dadaist school of creative thinking. The Dadaist poet, Tristan Tzara was famous for plucking words from the pockets his winter coat in a random manner and creating whole poems in front of audiences that way. Either technique has an element of chance to it, and as such offers an opportunity to push your creativity to help you write.

Ultimately, I encourage you to embrace *the total chance art approach,* as much of the random nature of dreamwork you are trying to use helps you get past all the clichés and platitudes that plague much of the writing we see in film and on the stage. It is not easy to let go of that control, and making sense of the random nature of what you pluck from your dream cache is very difficult and challenging at times. But give it a try and be patient. You are trying to *surprise* yourself with what may be bizarre, uncanny, and perhaps just plain crazy. But be aware there is a method in your madness because this kind of creativity – totally free of self-censorship – leads to new art that has never been seen before, and it's come organically from your own psyche. Remember that if you are surprised by the art you create, your audience will be astonished as well.

3   Step 3– Writing a Dream – Freeing Your Natural Creativity

Now that you've extracted material from your dreams, it's time to write your own dream. Telling a dream is like telling any story – you instinctively have, awake or asleep, what is called a *narrative engine* that is running all the time, with you as the star of your own movie. According to Bert O. States, the landscape of your dreams often follows one of three major tropes, not unlike the literary tropes that we all know. These tropes have grown out of the data collected by many different researchers in different dream research laboratories. And most importantly, these tropes are *suggested* here, but they are just that, suggestions – no police work involved. Remember that I never want you to accept received notions of anything – including from me! So, you may or may not find these dream tropes helpful, but sometimes a little bit of structure goes a long way to help you tell your story. You might allow the structure of one of these tropes as a form for your dream, or ignore them all together, and just flow with your inner narrative machine.

> ***Dream Tropes***
> – *Lyric Dreams* are a nonnarrative mode that express a state of mind in an orderly way. Lyric dreams explore a sudden emotional feeling for a place or object and explore it fully in terms of the five (or perhaps six) senses. While they have no story per se, they are intensive, introspective, internal, highly subjective, and personal. Nightmares and erotic dreams are usually lyric dreams. Lyric dreams are short form dreams.
> – *Epic Dreams* are a journey or a quest, linked by the desperate desire to find a person or object, commit an act of great import, or participate in a significant event. They are extensive, extrospective, external – an audience is often present. These social, communal (We) dreams involve human *activity* in the world (war, peace, work, etc.) or shared values (tribal codes of honor, patriotism, etc.). These are long form dreams.
> – *Dramatic Dreams* – take a "what if" scenario to the absolute, and perhaps bizarre extreme, finding linkage in images or objects and taking a dramatic action to its nearly illogical extremes. These dreams move from the banal to the bizarre, slowly unfolding as they move from quotidian reality to increasingly stranger occurrence. The flow from normal to weird is often precipitated by some single emotional event that triggers the change.

Your dream will begin with these words, "Last night I had a dream, and this is what happened ..." and from there you will remove one item from your dream cache, after first mixing up the cache thoroughly. Look at this first bit of language as a kind of incantation that allows you to start the dream: "Last night I had a dream, and this is what happened ..." Now you can extract a piece of paper from your *dream cache*. This is a *dream element*, a piece of the waking dream you are creating. Note your *emotional* reaction to it right away. This bit will begin your dream narrative. Let the dream element resonate with you for a moment – you can use it *literally*, as the word appeared on the strip of paper, or you can emotionally *free associate* with that item.

Sometimes the free association may be more powerful than the element itself. If you choose to use the dream element in its literal form, it will be harder, but it will also work your creativity more, strengthening that muscle. Incidentally, I do encourage you to try using the dream element as literally as possible at first, but then if that is not working at all, try the free association approach. The literal approach, which is essentially *chance art*, is a bit more difficult, but as I noted before, learning to work with what you have pulled out of your dream cache literally will really force your creative juices to flow.

When you work with this material, again think of the chance art of Dadaism – "The 'law of chance,'" Hans Arp, one of the founding artists of Dada, once wrote, "can be experienced only in a total surrender to the unconscious." If you allow yourself to work this way, it is not unlike the work done by an oyster when a grain of sand slips into its shell, irritating its soft flesh. In response, it covers the object with layers of nacre, to protect the oyster's soft innards from its roughness. What is created is a pearl! Treat each dream element that you experience by chance art to be that somewhat irritating grain of sand – and create your own pearl.

After you write the first sentence of your narrative; pause; and remove another strip of paper, another *dream element,* from your dream cache. Let it resonate with you, note its relationship with the first piece of paper, and see if you can incorporate this dream element in its original literal form – and if not, use the free association. Either way is fine, though the more literal approach will, again, stretch your creative response a bit more. Continue writing another sentence. Then stop and remove a third dream element – process it as well, then write another sentence. Choose a final bit of language from your dream cache – and then end your dream with this final item from your dream cache. You should have incorporated at least five to six items from your cache to create your dream narrative.

Read this dream out loud – what does it feel like? Where did it take you emotionally? What sticks with you? Bear in mind that these first created dreams are *gifts* from your unconscious. Consider writing three more dreams, write them on different days – and record the dreams that you have on those evenings. These dreams that you've created may be the beginning of a Dream Dramatic Concept Outline – an outline of a basic dramatic idea, which is the first step to writing a play or screen play, and a truly wonderful place to start your dramatic work – let's try one right now.

4   Step 4– Dream Dramatic Concept Outline – Germinating the Dramatic Seed

The Dream Dramatic Concept Outline is a way for you to process an idea for a play before you start writing it. It is a seed of the dramatic work – stage play or film script – that you hope to write. You are essentially testing the idea to see if it works for you in this present moment. The dramatic concept outline has essentially eight components: 1) The Working Title, 2) the Central Character, 3) The central character's Need or Desire, 4) the Obstacle, 5) the other Major Characters, 6) the Setting, 7) the Occasion, and 8) the Resolution. There are a few other additional dramatic components to think about, but these eight will give you the germ of the idea.

To incorporate your dream cache into this process, we'll start to plug in some of the *dream elements* from your cache into a basic dramatic concept – using the contents of the dream cache to create the dramatic components of your play idea. For each aspect of your dramatic concept, reach into your bag, and pull out something that astonishes you! You will pull one dream element out of your dream cache eight times. Take time with each one as you pull it from your dream cache; allow yourself to react emotionally to each item. Sense and ease into the interplay between the elements.

Again, you shouldn't feel that you must use whatever you pull from your dream cache in an absolute literal fashion. At times, consider taking a free associative approach to decide how to use each element. If the dream element you pull out of the bag simply makes you *think* of something *else* for each of these categories, just use that, and don't think too much about it. Sometimes a literal response to the dream element will work, sometimes the associative method will work. Just go with the flow.

Just remember that you can use *either* approach, no matter how illogical or crazy. Just keep pulling things out of your dream cache as you feel necessary – some may work one way; some may work another way. Some may be totally useless, and in that case, just return those elements to the dream cache. The most important thing is *flow* – any element that gets in the way of flow should be discarded and move onto the next. Sometimes dumping the whole dream cache in front of you, and just using what you feel works in the moment is the way to go. There is no police work here – do what feels natural, right, and easy.

1. Start with the *Working Title* of your script. Pull it out of your dream cache– right now. Yes, this is a totally backwards way to work on a script. The title before the concept?! But that's what we wanted – to surprise ourselves. And that title will help you pull together the entire dramatic concept. It provides a theme, an idea, a shaping element – try it!

2. Next, we'll pull the *Central Character* of your script out of the bag. Take a moment to fill out the character now that you have them in your hand. You want to pencil in a few physical details, nothing too elaborate – eyes, hair color, clothing, etc., and tab in emotional state and personality – and possibly consider more than one central character. And be aware of course, that the element you may pull out may not resemble a character at all – if that's the case, just work with it, and allow yourself to *free associate* a character with the element you pulled out. Or, using another technique, keep pulling until you hit the dream element that gives you the character that you want, working with your working title. Don't worry if that central character is a bit lean in description at this point – you'll find out much more about them in the next dream element.

3. Next pull out your central character's predominant, and perhaps desperate, *Desire* or *Need*. Again, the dream element that comes out may just be totally bizarre but see if you can associate upon it and come up with central character's desire or need. Or just pick through the dream elements until you hit something that works. Keep in mind your working title and the central character that you've now filled out – and be aware that this desire or need may suddenly cause you to shift how you see this character in your mind's eye.

4. Pull another dream element out of your bag – this is the *Obstacle* – and again, if you have pulled out something completely strange, no worries! You can just associate on that dream element to discover your obstacle – bear in mind the other dramatic components: the working title, the central character, the central character's desire, the other characters in the play, the setting, the occasion, bearing in mind this obstacle comes from both the dream element you have discovered and its relationship with these other dramatic components.

5. Now pull out about three or four dream elements –these will become the *Secondary Characters* in your script idea. Again, play with the dream elements and use them in either a literal or associative manner. Linger with these – they will become important characters in your dramatic work,

tied to the central character in some manner. Perhaps they are oppositional, or they may be supportive, to your central character's desperate desire or need. Fill out each of these characters with descriptions and start building relationships between them and your central character. Describe their physicality and personality more fully, and again keep in mind the working title of the play and how they might tie into that. Allow the previous elements to affect you as you start to compile your script concept.

6. Now comes your *Setting*(s) for the script – if it's a stage play, you might want to work with one or two – if it's a screenplay, you might want four or five, or even more. Each merits a substantial physical and perhaps emotional description. Again, the dream elements may work literally as they come out of the cache or if they seem too bizarre, then you can free associate on these elements to create your settings. Or just pull as many dream elements as necessary out of your dream cache until you find what you need.

7. The next component you need is your *Occasion* – that life event or series of life events that will help you shape your plot. Most dramatic actions take place around a major life event such as a birth, a death, a wedding, or a family event, a religious holiday, the start of a job, an anniversary, or a divorce. The elements you pull from your dream cache may again seem a bit bizarre and unusable, but if that is the case just free associate on the dream element to find what you want – or just keep pulling from the dream cache until you have what you need – and again bear in mind the working title of the play, the setting, and your central character's desperate need.

8. Finally, you pull out one last dream element from your cache, that will be your *Resolution*, and yes, it's important to know how you will end your play. You can again use this dream element as you have received, or as you associate upon it, or you can just keep pulling out dream elements until you hit something that works. I suggest you take advantage of serendipity and just work with what comes first, however. The resolution is important because it gets at the *major dramatic question* of the script – how you end the script is a big part of how you view the world of its drama, and what point you are trying to make about that world.

There are other dramatic components you might want to experiment with by pulling them out of your dream cache, so try these as well if you're settled into your dramatic idea. These are more oriented toward the structural shape of your dramatic idea and will help you later as you begin to craft your idea more thoroughly.

1. Pull a dream element out of your cache, this will be your *Character Change*. In other words, this is how your character will change by the end of the play, and it will affect the resolution and ultimately the major dramatic question you are raising. Some characters don't change at all – but the audience sometimes changes their point of view about the character. At any rate, your dream cache may have something to say about who your character is by the end of the script.

2. Finally, pull one more dream element to complete your play idea – this will be the What of your play, and it is a visual image that suggests a structure to your drama. Quite often this will affect the working title of your play, and offers a theatrical, magic, emotional, and mythic element to how your play or film will look visually and offers a structural suggestion of how it will work scene to scene. The What is an idea that comes from Jean Claude van Itallie, the off-off-Broadway playwright of the Open Theatre's production of *The Serpent*, and his *Playwright's Workbook*. The What might be the image that we see on a poster of your film or play, and have central role in your script's structure, tone, and how you tell its story through dramatic action. Again, feel free to either use the actual dream element you pluck from your cache, or associate on it, bearing in mind all the dramatic components we've explored thus far.

Be aware that there are many ways to use your dream cache for play ideas. One way might be to dump all the dream material into a pile, and just weed through it until you find the things you need, rather than allowing chance to give it to you. Or you could randomly choose six to eight dream elements and force yourself to create a dramatic concept outline out of just those elements using either the literal or associative approach. One last way is to create a different dream cache or each play you write – so that you combine that with your Ask at night and over a period of time as you think about a play, add to that dream cache and then create your dramatic concept outline out of that material.

Now that you have a basic idea for your dramatic script, you can begin exploring your characters, since at the heart of your drama, you must understand every aspect of your characters before you dig into writing a scenario, plotting the events of the script, or writing scenes. One way to explore character is to explore what your characters dream, and here, you'll use the same basic dream cache exercise for each of your characters.

5 Step 5 – Character Dreams – Exploring the World within Your Character

Exploring your characters' dreams enables you to explore the depths of their inner emotional life and to connect the dots of your characters' past using imagery and vision. You will work on this project *as if* you were the character. You will create your dream cache the same way you did for yourself, but on its paper surface, you will draw the symbols, images, words that help you think of your character. Writing your character's dreams, walking in their shoes, is the beginning of the second step of writing a dramatic work for stage or screen – which is the exploration of character, and this step is crucial. You can't write your characters' story until you know your characters so well that they try to break away from you and live their own lives in your imagination. That's how you know you're ready to move onto plot – because you know your characters so well, they practically force you to move into dramatic action! I suggest you choose a different day to work on each character in your play, since this is an immersive exercise in which you think, breathe, and live as your character and add dream elements that come from your character's life – not your own life.

Choose your dream menu of People, Places, Objects, Events: You will tear off all these brief dream elements into separate pieces of paper and put them into your character's decorated dream cache, just as you did in your own dream cache. I suggest at least five dream elements for each prompt, but you can choose as many as you'd like, perhaps up to ten, depending upon how deeply you want to explore the character.

– People: Select five people in your character's life, write them down with a brief but sensual description. These can exist in real life or be totally fictional existing within the world of your character. These people have a powerful emotional significance to your character.
– Places: Select five places in your character's life, write them down with a brief but evocative physical and emotional description. These can be real places or places within your character's world.
– Objects: Select five objects in your character's life, write them down with a brief but evocative physical and emotional description. These objects should have major significance within the world of your character.
– Events: Select five events in your character's life, write them down with a brief but emotional and sensual description. These events can be actual historical events or be fictional events existing within your character's world.

Consider a dream trope – either Lyric, Epic, or Dramatic. And again, only use these tropes if you find them helpful – and they may help you provide a structure or form for the telling of the dream.

Write Your Character's Dream

Without judging or thinking too much, allow your character to dream and have them start with "Last night I had a dream, and this is what happened" – keeping in mind a single desire running as an emotional thread in your dream. Allow a sense of the bizarre or the uncanny to prevail and write in a meditative state (using evocative music or white noise to keep you in the world of the dream). At regular intervals, select a new element (person, place, object, or event) from your character's dream cache and incorporate these into the world of your character's dream. Write a dream or several dreams for each of your characters. And if you write several dreams for a single character – consider different tropes – lyric, dramatic, and epic – for each dream.

6   Step 6 – Dream Adjacent Writing Exercises – Giving over to the Magic of Dreaming

These following exercises are useful in creating an entire dream play, or for adding theatricality to a play that has a more traditional linear structure. Each of these exercises can be based upon your actual dreams, but they certainly should be based upon your *dream cache*. Certainly, as I have mentioned before, the more frequently writers record their dreams, the more success they will have remembering them. However, it is also very useful to learn how to imitate the action of a dream regardless of whether you ever dreamed it – I call this *dream adjacent writing*. Dream adjacent writing is a useful way to segue yourself into the writing of nonlinear work; and it almost always serves as a meaningful way to fight writer's block.

1. Exercise #1: *Magic Overheard Voices.* This is a classic playwriting exercise to help you develop an ear for dialogue by learning to listen closely to human speech and transcribing it accurately. However, the goal here is to take a step beyond realistic dialogue transcription into dreamwrighting, by learning how to move from life to *art* by finding the *magic* in everyday life. Your task is to write eighteen lines of dialogue following these instructions:

- a. Listen closely to a conversation by complete strangers – see if you can mentally record it in your mind. DO NOT use a tape recorder – that is illegal (and cheating!).
- b. As quickly and as accurately as you can, write down six lines of the dialogue you just heard – make sure you get every nuance, every mistake, every pause, every mispronunciation, etc.
- c. Pay attention to the BEHAVIOR – what is the SUBTEXT of what you are listening to – what does the person really want? What do they seem to be hiding? What's at STAKE for the person.
- d. Then write six more lines of dialogue – trying to remain true to what the characters seem to want or are trying to do.
- e. Add a complication of some sort – and make it a bit *magical and a bit of an existential knot*. Is this real or is this dream? It can either be something within the characters themselves (a sudden idea or need), an external element, something physical perhaps – and write six more lines. Make it *subtle* – but make it *theatrical, magical, and dreamlike*.
- f. Bear in mind that you can bend the rules a quite a bit in this exercise – but even when you experiment in *non-realistic or non-linear style* you must find the *humanity;* you must find the *human situation* – adding the complication a bit earlier to see if you can fool us, so that we don't know where reality ends and where your *artifice* occurs.
- g. The goal is to write believable, honest dialogue – true to the characters you are writing, in their voices with whatever warts and peccadillos their language contains. And then to find your own *magic voice* – whatever that is!!!

2. *Exercise #2: The Chair Play.* The objective here is develop skills in "wrighting behavior" while exploring theatricality, dreamwrighting, and magic. You are also trying to avoid writing "spoken subtext" and learn how to keep an *audience* working as they discover and learn from the behavior of the characters. The exercise is to write a short play of five to ten pages following these instructions:
    - a. There will be two characters, a protagonist, Character A, and an antagonist, Character B.
    - b. Character A needs something *desperately* and *urgently* from Character B, who has her or his own strong reasons for NOT giving Character A what she or he wants. If Character A does not get what she or he wants from Character B, there will be *terrible consequences* and the *stakes are high*.

    c.   Character A and B are working on a physical activity of some difficulty and must complete the task at hand. They have *real, concrete, urgent* reasons for completing this physical activity.

    d.   Character A and B may only discuss the physical activity at hand. Character A *may not* ask directly for what she or he needs *desperately* and *urgently*, but Character A *must get what she or he wants* or there will be *consequences*.

    e.   THE CHAIR: You must use a chair in this scene, and the only rule here is that the chair can be anything *but cannot be used as a chair*. In other words, the audience must use its imagination to figure out how the chair is being used to represent some other object, person, prop, activity, etc.

    f.   Don't tell us what the chair is supposed to be in the stage directions. Let us figure out what the chair is through the *behavior* of the characters. Have the characters *endow* the chair with whatever special properties they need to create the imaginary thing or person the chair will represent.

    g.   Enjoy the theatricality of the scene, but remember to keep the play real, human, and work not just from the "trick" of the theatricality of the chair, but the deeper magic of the human heart.

    h.   Do what you can, and don't worry if you don't find an ending to the scene; just explore what the characters want, be true to their *real needs*, and let us figure out what is going on. Don't be afraid to be mysterious. We'll love it if your play makes us work our imaginations as an audience.

3. Exercise #3: *Single-mindedness.* Using your dream cache, create a dreamscape using all five senses, complete with image, sound, smell, touch, and taste. Choosing characters from your *dream cache*, allow a central action or theme to plant itself in your dreamscape and then follow it through in an imagined dialogue with yourself. You want or need something – "I desperately need a rose" or "I've got to get out of here" and write a dialogue with yourself. Make sure there is a real need behind the conversation. Allow the dialogue to move forward without conscious effort to manipulate; think of it occurring in an associational manner, as "sympathetic vibrations" or "enigma variations" adjusting to each unanticipated moment. Don't write down any characters' names, simply write down alternating lines of dialogue. Then go back and add as few or as many characters as you like to the dialogue you have written. Add the setting and allow it to flow and change as you feel necessary.

    a.   *1st Variation:* Select several mementos that have meaning to you – photographs, objects d'art, trinkets, even objects that disturb you – and place them in a box with a lid. Give the box a gentle shake, just to shift things around. As you write your dream play – and you allow the central theme to drive your character who is yourself – remove one object and allow it to become part of your dream (without looking or consciously choosing the object).

    b.   *2nd Variation:* Write down the milestone events of your life (or your character's life) but write them primarily in terms of your five senses and emotions – think of places, people, objects, emotional states, smells, sounds, textures, and images. Put these on small scraps of paper and fold them up into a box. Draw out a milestone every now and then as you work your way through your dream play – allow each milestone not only to enter the world of your play, but to transform the world you are creating.

4. Exercise #4: The *Harrison Ford Syndrome* is the dream experience described by Bert States in his book, *Seeing in the Dark,* of recognizing real life people in a dream, but noticing their physicality and personality keeps shifting, although the persona remains the same. So, using Bert State's example, in your dream you see Harrison Ford, but he sounds like your father, and he seems to be your father, but he looks, talks, and acts like Harrison Ford. Still, you *know* he is your father. With this in mind, write a simple two-person scene and allow one character to be yourself, and other to be a friend. As the conversation progresses, keep shifting your and your friend's physicality and characterization, at first being very specific about who or what that person is becoming, then allowing bits and pieces of many aspects of other characters to reveal themselves in your friend, using your dream cache. The interesting aspect of the exercise is that the conversation continues using the "singlemindedness" of dreams, following the same thread, the same desire, and the personas remain mostly themselves, but character aspects shift slightly as their visual and aural characterizations change.

    a.   *Physical Improvisation*: You can improvise this exercise using an even number of actors, six for example, with three taking the role of A and three taking the role of B. Set the actors up in a line and allow the actors to start the conversation and then at a certain rhythm dictated by the flow of conversation allow each of the actors to take turns at playing the roles of A and B keeping the conversation going as if it was being continued by the two original actors. Each actor should take on a specific persona for her/his version of A or B, so that there is a distinctly different quality as the characters of A & B change. Then allow the actors to take on bits and pieces of each other's physical and vocal characterizations as they move through the conversation, morphing in and out of their characters.

5. Exercise #5: *Dream Journeys*. Transform the situations and landscapes during this same simple conversation between two characters. Allow the changes to continue even as the situation becomes about a quest of some sort. The quest is for an unattainable essence, an almost impossible substance, or a constantly shifting object that is a mystery to you and the other characters in the play (never entirely define it). It should be something that keeps taking on different qualities, yet the magic at the center of it has a kind of consistency of emotional meaning. Allow the quest to go beyond the borders of the room, moving through space and time with no regard for waking logic.

   a. 1st Variation – *Journeys*: Select the settings in advance; write down detailed descriptions of landscapes, settings, and interior and exterior spaces on scraps of paper, including things such as specific buildings and rooms, geographic location, terrain, altitude, weather conditions, plants, animals, rooms, and all the sensory details of these various landscapes and interesting spaces. Once you've written these down, place them into a box and select them using a random process – and allow your dream play to flow in and out of these settings.

   b. 2nd Variation – *Journeys*: Like the variation of the singlemindedness exercise, allow a series of objects to serve as signals for a change of scene. Each object is a *call* – a kind of talisman that becomes a portal into a new world – Paul Castagno invented this term in his excellent book, *New Playwriting Strategies*. A character might just randomly pick up the *call*. Then allow that character to disappear into the world of that *call*, whether it is a painting, a photograph, a book, or even a graphic image on a soup can, and then that unique world becomes the next scene in your dream play. Let the *call* dictate the shift of the landscape – and the emotional truth of that *call* to suggest the emotional state of the characters in that world.

6. Exercise #6: *Time Mutations*. Allow time changes in the scenes; slow the action, speed up the action, repeat the action of a scene. Reverse the action of the scene; reverse it quickly, slowly. Keep the scenes simple though, keep the conversation between yourself and your friend on a consistent basis, following a powerful emotional need, but one that has

some unexplainable quality to it. Allow the time morphing to speed up the conversation, to jump ahead to newer or older sections of the conversation, leaping over times and returning.

7. Exercise #7: *CHARACTER DREAMS*. Write your character's dreams (see *step 5* above). Have your character tell us a dream they've had. Choose very powerful dreams, dreams which foretell something, or have a profound effect on the dreamer and are tied to an important event in your character's life. Also create your character's childhood dreams, recurring dreams, or dreams that occur in the middle of a crisis. Write a scene in which it isn't entire clear what is the character's dream and what is the character's reality. Tie the character's dream world to the real world and let the barriers between the two worlds drop. Let the images, bizarre occurrences, strange juxtapositions, odd quests, fall into the life of the living character; let the props and symbols of the dream world drift into the real world and vice versa.

8. Exercise #8: *Dream Scenes*. Write out a dream from your character's childhood, then write a recurring dream. Create a scene from these dreams. Try to recreate the elements of bizarreness through theatricality; use minimal props, settings, and rely primarily on the use of actors' voices, bodies, and movement through space to create the bizarre elements. Allow the scene to progress in an associative manner, allow events to occur that drift in and out attached to a common theme. When you write the dialogue don't even include the character names; write the scene as a series of lines reacting off each other and add the character's names later (this is how the famous playwright/director Richard Foreman created works for his New York-based Ontological-Hysteric Theatre).

9. Exercise #9: *Dream Monologue*. Write out a monologue that allows a single important desire to flow through it, but write it in imagistic, descriptive language that makes no logical sense. Use your dream cache, pulling out dream elements as inspiration along the way. Key, however, is to keep coming back to the *original powerful desire or need* in the speech; why is your character making this speech? What is at stake in their doing so? What are the consequences if they don't make this speech? Make them the consequences substantial, but perhaps nonsensical. Allow the language to work as a collage – a flow of images that connect associatively, not necessarily logically. There's something your character desperately wants but is lost in a world of images flowing through this need. Allow the language to flow from alliteration, puns, emotional slides, rhythmic effect. Choose all nouns, or all verbs, or cliché phrases turned sideways – and again, allow your dream cache elements to give you associational

hints along the way. Just always keep the *need* in mind; and make sure it is a powerful, and perhaps *unexplainable* one. Don't worry about making sense, worry about your attaching to that need, understanding it yourself in a profound and real way – to discover the emotional state of your character and their desire.

10. Exercise #10: *Magic abilities/disabilities*: In a scene write characters that have sudden gifts of strange physical powers; they can fly or are enormously strong, or can speak in foreign languages, or can perform elaborate martial arts. Create a scene where the characters can float on air, speak sonnets, limericks, or in a language that makes sense only through the accretion of specific images (see dream language above). Perhaps they can only run in slow motion or are suddenly paralyzed or find themselves suddenly falling off the edge of precipice. Dream disabilities include uncontrollable laughter, being only able to talk like a child, suddenly having limbs or parts of the body that are like those of an animal. Characters may only be able to talk through dancing or singing or through rituals that have no basis in any waking ritual. The disabilities could also take the form of transformations; whenever a certain character says a specific word, she or he is forced into becoming a certain person or animal. Suddenly the senses become overwhelmed by a particular taste, smell, sound, image, or touch or the character develops a strange allergic reaction to something or someone. At the base of each of these abilities/disabilities is a deep, mysterious desire that is framed by its desperation and consuming, though vague, need.

The Chapters Ahead – Exploring Dreamwright Styles

Here we take a pause and begin to focus on our next steps – you have played with your basic dramatic concept outline for one or more projects; you are getting to know your characters through their dreams and in many other ways. You are playing with dream adjacent exercises, that allow you to create scenes that have the look and feel of dreams. Now we'll step back and look at the bigger picture, while still exploring our characters as they enter the world of the play. From this point on, as we move through the chapters of this book, we'll look at some of the major dramatists of both the stage and screen, exploring their non-linear, non-traditional techniques and how those techniques tie into the world of the dreamwrighting. I call these kinds of writers *dreamwrights* and this is because in each case they work in ways that suggest the form, content, and technique of dreams. Bear in mind, you *don't* have to read every play or screenplay suggested in this book and/or attempt every exercise. Some will be more useful to the specific project you are working on, and some will not. I do suggest *eventually* adding all these dramatic works for stage or screen to your reading and viewing lists, because as dreamwrights, they are seminal writers in the realm of non-linear, non-traditional dramatic writing technique.

For the instructor using this book to build a course in non-linear, non-traditional dramatic writing, each week will provide an entry into a different aspect of this kind of dream-based dramatic writing. Chapter Two through Chapter Six will provide mostly character exploration, or to use the term made popular in playwriting books by Michael Wright in his book *Playwriting in Process*, "character etudes," which help the writer tease out the more complex aspects of their characters in preparation for those characters' entrance into the world of the drama – whether for stage or screen. Chapter Seven through Chapter Fifteen are designed to help the dramatist to build their plot, again using dream techniques that create unexpected twists and help to keep both the dramatist and their audience on the edge of their seats. The trick being that in the writing process if the dramatist doesn't know what will happen next, neither will their audience. Key to all of this is the use of the *dream cache*, which I really encourage to continue to be updated with new *dream elements* as you work your way through the course.

With these plot techniques, the dramatist can then develop their play or film treatment, and again, we'll be using the *essences* of several difference plays and screenplays by a diverse canon of playwrights and screenwriters to provide insights into the various non-linear techniques and theories that can help evolve the plot, including the use of what I call *"magical" plot cards*. When we reach that point, we will be layering in different structural images to help flesh out the non-traditional plots we hope to create, and the often scraping back some of those layers to reveal uncanny linkages, not unlike the work of certain oil painters, who cut through the layers of paint to unmask a palimpsest of images below.

While some might consider my use of other playwrights and screenwriters' work a bit too literary, I have always felt that writers build on each other's work – and frankly, if you are going to steal technique – steal from the best. This is certainly what Shakespeare did, and my own background in studying the history of New York City off-off-Broadway theatre, shows that a generation of playwrights, including Sam Shepard, John Guare, Lanford Wilson, Adrienne Kennedy, and Irene Fornes, were all deeply engaged in each other's work – quite often borrowing techniques from each other on a weekly basis, as well as from the absurdists Edward Albee, Jean Genet, Harold Pinter, and Eugène Ionesco to create work that was uniquely their own.

Chapter by Chapter Summary – Dreamwright Styles

After the initial dreamwrighting workshop, this book follows a 15-week course of dramatic writing with several major projects along the way. However, work with the text in any way you'd like. If you are using this text to complete a single new project, then feel free to move chapter by chapter, and work your way through each step. Or feel free to just dive in and use the book to explore useful nonlinear techniques. I even suggest you just use a random approach and explore a chapter out of order as your curiosity is whetted– which is very similar to how a dream might work.

Each of the next chapters featuring specific dreamwrights will also focus on their non-linear techniques that grow out of the structure, form, or style of dreams, but also have a unique, important, and historical precedent in non-linear dramaturgy. Each chapter will feature at least one playwright and one screenwriter, moving from stage to screen in our exploration of non-traditional structure. There are so many ways of bursting through traditional Aristotelian dramatic structure, and even the Greeks themselves were far more experimental than we normally suppose. Think about all the variations through time, even before there was realism and naturalism there was romanticism, which posited an ideal world beyond the quotidian realm. Then in reaction to and simultaneous with the stranglehold of realistic art and drama came symbolism, impressionism, pointillism, modernism, expressionism, dadaism, surrealism, epic theatre, absurdism, new wave cinema, post-modernism, pastiche, etc. Each of these non-realistic, non-linear, non-traditional "isms" reacting to realism in art and drama explore techniques that have roots in the form, structure, and content of dreams. Because there is no point in reinventing the wheel, I think it's always useful, and deeply inspirational, to get at the *essence* of other artists techniques, and experiment using our own organically created dream elements using these techniques as a jumping off place. You won't be imitating these artists; you'll be allowing yourself to be stimulated by the *essence* of their experimentation to create your own wholly new forms of drama. Within the realm of phenomenology, the exploration of essences is very common, and a definition of an essence can be: "a structure of essential meanings that explicates a phenomenon of interest."[2] In a more practical manner, for each dramatist's "essence" of non-linear, dreamwrighting technique discussed, I will

---

2   Karin Dahlberg (2006), "The essence of essences – the search for meaning structures in phenomenological analysis of lifeworld phenomena," *International Journal of Qualitative Studies on Health and Well-being*, 1:1, 11–19, DOI: 10.1080/17482620500478405.

provide a practical exercise, so that you can experiment with that technique in your own writing.

After we are done with the dreamwork workshop in chapter one, we move into the first set of non-linear dramaturgical essences in Chapter 2, "Structure of the Dream Work, Myth, Ceremony, & Ritual." Here, we'll exploring the powerful tools of ritual, myth, and ceremony to build a unique structure to your non-linear dramatic writing. One of the challenges of working off the grid of traditional dramatic structure is that there is a myriad of ways to break Aristotelian form – so using the powerful roots of myth provides a story structure that quite often takes the writer into new places. We'll begin with August Strindberg's classic non-linear drama, *A Dream Play* which provided a unique map for creating non-linear technique based upon ancient Hindu and Sanskrit mythology through his fractured mind-state, during his Inferno period. From there we'll dig into the highly ritualized, and fragmented noir detective film structure of Orson Welles *Citizen Kane*. Both are seminal works that use a sense of ceremony to capture the lives of Agnes in *A Dream Play* and Kane in *Citizen Kane* within specific dream structures that have become classic techniques of form. Strindberg goes so far as to define what a dream play is, providing a paradigm of mutation, time fragmentation, and malleability tied to the uncanny sense of the dreamer's will driving the engine of narrative. Welles leads from the reverse deduction model of detective fiction, starting with the death of a great yet deeply flawed individual, and working back through highly subjective and unreliable narrators to get at a truth that can be uttered with one word.

In Chapter 3, "Ancient Dream Structures: Myths and the Greek Chorus," we explore the unique non-linear, and dreamlike role of the chorus in Sophocles' *Oedipus the King*, and with Paula Vogel's *How I Learned to Drive* we learn a fundamental non-linear feminist circle structure that ruptures the patriarchal hegemony of crisis-based drama complemented by her brilliant post-modern reimagining of the Greek chorus. We also explore how that same chorus can become useful in the very non-traditional aural symphonic creation of setting with Lanford Wilson's lyrical *Book of Days,* and finally, we explore how ancient Greek mythos works in film as we deconstruct the myth of Orpheus and Eurydice in Marcel Camus' *Black Orpheus*, seen through the highly ritualized lens of Vodun in Brazil.

In Chapter 4 "African-American Dream Funhouse – Creating Ritual Liminality," we examine two seminal African-American dramas, Adrienne Kennedy's stage play *Funnyhouse of A Negro* and Julie Dash's film script *Daughters of the Dust* create fluid, liminal, structures that in their essence evoke an anti-racist, activist approach to drama that is particularly powerful because it is indirect, subliminal, and emotionally engaging. Both writers have influenced generations of black writers, and their work provides a leaping off place into a highly spiritual, profoundly otherworldly style of non-traditional dramatic structure that I have found deeply influential in my own work. Having directed Adrienne Kennedy's *Funnyhouse of a Negro* at the University of Missouri and corresponded with her for years on the importance her dreams are for her work as a dramatist, I feel that she is a particularly meaningful source for understanding dream work. Julie Dash, being the first major black female film director and screenwriter to have her work produced in the United States, holds a particularly important place for those who are interested in exploring her unique storytelling methods of using African-American ancestor worship and the veneration of the dead to write transcendent narratives in a powerful meditative manner.

In Chapter 5, "Transfiguration of Gender and Identity- Transformations, Mutability, and Androgyny," we switch gears and explore two major writers whose work transcends traditional notions of gender, in order to get at a kind of subversive sexual slippage in dramatic writing that yanks its audience from its cis-gendered hegemony and thrusts into a powerful transmutability that is both freeing and thrillingly dangerous. Jean Genet's *The Balcony* takes us to a new level of gender performativity that offers trans-strategies of subversion that are as enlightening in terms of character exploration as they are in standing societal roles on their ear. And in Sally Potter's screenplay for *Orlando* which is based on Virginia Woolf's world-changing novel, we encounter something entirely different, a filmic and image-laden view of human history where we discover how dynamic gender can be in terms of setting us loose from our moorings in traditional roles, and uncovering new realms of freedom.

Moving to Chapter 6, "The Dreamer's Heart – Thinking Backwards First: Character Dreams and Storytelling," we will look at the essence of two major dramatic works that take Orson Welles' idea on reverse structure in non-linear writing, and twists it into something shatteringly comic and profound, In Martin McDonagh's *The Pillowman* takes on the nature of storytelling itself, but as we move backwards to the truth of the central character Katurian's children's stories we uncover a level of horror that shakes us to the core, even as we find it impossible to stop laughing at its almost reprehensible levels of nerve-racking comedy. With Christopher Nolan's: *Memento*, his screenwriting insists upon a unique architecture that takes on the narrative shape of a hairpin turn, and twists it into a fresh approach on the ancient non-linear detective story, arcing backwards to truth from the moment of homicide, even as we simultaneously race toward murder with an impossible, and relentless blinded energy of enigmatic tattooed revelation.

With Chapter 7, "Magic Plot Cards –The Dreamwright as Story-teller," we encounter three masterful dramatists Tony Kushner, Charlie Kaufman, and Guillermo Arriaga who provide revelatory non-linear tools based on tangible and incredibly useful sources. One of very important aspects of this chapter is the work on exploring plot with *Magic Plot Cards* which help you work through the complexity of a non-linear plot outline considering *story, structure, and performance*. For those writers who have never worked through a plot for a full-length dramatic work before, I highly encourage you to dig into *Magic Plot Cards* once you have fully explored your characters. In Kushner's *Angels in America,* we channel the essence of the prophets' vision, with Kushner's gay revisioning of Joseph Smith's *The Book of Mormon*. In Charlie Kaufman's brilliant *Eternal Sunshine of the Spotless Mind* we find the screenwriting essence of the lacuna or gap to provide a mind-bending "knot" to be untangled in the audience's mind. Kaufman's gentle, human, and yet radical approach to our own fragile understanding of memory unleashes one of film's most haunting tales of lost romance, told with an uncanny quotidian reality and generated by the unbearable pain of a broken heart. Mexican screenwriter Guillermo Arriaga Jordán's partnership with film director Alejandro González Iñárritu has unleashed many internationally acclaimed non-linear films tied to the nature of death, most famously, *Amores Perros,* and in their movie *21 Grams*, we encounter a technique that I would call a triple narrator pastiche that allows a dreamlike filtering of the stories of three intertwined individuals to be unveiled in a manner that forces its audience to rethink all their presumptions even as they make sense of a unique world tied to the unmasking of the human soul at the limits of mortality.

By the time we arrive at Chapter 8, "The Snap of the Heartstring – Symbolism and Romanticism," we have experimented with many of the classic nonlinear techniques that may be slipped into traditional narratives to encourage audience members to dig deeper into the character. In Anton Chekhov's *The Cherry Orchard* we are whisked into the realm of symbolist traditions, that heralded a sea change in complexity in how we perceive character in drama. Chekhov, the dramatic master of character complexity, uses a single strange moment, a snapping string, to unveil the heartbreak and loss at the center of his play. With José Rivera's *Cloud Tectonics,* there is an entire world located within the nature of time, tied deeply to the impossible logic of Rivera's own brand of Latinx magic realism which resonates with the profoundly mystic Catholic resonances of Santeria and its noumenal-based romanticism. Moving to film, we dig into the essence of nuclear horror in Marguerite Duras' *Hiroshima Mon Amour* which shudders with the uncanny and the grotesque as its European and Asian lovers embrace even while they slip into their shared horrific memories of post-WWII trauma. In so doing, Duras reveals the depth of how profoundly the second world war transformed a generation – and reveals the power of an inexorable, unending voice-over, and a scene that never ends.

Continuing with some of the classics of non-linear technique in Chapter 9, "Realms of Theatricality – Surrealism and Waking Dreams," we will unpack the profound experimentalism of Thornton Wilder's dream-like vision of America's early twentieth century past in his heartbreaking, lovely *Pullman Car Hiawatha* – a play I almost always read out loud with my classes because it inevitably makes me cry. Because of the *Saturday Evening Post* homespun nature of Wilder's profoundly important play, *Our Town*, we often forget that he was the dark master of an extraordinary oneiric approach to theatricality, using just tables, chairs, and a shaman-like stage manager, that is at once profoundly simple and mind-bogglingly complex. He is matched with filmmaker David Lynch, whose weird rabbit-hole surrealism has a similarly deceivingly unpretentious quality that turns reality into a place filled with strange black holes into which characters disappear at the drop of a coin. In our exploration of his *Mulholland Drive,* we'll explore how Lynch transforms a slamming, slippery, and ugly ungluing of a profoundly disturbed actress's deep dive into madness and self-destruction into mercilessly muck-racking exposé of the cult of Hollywood's movie-making magic.

To my mind one cannot explore Thornton Wilder without immediately looking at how his post-modern progeny, Sarah Ruhl, has expanded on his gently insistent subversion of Americana. This we do in Chapter 10, "Inside Out – The Expressionism of Dreaming." To my mind Ruhl is the inheritor of his tender, soft-touch radicalism and so in Chapter 10 we'll explore another classic non-linear technique, expressionism, which employs the deep dream tool of peering through the twisted vision of the dreamer who can't seem to escape their own nightmare. In Sarah Ruhl's *Eurydice*, we once again encounter myth as a non-linear tool, but this time using a relentlessly feminist rethinking of the myth of Eurydice. In this chapter the subversively simple notion of rethinking an ancient myth by switching the focus onto the woman's point of view becomes tantamount to an entire new way of writing drama. Expanding upon this neo-feminist technique, in Karen Moncrieff's film script for *The Dead Girl,* we are forced to experience how multiple women have been torn away from their personal realities by the death of their murdered daughter, friend, lover – and working from the corpse back in time, we experience the sudden stubborn changes in their lives as they are transformed forever by their deep relationship with the eponymous dead girl.

In Chapter 11, "Epic Theatre and The Lucid Dream," we explore another of the classic non-linear approaches, tied to expressionism, which is Epic theatre, and which is itself an expansion of Shakepeare's own tried and true non-linear device, the play within the play – or what is known as "metadrama" – drama which is aware of itself as drama. In terms of dreamwork, this technique ties deeply and directly into the fascinating and rapidly expanding realm of lucid dreaming – dreaming where the dreamer not only *knows* they are dreaming, but actively engages in the *shaping* of their dream reality. In Chapter 11, "Epic Theatre and The Lucid Dream," we explore how metadrama and meta-cinema are closely tied by feasting on their essences in Bertolt Brecht's fascinating musical collaboration with Kurt Weill, *The Threepenny Opera* and Lucy Alibar's extraordinary *Beasts of the Southern Wild* – both of these works expand the range of non-linear technique by fracturing the empathetic nature of dramatic engagement and instead force audiences to acknowledge their own participation in the theatrical fantasy by awakening their lucid dreaming selves within the narrative and raising the question – what would I do in the shoes of the protagonist? The strangeness of these two works of drama, for stage and screen, comes from the insistence that one engages choice rather than empathy in the process of making narrative sense.

One of most important voices in non-linear dramatic technique was an Italian dramatist, Luigi Pirandello, who forced his audiences to understand that their notion of reality was painfully subjective and in fact within the world of drama he essentially created the postmodern notion of the unreliable narrator, and so in Chapter 12, "Postmodernist Worlds of Slippage," we fully investigate Pirandello's *It Is So! (If you Think so)* which takes one story and twists it through an excruciatingly detailed balancing act of twinning narratives that bounces its audience back and forth over the revelations about the mysterious Giulia Ponza between her heartbroken husband, Signor Ponza, and his relentlessly truth-driven mother-in-law, Signora Frola. This is paired with the extraordinary film adaptation of John Cheever's *The Swimmer* by Eleanor Perry in which its central character, Neddy Merrill, swims his way through a lush Westchester landscape, moving from suburban pool to suburban pool, as his privileged sunny WASP existence is twisted and morphed into dark reflection of his truly awful inward reality, and brilliance of Perry's writing is reflected in how horrifyingly banal Neddy Merrill's slipping descent into gothic horror becomes.

With Chapter 13, "The Absurdist Nightmare and the Dramatic Wet Dream," we move into the final chapters of the book which focus on absurdist technique, which to my mind makes some of the most radical departures from realism into the world of dream. For me, the absurdist movement is forever tied to what I consider to be a reaction to horrors of World War II and Nazism, when all the institutions of European humanity – the church, the state, and fundamental nature of a humane society – descended into the primeval darkness of the Holocaust. At base of absurdism was the essential distrust of language twisted and corrupted by Joseph Goebbels' German Nazi propaganda machine during the war as well by the double-speak of Stalinist communism as the Iron Curtain clamped down throughout Eastern Europe at the war's end. European absurdist theatre encapsulated the privations, violence, rationing, and human loss in World War II's aftermath, as each country slowly recovered in the late 1940s and into the 1950s from the bombings and carnage in a lingering hellscape of crime, hunger, sickness, and loss of critical infrastructure. This chapter begins with a focus on Eugène Ionesco's wildly funny yet utterly heartbreaking *The Bald Soprano*, which extends Bert State's notion of the dramatic dream, a dream in which the ordinary devolves into the deepest trenches of irrationality ending with a nonsensical utterance of nothing but vowels. Ionesco was one of the more important influences on my writing this current book, because of his reliance, particularly in his later plays, including *Journeys Amongst the Dead* and *Man with Bags,* on the use of dreams to create his drama. Chapter 13 also digs deeply into Samuel Beckett's short script *Play,* which dramatizes how far people may find themselves horrifically subjugated and still want to carry on, defiantly maintaining even the tiniest semblance of humanity. Beckett's minimalist technique is built on structure of subtraction – how much can you take away from a human being and still have them want to survive? The chapter ends with an exploration of Quentin Tarantino's film *Pulp Fiction* and his own single-mindedly bloody, brutal and extremely funny vision of absurdity, tied to Tarantino's incredible love and knowledge of film and filmmaking, subverting and parodying genre into a kind of club with which to beat the cliché out of film noir.

With Chapter 14, "The Breathing of a Play: Music and Ritualized Sacrifice" I explore the work of my personal mentor, Edward Albee, and his own relentless and terrifying form of distinctly American Absurdism, built the deep ritualized form of Ancient Greek religious sacrifice that informs his utterly mysterious *Tiny Alice* and really, all his plays. Using ritualized sacrifice, Albee invests a kind of dissonant structure to drama, using the punctuation of dialogue as a form of musical notation, providing dramatists with entire new tools with which to build dramatic action. We take that notion of dramatized sacrifice a step farther with Agnès Varda's *Vagabond,* in which an enigmatic young woman, Mona Bergeron, aimlessly wanders the French countryside, culling vines, barely surviving hand to mouth, only to die in a strange Dionysiac frenzy that calls forth the death of Pentheus in Euripides *The Bacchae.* Once again using the classic non-linear technique of beginning with a corpse in a ditch, Varda, using her signature non-linear technique of flashback-driven cinécriture, finds a distinctly fractured manner to get at Mona's inexplicable desire to descend from the quotidian life of a Parisian office worker into complete and utter homelessness and death.

In Chapter 15, "Comedy Shock: Rhythms of Menace and Joy," I focus on three unique absurdist dramatists who derive the strength of their nonlinear technique from the brutality of their comedy. Key to this chapter is Harold Pinter's *The Birthday Party,* and we delve into his masterful depiction of a man, Stanley, driven mad by two ominous yet utterly clownish thugs, Goldberg and McCann, who insist upon his having a birthday party Stanley does not want. In moments banal and serene, Pinter derives his power from his ability to switch dramatic from the quotidian instantly into stultifying terror. In Irene Fornes' *Conduct of Life*, Fornes' extraordinary ability to make language itself strange, detached, and ironic helps to dramatize the rise of petty Latin American thug into a monster as she uses a kind of twisting, senseless domestic violence to flow his bizarre and appalling transformation. The chapter ends with Jean-Luc Godard's astonishingly ruthless and extremely funny film *Weekend*, in which we follow a stunningly heartless and violent couple, Roland and Corinne Durand, as they each connive their family inheritance from Corinne's dying father while plotting to murder each other, and simultaneously harboring a secret lover. This French New Wave film is perhaps emblematic of Godard's famous quote, about non-linear narrative, "I agree that a film should have a beginning, a middle and an end but not necessarily in that order," and provides the perfect non-ending to our exploration of dreamwrighting technique.

The last chapter of the book and its conclusion, "The work of a DreamWright," we take a moment to pause and think about where we have been in the non-traditional, non-linear world of dreamwork for dramatic writing – and our own evolving technique. One clear message I hope I offer, is that your own way of exploring your dreams, both at night and during your waking hours, is wholly your own business, and that I offer all of these other writers' essences as a way of extending that technique in a manner that is uniquely your own. There is a vast array of non-linear technique awaiting you, and its history dates back through time to the earliest forms of storytelling dating back to the Sanskrit and Vedic traditions of the Mahabharata and its use of flashback. I encourage you to read all of these plays and screenplays, and then if you try the essence exercises I have created, feel free to use what is useful to you, and discard the rest – it is your dreamwork that matters!

Finally, I use all the material in this book to teach my advanced courses in dramatic writing (both playwriting and screenwriting) at the University of Missouri and have for many years. However, even if you are just starting out, I hope that you'll find many of the exercises useful, especially the initial dreamwork for dramatic writing workshop, and perhaps even a game-changer as you conceive of your dramatic ideas, characters, plotting, and technique. I have seen my students transform their writing with these exercises, and suddenly win awards with their work, after years of struggling to find their own voice. So, let's dive in, and allow some old hands at the dream ranch, August Strindberg, and Orson Welles, lead the way to help us discover our own non-linear, non-traditional voices.

CHAPTER 2

Structure of the Dreamwork, Myth, Ceremony, and Ritual

August Strindberg's Dream Play *and Orson Welles* Citizen Kane

In this chapter, we'll learn how to develop ways of bringing dream elements to your scripts using both ancient and contemporary myth & folklore while using the structure of ritual and ceremony to provide structure. In the process we'll be exploring two great dramatists who uniquely transformed the landscape of drama on stage and on film – August Strindberg, the nineteenth-century Swedish playwright of *The Dream* Play, and father of expressionism in the theatre who essentially created the notion of the dream play itself, and so deserves primary mention in this book; and the seminal work of American director, performer, and screenwriter Orson Welles, whose unique, moody, non-linear work in his *Citizen Kane* remains fresh, innovative, and cutting edge even after more than 80 years. Both are key figures in non-linear, dream-based technique at the early part of the twentieth century who were highly influential on later dramatists of the stage and screen. While these writers (and in the case of Welles, he was also an amazing magician!) may seem to make odd bedfellows, each brought a unique, expressionistic highly ritualized dream technique to their nonlinear dramatic writing, and both used ceremony and myth-making to create their famous artworks.

1 *A Dream Play*: August Strindberg's Growing Castle of Suffering

In the case of Strindberg's *A Dream Play,* we follow the adventures of Agnes, the Daughter of Indra, originally played by Strindberg's actress wife, Harriet Bosse, as she descends to the earth to witness the suffering of man. Strindberg based the structure of his play upon his own interpretation of Hindu and Buddhist beliefs, most of which he taught himself as he learned Chinese and Japanese. Strindberg also studied alchemy in Paris, a strange kind of metaphysics to gain control over the atoms of metals with the goal of being able to transform them, and so his play used a blend of this technique along with the rituals of Eastern thought and Theosophy. If this sounds strange to us now, it was not very different from the New Age philosophies of our present time, and in these occult mysteries, Strindberg was able to find structure and meaning for his art.

The Daughter of Indra, the central Hindu figure in his play is a Christ-like figure who is bent upon learning the nature of suffering in humanity, and the structure of *A Dream Play* is built around the various "stations" of suffering she encounters. Built in fourteen scenes, Agnes, the Daughter of Indra, charged by Indra to enter a world of suffering, moves from one weird location to the next, beginning with the "growing castle" and moving through various realms of both domesticity and the work day world, encountering with forty archetypal figures, the Lawyer, the Officer, the Teacher, the Portress, etc., enduring a miserable marriage at one point, moving through life in order to experience the full range of human suffering. Locations shift and transform into other locations, including the aforementioned castle, a theatre, a lawyer's office, Fingal's cave (a famous Scottish lair), with each location becoming a kind of "station of the cross" in Agnes's attempt to understand human suffering.

The nature of dream logic in playwriting was most famously elucidated by August Strindberg in his "Preliminary Note to A Dream Play" who offers his own expressionistic essences for the phenomenon of the dream play structure:

1. A dream play imitates "the incoherent but ostensibly logical."
2. "Anything can happen, everything is possible and probable."
3. "Time and space do not exist."
4. "Insignificant real events" provide the "background" and these events are woven into "new patterns;"
5. Characters are malleable: they "split, double, multiply, dissolve, condense, float apart, coalesce."
6. One mind stands over all: "the mind of the dreamer" and for this dreamer there are "no secrets, no inconsistencies, no scruples, no laws."[1]

Strindberg's distillation of the nature of the dream play provides useful guidelines that resonate beautifully for the exercises that follow. His *Dream Play* was the eldritch result of his "inferno" crisis, occurring in 1891 after Strindberg moved to Berlin following his divorce to Siri von Essen, where he was briefly married to the Austrian journalist Frida Uhl. He and Uhl had a daughter but separated quickly, and Strindberg moved to Paris. There he entered a period of his life in which he was tormented by invisible enemies and hallucinations, his infamous Inferno crisis. Written in 1901, *A Dream Play* seemed to have been created out of Strindberg's tremendous psychic pain, and yet, it reveals a deep sense of peace and compassion, even as the journey of the play is built on suffering.

---

1   August Strindberg, "Author's Preliminary Note to A Dream Play" in *Dramatic Theory and Criticism: Greeks to Grotowski*, Bernard F. Dukore, ed. Holt, (New York: Rinehart and Winston, Inc., 1974), 575.

Exercise 1: The Coalescing Essence of Strindberg – Dream Play Variations

Useful to these exercises is reading Strindberg's *A Dream Play*. Take notes as you do so, pausing to experience and acknowledge the moments that are bizarre, uncanny, and surreal. Always trust your gut responses to dramatic work – note where the play affects you emotionally. Then try some of the exercises below.

1. Time Mutation: Write a single scene that allows the characters to speed up or slow down the action during its action.
   a. Allow the scene to slip from ancient past to the present to future shock.
   b. The characters shift in costumes, props, and setting as they move through time, continuing a single conversation.
   c. Make sure there is a persistent need or desire that links all the presents, pasts, and futures.
2. Dream logic: Choose an impossible situation based on an evocative image of your choosing – perhaps a famous painting that has always affected you (like Edvard Munch's *The Scream* (1893) or Hieronymus Bosch's *The Garden of Earthly Delights* (1490–1510), or a famous photo, like Dorothea Lange's *Migrant Mother*, (1936) or *The Most Beautiful Suicide* by Robert C. Wiles (Evelyn McHale's death jumping off the Empire State Building)).
   a. Explore your image as if you are the character transformed.
   b. The *where* is a setting or location suggested by the image, but perhaps physically impossible.
   c. The *what* is a desperate but impossible need.
   d. The *when* is the event, perhaps end of the world.
   e. The *how* is tied to *how* you tell the story, perhaps your story will use the shifting associational logic of a dream.
   f. Follow the logic of the world created by the central image carefully, being careful not to break the internal rules you have developed.
3. Character to Characters mutations: Write a scene where characters transform.
   a. Start a scene with two characters.
   b. Then allow the two characters to begin an involved argument – tied perhaps to a desperate, immediate need or desire of one of the two characters.
   c. The second character is opposed to that first character's need.
   d. Allow the two characters morph into multiple characters (based upon a trigger word of some kind), individually at first, then have both characters transform, perhaps they double, growing to four,

then perhaps eight, each pair the product of the original two characters.
e. The transformation may be tied to argument itself.
f. Perhaps grow the pairs to triplets with off-stage voices. Continue the argument.
g. Make sure each character is still attached to the original two characters and voices their original needs in some way.
h. Allow these characters to occasionally disappear and reappear.
i. Allow the characters to return to the single characters.
j. Have them speak as a chorus, at times in unison at times not.

Now you've experimented a bit with Strindberg's own dream technique, how all does this translate into non-linear dramatic writing technique that you can use to explore your characters and write your play? It begins with a challenge – and requires that you create your own ritual or ceremony as the structural spine of your storytelling – and you'll find that as you explore these structures, you'll be also exploring your characters as they are forced to bend and change to live within the realms you are creating. Ritual and Ceremony provide the structure to tell a story – think about how this occurs in everyday life. A ceremony is a dramatic event in and of itself, and a good example of this might be a Passover Seder, which retells the story of the Exodus Ceremony over a meal, or the Catholic Mass which celebrates the supernatural corporeality of Jesus Christ.

A ceremony incorporates symbols from the story and provides a series of steps by which a new understanding of the story or a certain state of mind may be achieved. Rituals are created through monologues & dialogues between the performers and the audience which are enhanced using symbolic objects, spaces, chanting, musical instruments, and dance. While in traditional dramatic structure, there is the basic sonata form of setup, struggle, and solution – ritual and ceremony offer an alternative structure. Sonata structure can be translated into a "hook" at the beginning, a high moment before intermission, a climax a few pages before the end of the second act, and a striking image at the end of the play. However, the shaping of the play can be also based upon the steps and arc of a ritual or ceremony, in other words, upon a *structural image* which is a shaping of the play that ties powerfully into an emotional image of the ritual or ceremony but has a purely structural effect on the story. We'll experiment with several kinds of ritual and ceremony as we move through the book.

Bear in mind that while you're experimenting here, allowing the story you are creating to come up against a structure that may be alien to it – it never hurts to find a strong connection between the story you are telling and the dramatic structure you're using to enhance it. You are playing a writing game with yourself, a challenge, to allow the structure to affect your storytelling in a way that will be surprising and unique.

Exercise 2: Exploring Ritual and Ceremony to Reveal a Dramatic Action

Method: Write a basic story (i.e., a love tryst, revenge story, mystery play). Keep it to a few paragraphs or simply outline it and consider using your *dream cache* to create it.

Write out a plot treatment of that story, but consider building the story using the form of a ritual to tell it:

a. Religious Ceremonies and Everyday Rituals – Consider:
   – A religious service: a mass, exorcism, baptism, wedding.
   – A social, legal, or business situation: court case, music lesson, geometry class, an interview, a firing.
   – A seasonal ritual: harvest, summer and winter solstice, May day, Midsummer's Night Eve, Twelfth night.
   – A holiday or family or life ritual: Christmas, Thanksgiving, Mother's & Father's Day, Valentine's Day, a graduation, a cousin's club, moving day, a break-up, a marriage or a divorce, moving into new house

b. A structural image to tell the story. Consider:
   – A geometric form, descending spiral, circle, cube, figure eight,
   – A natural form: a waterfall, a rose, a cavern, a balancing rock, a canyon, a river,
   – A physical structure: i.e. a cathedral, a stadium, a baseball diamond, a skyscraper,
   – Physics: particle theory, entropy, a black hole, a worm hole,
   – A musical form: ballad, minuet, sonata, opera, symphony
   – A dance form: a modern dance, a ballet, a jazz combo, or a highly ritualized dance from another culture.

Remember that your *story* may be a series of events that begins far earlier than the events of the play, which is your *plot*, and the *story* may end far later. The basic definition of a *plot* are the events which occur *during your play* or, in other words, the immediate dramatic situation of your drama in the present moment occurring on the stage or in the film you have written. Allowing your plot to flow around these alternative dream structures like water moving around rocks, will change the quality of your story telling – and you may be using a combination of these ritual, ceremony, and structural images to transform your plot into something that is non-linear and non-traditional. Now that you've looked at how ritual and ceremony can affect the structure of your story, let's go a bit deeper into where those rituals and ceremonies come from – and reveal yet other tools for building your oneiric dramatic writing technique.

While it's important to always find structures that are organic to you, the story you want to tell, and ultimately, the dreams you want to share in your drama, there is a rich supply of dreamwork that has come down to us in the form of myth, stories, and biblical parables. All these elements are at the beck and call of your imagination. Parallels between these archetypal stories already exist in your consciousness as part of the collective quality of culture flowing through your mind. Carl Jung wrote extensively of the "collective unconscious" and while that kind of positivist and unblinking acceptance of broadly suggested archetypes could be easily questioned as the notions of the white, privileged, male mind, there is quite a bit of truth that story generation can be gleaned from the ancient myths and stories coming from a diverse multitude of cultures, which we have been exposed to in our new global, digital hive mind.

Exercise 3: A Play Built on the Mythic

Many stories and myths are repeated in various cultures and become archetypal in both structure and meaning. These stories are very powerful means to creating a ceremony which will enhance a play script. Your plot can wrap around the structure of a myth or fairy tale, or even an urban legend, adapting to it, allowing the myth to flow through and become a counter current in your play. Examples of categories of myths are:

– Creation Myths	– Dragons & Serpents
– Star Lore & Astrology	– Aliens/UFOs
– Floods & Disasters	– Crones & Sages
– Earth Goddesses & Gods	– Trees & Plant Lore
– Sky Goddesses & Gods	– Tricksters
– Fairy Tales/Urban Legends	– Shamanism

As you consider working with myths, look first at the ancient stories tied to your own family, religious, ethnic, or cultural background – go deep – and look also for family stories that verge on the mythic, but then consider myths, folk stories, and even bizarre internet memes and urban legends that come from the broader swath of the culture you grew up with. Consider also urban myths and legends that have grown out of popular culture – or even a town legend, something that people still talk about where you are from.

Bear in mind that if you are going to explore and borrow from the cultures from backgrounds other than your own, just be aware that you'll need to do serious research before plucking your ideas. Working with myths from other cultures comes perilously close to exploitation – which you certainly don't want to do. However, you can and should celebrate diversity in your writing, and so, do your homework, and consider your own personal connection to the myths and folklore of other cultures before you incorporate them into your own work. Be particularly careful with material from indigenous peoples (unless, of course, you have that background) and be sensitive to how your work engages with those specific myths and folklore. Consider contacting and collaborating with those who share that background and heritage.

Another source of ritual theatre material is the Bible. In Jean Claude van Itallie's *The Serpent* (1968), the Open Theatre created a stunning piece of theatre based upon the story of Genesis. Jean Claude van Itallie, the off-off-Broadway playwright who created *The Serpent*, wrote a wonderful text on playwriting, *The Playwright's Workbook*, and was highly influential, most famously on Tony Kushner, and his play *The Serpent*, as performed by the Open Theatre, had a profound effect on me as a writer. Interspersed with the story of Genesis, using ensemble performance techniques, *The Serpent* brilliantly comingles ancient biblical scenes of creation with horrific moments from the modern tragedy of the Kennedy and MLK assassinations. The scriptural stories are at times subverted, enhanced, distorted, and made relevant by their mixture with scenes from contemporary life.

Exercise 4: Creating a Ritual Play from the Bible

Create a ritual using the original biblical stories listed below (or a biblical story of your choosing) and intersperse it with scenes from an event from a contemporary life, a personal story, or even a playscript one which you are currently working. Some suggestions for stories are:

- Adam & Eve
- Jonah and the Whale
- Abraham & Issac
- Jacob and Esau
- David & Goliath
- Noah's Ark/The Great Flood
- Joseph and his coat of many colors
- The Story of Esther
- Samson & Delilah
- The Exodus

Ceremony: Now that you have your myth, the next step is developing your ceremony! Think about its guiding principles and intent. A good example to borrow from is the Catholic Mass, which has distinct prayers and liturgy, physical rituals, sacred objects, and incorporates the shape and stations of the cathedral. Consider these elements as you create your ceremony:
- What kind of time sequence will it follow, how will you divide up its segments? What is the order of events? How does it start?
- Is it a ceremony to someone/thing or tied to some historic/mythical event?
- What is the language, poetry, liturgy for the ritual?
- How formal is the process?
- Who leads the ritual and how?
- Kind and placement of ritual objects?
- What are the levels of participants, and how should they behave and respond?
- What is the space for the ritual – define each location and how it is used?
- How do you establish order and set a meditative tone?
- Order of events of ritual: How do we move from Beginning to Middle and finally to End? How is the ceremony to be ordered – perhaps based on the events of the myth?

Contemporary Drama Element – Once the ceremony has been established, how can you disrupt it or blend with it, the scenes from a play or contemporary event and/or current issue that will at once complement the ceremony and comment upon it? When writing the Drama consider these theatrical elements:
- Actors in the scene are the celebrants of the ceremony. They freely mutate between ceremony and drama with no seams.
- The central conflict of the drama should touch upon the central idea of the myth/biblical story presented.
- Perhaps there is a controversy among the characters performing the ceremony; some disagreement over how the ritual should be performed.
- Consider using a major political or social event as part of the story, i.e. if the ritual uses Noah's Ark (or another flood myth), perhaps the drama could be about a recent flooding or a local flood in the area, due to global warming.

Perhaps the Drama could be contained within the Ceremony, or the Ceremony contained with the Drama. In creating your piece, decide where your story lies – perhaps retelling the myth is strong enough alone – or perhaps the ritual you created around the myth has taken on a life of its own, and that will become the focus of your work. In either case, your final play should embrace elements of both, with either the original drama, the myth, or the ceremony dominating specific moments.

Taking a moment to go back to *The Serpent*. You should try to watch the Youtube video selection of the Open Theatre production, directed by Joseph Chaikin and consider how you might pair a contemporary subject in your play with a mythic one. After you watch the video, you'll find below another exercise that I'd suggest – *Pick-up/Persephone*, which looks at an everyday ritual – the pick-up at a bar, and the ancient myth of Persephone and Hades.

Exercise 5: A Ritual Play – Mixing the Mythic & Contemporary: Pick Up/Persephone

About The Myth of Kore/Persephone

In Greek myth, Kore is the original name of the young maiden of spring, daughter of Zeus and Demeter. Zeus promised Kore to his brother, Hades, without telling her mother. After Hades kidnapped her and brought her to the underworld, she was known as Persephone, Queen of the Dead. According to some versions of the myth, Kore strayed too far from her companions, enticed by a bloom of narcissus. In his horrific chariot pulled by coal-black horses, Hades rose through a chasm in the earth, grabbed Kore by the wrist, and sat her next to him, and descended into the Underworld. Her mother, Demeter, wandered the earth for a very long time looking for her daughter until she came to the sun, and he told her what happened. Demeter then went to Zeus who declared that Persephone be returned to her mother – only if she hadn't tasted the food of the dead. But Kore had eaten some pomegranate seeds, so she could only return to her mother for two thirds of the year and spent the other third at Hades side as his wife. While Kore remained in the Underworld, her mother Demeter pined and forgot about the world, as it slid into the Winter of cold and ice; once she returned to her mother, Spring came and the earth was once again, verdant, green, and abundant.

While the myth explains the seasons, the students in my class were interested in both the social mores and political overtones of the Ritual of the Pick-Up – which they decided to pair with the first part of the story of Hades and Persephone – and in the process found a different kind of resonance – is there aggression in the whole notion of the Pick-Up and the infamous Pick-Up Line? Does this aggression point to a much darker interaction between the young man and woman in our scenario – and how did that tie into the darkness surrounding the Myth of Persephone and the politics of dating? We wanted to explore all of that, so we created two sets of story points/events and had two sets of actors improvise simultaneously with both – allowing them to overhear and improvise on each other's cues.

Pick Up/Persephone – Improvisation/Ritual

RITUAL	MYTH
Ceremony of the Pick-Up	Kore/Persephone/Prosperpine
1. The Look	1. Persephone wanders too far from her companions, falls in love with the flower Narcissus
2. The Walk Toward Each Other	
3. The Line	2. Hades appears in his chariot
4. The Response to the Line	3. Persephone succumbs to Hades
	4. Persephone enters Tartarus
5. The Ordering of Drinks	5. Hades seduces Persephone to eat the seed of the Pomegranate
6. The Dance	
7. The Conversation of the Dance	6. Persephone falls in Love with Hades
	7. Zeus demands Persephone return to Demeter
8. The End of the Dance	8. Hades demands she stay
9. The Second Drink	9. Zeus decides to allow Persephone to live in both worlds
10. The Exit	
	10. Persephone leaves Hades

1. Breaking out the Contemporary Scene: We first created our ritual/ceremony of "the Pick-Up" noting some of the everyday steps of what seems to happen when two strangers meet in a bar. Each moment of the ritual received a number, a brief title, and a description of the action.
2. Itemizing Mythic Events: Then we created a series of similarly numbered events for the part of the myth we wanted to ritualize – which also had numbers, titles, and descriptions.
3. Improvisation: For each moment, we had our actors improvise and then "freeze" at what we felt was an iconic moment. We listed what those freeze moments looked like and created a kind of frozen image in our minds, so that we could come back to those freezes in a kind of "essence" of those dramatic moments.
4. Dialogue: We distilled dialogue from each of our frozen essence moments – so that these became a kind of poetic outburst from the actors – not necessarily making literal sense but having an emotional truth.
5. Dancing through Essence: We then had the actors play through both the Contemporary and Mythic elements separately – with the Man and the

Woman moving from one frozen essence moment to another – creating a kind of physical abstraction of the story and adding vocalizations from our distilled dialogue.
6. Bringing it all together: Finally, we started to weave the two "dance-dramas" together – creating a kind of dream dance drama – with the increasing abstraction of the two realms of contemporary and myth moving in and out of each other in a combined, unified artwork – and it was a mesmerizing thing to watch – and suddenly all of our questions about both the Pick-Up and the story of Persephone began to have some intriguing answers.

2 Orson Welles and the Flashback Dream Structure

Moving from Strindberg's rather rarefied, expressionist world to the black and white realm of Orson Welles' *Citizen Kane*, it is important to note that both of these artists were innovators whose work took the art forms of theatre and film into new directions, highly influenced by myth. For Strindberg, this was tied to the Hindu divinity of the Daughter of Indra, but for Orson Welles, it was the myth of quintessential American Dream as personified in the great capitalist, William Randolph Hearst. Key to both writers is their interest in the subjective experience of their protagonists – working from an expressionist viewpoint – that is, the twisted, subjective view of a protagonist crippled by broken, warped, and perverted society. Working closely with Herman J. Mankiewicz, Welles built his non-linear *Citizen Kane* from his years of radio theatre working from "the first person singular" (which became the title of his radio series). Welles starts *Citizen Kane* at its ending, insistently non-linear, telling the story *backwards*, turning the film into a subjective, twisted, and highly ritualized journalistic investigation of Charles Foster Kane's final word, "rosebud." What follows then is the journey of an anonymous reporter, Jerry Thompson, interviewing the various characters from Kane's life, some of whom, clearly opinionated about who Kane really was, are unreliable in their storytelling. The film narrative, following Kane's life backwards expressionistically, has a kind of slippage, dreamlike and a bit dicey. Yet even if it's nearly impossible to get anyone to say who Kane really was, his lonely, sad story of ambition, fame, and finally, loss, slips through, and Welles' process of filmic storytelling becomes a powerful and still revelatory nonlinear, storytelling paradigm.

What is key to understand is Welle's notion of the subjective camera. This was his idea of the camera that sees the world of the film from within the twisted mind of the protagonist – and so, like a dream, it is a realm that unfolds guided by the single-minded desire of the dreamer. Because of this, much of film has an oddly angled, chiaroscuro, yet diamond-clear quality. One feels that the world of the film is haunted by each narrator's particular prejudice toward Kane, each one lending a kind of obscured facet of Kane's life, even while the ritual structure of the investigative reporter's drive to tell Kane's story – and get at the mystery of "rosebud" – powers us through the film. In other words, a *Citizen Kane* becomes a sacramental exploration of a capitalistic "great man" in which investigative journalism is transformed into a ceremony of interrogations, with each figure in Kane's life, the Benefactor (Thatcher), the Partner (Bernstein), the Friend (Leland) the Lover (Susan Alexander), the Butler (Raymond) providing one more key to the mystery of Kane's final word.

What follows then is a series of exercises that explore the essence of Welle's classic nonlinear, dream storytelling strategy, and it shadows closely Strindberg's own expressionistic station drama – as the locations and realms that Thompson's investigation explores – Thatcher's Library, Bernstein's office, Leland's Nursing Home, Susan Alexander at the El Rancho Nightclub, and Raymond at Kane's strange, dreamlike estate, Xanadu, provide a warped, distorted landscape. We will start, however, with a single physical object of great meaning to your central character – in *Citizen Kane*, this is Kane's sled, Rosebud. And don't forget, start from the ending – like any great mystery, the story often starts with an exquisite corpse, and in classic non-linear fashion moves *backwards* to the truth.

Exercise 6: The Rosebud Exercise – The Jigsaw Shard of Citizen Kane

If you are exploring characters in a film of your creation, one of the important exercises in this book is to write a series of scenes and monologues based on the dreams your characters have – and creating those dreams using elements from separate *dream caches* for each character. Key to all this work is the idea of a *dream cache* from which you can extract creative clues. In this exercise, it is going to be assumed that you have already worked on Step 5 – Character Dreams – Exploring the world inside your Character.

- Step 1 – *Identify the field of objects* – If you have done so, gather three of the five dream elements you have already identified as emotionally important to the central character in your film. Bear in mind that you are investigating these things to find an object with which to *start* your film, tied to your character's final moments of life – before they become the *corpse*. Spend some

time investigating each of these objects and allow your character to discuss the objects with all five senses in a monologue directed to you, specifically.
- Step 2 – *Isolate the most important object* – Of the three objects that you have whittled down from the first five, choose a single object, the most important object, that your character has not already explored in a dream. Have your character tell you the story of that object's emotional importance to you, using all five senses.
- Step 3 – *The Object – Originating Scene* – write a scene, using what your character has already told you about the object which may be, in fact, the origin story for the object – incorporate as many characters from your film in this scene as you can. And bear in mind they may have very false information about that object and its importance, and the information they have will be unreliable, especially because *your central character may have lied to them about the object* (though *never* to you the writer).
- Step 4 – *The Object – Four Points of View* – write four scenes, one from the beginning of your plot, two from the center struggle of your plot, and one from the end of the plot that involve the object and tie into its origin story. You should try to incorporate as many characters from your film as you can in these scenes, but each scene should come from the different point of view of four of the most important characters of your drama, but none of them the protagonist.
- Step 5 – *The Object – Protagonist's View* – Write a final scene about the object from the point of view of your protagonist and incorporate that object in the final moments of your character's life. But now go back and *start* your drama *here*.
- Step 6 – *The Object – The Resolution* – Think about what the drama will say in its resolution, keeping in mind that the object is key. How does that resolution of that object's meaning tie into your central character's final emotional response in your audience? How is it obscured in the end? And consider all the other objects your character discussed – how to they tie into that most central object? Write the final scene of your film narrative – bearing in mind that the truth about this object may never be known to any other character in the film but may be clear to the audience (though not spelled out).

One of the major structure devices of Welle's *Citizen Kane* is the role of the reporter/ investigator hunting for the one true interpretation of Kane's life. Instead of finding the truth, we are left with many different fractured truths of a highly mediated personality. Kane's identity is as fractured as the depiction of him in the Hall of Mirrors in Xanadu. Kane becomes an image in multiplication, absorbed by his own empire of corporatized meanings, haunted by not only his failings and those who are left behind, but also his uncanny successes, overabundant, excessive, and ultimately spoiled. Jerry Thompson, the reporter, becomes a stark silhouette against the figure of Kane; he is our own anonymous desire to know, our unfettered curiosity, itself stained by American voyeurism, prurience, intrusiveness, and a collective if seedy schadenfreude.

Exercise 7: The Investigator/Detective – The Inner Landscape of Kane

In this exercise you'll establish a character who may or who may not inhabit the world of your drama – this character will be the Investigator, who, like Jerry Thompson, will be an anonymous figure, digging deeper and deeper into background of your central character. Here the structure will be built on dream settings that grow out of the settings you unpacked from your character dreams exercise for your central character, and again, we'll start from the end and work back toward the beginning.

Step 1 – *Choose your Investigator* – Digging into your central character's dream cache, find a dream element to inspire your Investigator – this may be a dream element wholly unrelated to an actual person, but inspires you enough to create a character who is very, very curious about your central character. Then choose another dream element that provides a reason why your Investigator needs to investigate your central character. Allow the world of Noir to affect you – and bear in mind that your Investigator can be highly flawed, strange, difficult, and not necessarily a genius. They *should* have, however, an uncontrollable need to investigate your central character.

Step 2 – *Unmasking the Obvious* – Choose four to five settings tied to your central character's dreams – after first creating a *dream cache* for your character. Have your central character describe these settings using all five senses and tie each setting to a period in their life – and to a specific person (or persons) in their life (choose those characters from your central character's *dream cache*). In each setting, allow the description to include a deeper description of the setting and the person, unmasking some secret aspect of their relationship to your central character. Make sure the characters being queried react personally and specifically to the detective or reporter investigating – they may not like all these questions and may or may not be cooperative.

Step 2 – *The Spectral Interview* – Now allow your detective to go to work interviewing each of the four to five persons in your central character's life, in the locations your central character has given you. Allow the interview to be straightforward, but make sure the detective and the witness interacts with their location in specific ways during the interview – and don't be afraid for the

STRUCTURE OF THE DREAMWORK, MYTH, CEREMONY, AND RITUAL   67

interview to have aspects of it that are uncanny or strange. For the interview location for example, you might have the interview take place over lunch, or a happy hour, or a sporting event, or even from the grave. In the interview, that witness's specific memory of interacting with your central character is revealed; it is a memory that haunts the witness for either good or bad reasons. Is there something very wrong in this world? – something broken, twisted, or just bizarre? Don't back away from that!

Step 3 – *The Memory Scenes* – The next scene involves an interaction between the central character and each witness, mentioned in the memory of the witness. It takes place in either the actual location of the interview, or in a new location – the scenes should somehow be linked – emotionally, symbolically, associatively, so that each scene provides a key into the central character. Find a linking moment or event tied to each witness that provides the ideal reason and setting for the scene you want to write between central character and witness.

Step 4 – *The Fireplace Revelation* – The detective brings together all the witnesses he has interviewed, revealing the memory scenes to them all. Write this scene and include their reactions to each other's memories – rediscover the link that pulls all the characters and locations together. Think of this as the final scene in a detective drama, when the detective gathers the suspects into one room, and reveals to all who the actual murderer is.

Step 5 – *The Dreamer Awakens* – The detective returns to the central character who may be alive or dead at this point – and in one of the locations where the interviews took place – or in another location entirely. The detective reveals all that they have discovered to the central character – who can deny, affirm, or remain silent – but the central character does have a clear emotional reaction to what the detective has revealed.

Finally, there is one last essence of Welle's *Citizen Kane* that should be explored in the dreamwork of your dramatic experimentations, and that is tied to the obscenity of the massive size of Charles Foster Kane's art collection, which is revealed at the end of the film. The sheer magnitude of Kane's obsessive need to hoard masterpieces provides its own structure that begs one last exercise – which brings together the objects, locations, and people in a kind of museum of the soul of your central character.

Exercise 8: The Cryptic Museum – The Collection of Crises

In this exercise inspired by Kane's crated collection of artworks, you'll pull together series of dioramas that will serve as the medieval theatre mansions or perhaps dioramas of your central character's world – there will be four to five of these mansions, with your detective moving from one to the next gathering information that pulls together everything you have discovered about your characters.

Step 1 – Museum of Objects – in this step, your detective walks through a series of four to five empty diorama cases, joined by the central character – who places an object in each case from Exercise 6, The Rosebud Exercise.

Step 2 – The Flowering of Setting – now the central character, with the aid of the detective, puts the scenic elements of each of the dioramas in place, assisted by the characters in Exercise 7, The Investigator/Detective Exercise, the settings may or may not be from the memory scenes in that exercise, but should include an aspect of the interview location.

Step 3 – Character Inhabitation – all the characters from the previous scenes now inhabit their specific dioramas – and move into a frozen state.

Step 4 – Fragmenting the protagonist – With a question from the Detective, the Protagonist steps into each diorama, and a scene ensues – these are different scenes from Exercise 7, but they are related to those scenes – perhaps at a different time of the characters' lives. Each scene ends with a question, as the protagonist transforms, moving from one diorama to the next.

Step 5 – Switching Personas – The characters then scramble and move into each other's locations – and inhabit those worlds as best as they can – and once again, a scene ensues in this new location between the characters and the protagonist – with new questions from the detective to start each scene.

Step 6 – Report from the Grave – After the last set of diorama scenes – the detective gives a report to the audience, tying together the clues that they have compiled – into a final post-humous monologue about the Protagonist.

Each of these exercises in this chapter have helped you enter the dreamscape of your protagonist and the other characters of your drama – for you to begin your journey of exploration with them. Using the tools of expressionism, both Strindberg and Welles, used non-linear technique to build interiority of character, fleshing out the realm that most traditional dramatic scripts ignore, or are only able to hint at with linear technique. In the next chapter, we'll go back a bit further in time – all the way back to the Ancient Greek Theatre – which was decidedly non-linear and non-realistic. At the heart of this dreamlike dramatic technique, that most primeval of oneiric drama devices – the Greek chorus!

CHAPTER 3

Ancient Dream Structures: Myths and the Greek Chorus

Sophocles' Oedipus the King, *Paula Vogel's* How I Learned to Drive, *Lanford Wilson's* Book of Days, *and Marcel Camus'* Black Orpheus

In this chapter we'll look at how ancient dream structures from Greek Myth and Drama can provide a useful interface with our own contemporary dramatic storytelling for stage scripts and screenplays – this is particularly true of non-linear, non-traditional technique. We'll be using two stage plays, Paula Vogel's *How I Learned to Drive*, Lanford Wilson's *Book of Days*, and the screenplay of Marcel Camus' *Black Orpheus*, to provide us with insights and essences on now to do this. Digging into the past, our heritage as dream dramatists conflates intriguingly with Ancient Greece and the fundamental notions of Aristotle and his hugely influential *Poetics*, circa 335 BCE. Though we think of Aristotle's *Poetics* as the basis of *traditional* playwriting technique, which is perhaps the opposite of what we're proposing in terms of dream dramaturgy, his work also provides the background for a larger understanding of drama.

1 The Ur-Detective Story: Sophocles *Oedipus Rex* and the Importance of Working Backwards

The *Poetics* has guided the discussion of the writing of drama and specifically, tragedy, for centuries. Sam Smiley's important book *Playwriting: The Structure of Action* is a brilliant distillation of the *Poetics* and provided the structural backbone for playwriting technique and classes for years. And like Aristotle, I'm particularly impressed by Sophocles' one act play, *Oedipus Rex*, which is built on the classic detective structure, working backwards (and in a somewhat non-linear fashion!) from a problem to a solution – with King Oedipus carefully hunting down the criminal who has angered the Gods, and brought a plague upon the City of Thebes. Key to understanding Aristotle's work, however, and his condensation and analysis of *Oedipus* is that it is an inductive process; Aristotle was describing what tragedy *can* be in his *Poetics*, not delimiting what tragedy and thereby, drama, *should* be. In the *Poetics*, Aristotle unmasks and investigates the elements of drama (plot, character, thought, diction, spectacle, and song), and notes what seems to work well, but seeks to *describe* what he found, not *prescribe* how a play *must* be written.

What is so powerful about *Oedipus Rex* for me, however, is not its central character, but its chorus – a multiple performer entity which was a vestigial limb of Greek's evolution from dance and ritual. It is always important to remember that because of the chorus, a Greek tragedy is essentially an offering to the Gods, an extended prayer, and therefore something holy. In a sense, this is true of any dramatic work, but this was specifically true of the Choric Dithyrambs from which the Greek Chorus evolved, as they were tied to the death and resurrection of Dionysus, who was the God of wine, fertility, and theatre. The chorus is also something that grows out of the dreamer, as it is facets of a dream self – fractured, transformed versions of the dreamer, multiplying, and twisting to fit within the associative logic of a dreamer investigating themselves. In the realm of drama, the chorus has numerous functions, and it's important to our conversation to examine those functions here.

1. First the chorus has a *narrative* function – to assist in the telling of the story, the chorus can have a conversation with the protagonist or even itself, determining why the story about the hero must be told, justifying its own existence, challenging and haunting its protagonist as if within the periphery of a dream.
2. The chorus provides *interiority* of character; it can slip and slide in and out of the central character, and even contain multiple characters within itself, which can compartmentalize and step out as separate characters at any time.
3. Working within the dramatic action, the chorus may become a character itself, directly involved as an *antagonist* or as a foil, splitting and transforming as necessary, or the chorus can move to outside the dramatic action, providing commentary as a kind of raisonneur – the reasonable side of the protagonist, perhaps as a stand-in for the playwright, the audience, or the community – attempting to keep the less reasonable side of the protagonist in check.
4. The chorus is also a kind of *ideal spectator*, raising questions about the actions of the protagonist providing both specific commentary, questions, concerns, and warnings as it crystalizes and specifies the experiences of the protagonist, but then also sympathizes with their victims or enemies, and/or providing facts as a range of sympathetic supporters or as the mouthpiece of a crowd of conservative, contrary community members.
5. The chorus *embraces and represents the audience*, drawing it closer to the action of the play, and intensifies the dramatic and emotional experience.

6. The chorus *creates a state of ceremony*, unreality, formality, shifting the landscape, changing the mood through lyricism, rhythm, chanting, and dance.
7. The chorus *has its pulse on the passion of the dramatic action*, as it connects actors and audience in call and response, digging into the questions the audiences want to ask, as well as unifying and pulling together the disparate elements of plot, dance, speech, music and provide the thread between segments and episodes.
8. The chorus *operates as a kind of punctuation on the play*, using elaborate masking, dance, singing, and musical instruments to move the play between ode and episode.

Now it is your opportunity to experiment with a Greek chorus in your dramatic work – whether it is a stage or a screen play, allow a scene of your script to include several characters who provide a choral effect to the drama. At first, these characters may have nothing to do with each other – but allow them to take position in reaction to your protagonist and/or antagonist. They may be henchmen, members of the public, team members, or officemates – but something in the language of the scene transforms them, and they take on the role of the chorus. Bear in mind that acting in unison is but one way to work with a chorus – and in fact, you might find that your chorus works in reaction to each other, rather than in simple unity.

Exercise 1: Oedipus Rex – Chorus Experiments – Language

1. Write a scene with your protagonist seeking something, pursuing a specific, immediate, and urgent need, and involve at least three chorus members, but feel free to use more.
2. The Protagonist should have specific, detailed relationships with each of the choral characters – and each choral character can have a very unique personality and look – or all three may share a unified choral presence; either or both is fine.
3. The choral members can have the following qualities:
    a. Choral members can be individual characters or become one unit. If they are dressed similarly, you might want to have costume pieces that allow them to individualize at times.
    b. Choral members can be antagonistic or an extension of the protagonist.
    c. Choral members can transform, shift their roles with the use of a mask, each taking on a specific role – sharing it at times.

d. Experiment with the chorus, allowing it to drift in and out of choral action.
4. Choral Members can:
   a. Speak in unison, all at once, varying timber, loudness, or devolve into gibberish.
   b. Speak different parts of one sentence, pulling it together.
   c. Repeat certain significant words, certain sounds.
   d. Emphasize specific *sounds* of words in unison.
5. Include chorus participation several times in the scene, as narrators or commentators.
   a. Chorus can become involved.
   b. Chorus can disengage.
   c. Chorus can split, extend, diminish.
6. Speak chorally at least once at significant moments.
   a. Find moments that are integral to the plot.
   b. Choose climatic moments.
   c. Consider using personal moments – attach the chorus to specific characters.
7. Imagine *MASKS* similar in appearance for the chorus. Describe them simply but evocatively. Perhaps the actors mask themselves in the process of transforming into a chorus. Bear in mind the more elaborate the mask, the more specifically that character is defined – the simpler, the more flexibility you have.
   a. Masks also can change, flip, morph. They can be handed around at random, or in specific ways to provide transformational meaning.
   b. Masks provide teams, groupings, soldiers.
   c. Masks create environment, worlds, obstacles.
8. Imagine music, played by chorus members, to emphasize the action and/or provide transitions.
   a. Music can be songs that emphasize the moment in choral fashion.
   b. Music can have lead singers, choral parts.
   c. Music can be instrumental using traditional or found instruments.
   d. Music provides the basis for dance, which gives the chorus an outward physical means to express their innermost feelings.
9. Tableaus – Imagine your characters freezing into a tableau during a scene.
   a. Then, one character vocalizes an emotional state (for example, depressed) and matching it with a physical gesture.
   b. Then the entire group of characters repeat the language and the gesture.

ANCIENT DREAM STRUCTURES: MYTHS AND THE GREEK CHORUS   73

  c. Evolving, another character else will call out a different emotion (for example, triumph) and the group must start chanting that, but slowly evolving the gesture in unison to match the word.
  d. Do this until every character has had the opportunity to flow into the tableau, evolving it into something else, or even allow it to transform into dance.
10. Complete a scene of about 5–10 pages, allowing the piece to come to an ending, but be aware that you can extend the scene with the next exercise:

Exercise 2: Chorus Experiments – Ensemble Movement

In this next exercise, you can begin an entirely new scene, or extend the one you have just written – and you might even incorporate both exercises into different sections of a longer work. In this exercise we'll be working on moving your central character and chorus, moving them through space.
1. Flocking – Characters move within a space, slipping in and among each other rapidly, aware of each other. Without overtly signaling, and with no single character leading, allow the chorus to find common impulse to stop. Allow language to flow with this energy to move and stop. Characters come to a complete stop, rather than gradually slowing. Then, allow the characters to find a common instinctive urge to move again together, without a leader, feeling the impulse.
  a. Morphing – Allow other physical actions and movements to occur with the flocking; add voice to this – allow the characters to extend the flocking with their voice and movements, morphing into different kinds of chorus creatures; transforming. The morphing can allow many characters to become one thing, and then disperse as many things as possible.
  b. Scenic state – After flowing and flocking, the chorus can freeze into an environment, becoming the trees, rocks, buildings of a world – shifting into a scenic state around which your central character and protagonist can flow. This is something that playwright Lanford Wilson experiments with in his *Rimers of Eldritch* where the characters become a forest near the end of the play, becoming the backdrop against which the play's final moments occur.

After experimenting a bit with a very ancient dream structure like the Greek chorus, it is intriguing to see how it might be used in a more contemporary work, and below, I'll provide examples from two different playwrights, Paula

Vogel and Lanford Wilson, both of whom are gay playwrights whose innovations have led the field in dramatic literature, to examine how a chorus can be a subversive tool to get at the uncanny and bizarre in dramatic action.

2 *How I Learned to Drive* – Paul Vogel's Contemporizing the Chorus

In her brilliant, Pulitzer prize-winning play, *How I Learned to Drive,* Paula Vogel uses the tools of a Greek Chorus to delve deeply into the mind of Li'l Bit, Vogel's protagonist. Vogel's chorus can easily transform into characters in Li'l Bit's past, as well as narrate Li'l Bit's story, as well as the landscape of her mind. The chorus drifts into Li'l Bit's arguments to the audience, to lend those dialogues extra dimension and amplifies Li'l Bit's temptations in the final moments of the play.

Using a uniquely circular structure Vogel's uses the chorus to get at the horrifying, all too real experience of sexual molestation mostly from the point of view of the molested child, Li'l Bit. However Vogel also does this at times, and uncomfortably so, from the point of view of the molester, Uncle Peck. It is a play that challenges its audiences to go places where no one would want to go, and it asks its audience to consider the nuances of an incestuous, pedophilic relationship that becomes unnervingly close to a romance. The overall structure of the play is built on a series of PowerPoint slides that, in a distinctively Brechtian fashion, suggest the kind of awkward, utilitarian presentation of a driver's education course. While the focus of this book is not primarily to provide an analysis of dramatic literature, it is useful as we explore dramatic writing technique to look at how Vogel structures her play to play with our prejudices.

At the beginning of the play, when we first encounter Uncle Peck, and his victim, his niece Li'l Bit, she is seventeen years old, and in this moment his sexual advances seem to be almost consensual. Intriguingly, using a minimalist technique that recalls the theatricality of Thornton Wilder, Vogel throughout the play only *suggests* these moments of physical intimacy, without forcing the audience to view them in their full obscenity. Peck draws circles in the air where Li'l Bits breasts might be; he never touches her; they sit in two separate chairs. Yet, in this first scene between them, there is a clear sense of Peck's intentions, and as uncomfortable as these may be – we have the sense that Li'l Bit has some agency as to how far she might be willing to go.

However, even as the play dips in and out of the past, hurrying to moments that get at some of the complexities and idiosyncrasies of Li'l Bit's life permitting a culture of molestation, we are never far from this ongoing intimate relationship of Peck in the car with Li'l Bit. It seems like they are always in the car together – on the verge of intimacy. Using the placards and slides that work like intertitles in film to move us back and forth in time, Vogel can tease out missteps along the way, those of Li'l Bit's grandparents, her mother, her aunt, all provide a gateway for Peck, the predator, to make his way to his victim.

A basic structure of the play is provided below, with an indication of the various placards, projections, or slides as Vogel provides them as context for the dramatic action:

How I Learned to Drive – A Circular Structure of Revelation

1. *Prologue*: Sometimes to Tell a Secret, You First Have to Teach a Lesson.
2. *1969 in the Maryland Cornfields* – "Safety First – You And Driver Education" – Intrusion: The moment Peck fondles Li'l Bit? Lil' Bit is age seventeen in this scene – and the suggestion here is that she is complicit in her undoing.
3. *Idling in Neutral Gear* – A narrative about names – and about differing senses of reality.
4. *Shifting Forward from First to Second Gear* – About Li'l Bit's disastrous college career.
5. *You and Reverse Gear* – 1968, Eastern Shore, Celebration Dinner (About Drinking)
6. *Vehicle Failure* – Li'l Bit is drunk in Peck's car.
7. *2nd Idling in Neutral Gear* – Peck and Cousin Bobby; Teaching Bobby How to Fish – revealing that Li'l Bit isn't the only child Peck has molested.
8. *Talking about Sex*: With Mother and Grandmother.
9. *When Making a Left Turn*, You Must Downshift While Going Forward (1979 – A long bus trip with a horny boy, Upstate NY).
10. *Back to Sex Talk* – Does It Hurt?
11. *Before You Drive* – And the Bodies of Small Children – Serious Driving Lesson.
12. *You and Reverse Gear* – 1967 – Peck Teaches L'il Bit about Driving.
13. *You and Reverse Gear* – Allergy to Foam Rubber.
14. *Good defensive Driving* – In the Showers.
15. *Were you Prepared?* – The Sock Hop.
16. *You and Reverse Gear* – 1965 – The Photo Shoot.
17. *Implied Consent* – What will Peck do with the Photos?
18. *Idling in Neutral Gear* – Mary's Monologue on Uncle Peck.
19. *You and Reverse Gear* – Lil Bit's 13th Birthday, Christmas, 1964 – Uncle Peck Does the Dishes.

20. Shifting Forward from Second to Third Gear (Days and Gifts 1969).
21. *Shifting Forward from Third to Fourth Gear*, December 10, 1969, hotel room Philadelphia – *Climactic scene.*
22. *You and the Reverse Gear* – Summer 1962, On Men, Sex and Women, Part III (Fight about Uncle Peck), Mother hold's Lil Bit responsible.
23. *1962 On the Back Roads of Carolina:* The First Driving Lesson.
24. *Driving in Today's World*: Coming to terms with Peck's Ghost.

When we reach very nearly the end of the play, at the scene titled "1962, On the Back Roads of Carolina: The First Driving Lesson," we have come full circle on Peck's molestation, and we are, once again, in the car with Peck and a much, much younger Li'l Bit, a little girl of eleven. However, in this moment we see that this young girl really had no say, no agency, no escape from her much older, more powerful Uncle. His physical abuse of this little girl touches us deeply; it is a moment of horror – horror not only at the obscenity of Peck's molestation, but at our own previous willingness to blame the victim, to ascribe to Li'l Bit complicity in her own corruption. It is at this moment, and the moment directly after – the moment when we realize how terribly scarred Li'l Bit truly is – that the full circle of this moment hits its full dreadfulness, and our revulsion is not just for Peck, but for ourselves, having bought into the same kind of blind acceptance of this victim-blaming.

In Vogel's hands, the ancient structure of a full circle of retribution, which is in fact what happens in *Oedipus Rex*, becomes the driving force for engagement of the audience in *How I Learned to Drive*. In Sophocles' play, Oedipus's parents King Laius and Queen Jocasta have attempted to thwart fate and destiny by cruelly abandoning their baby son, his heels pinioned, only to have him live and return to murder his father and marry his mother. This fate is then sealed when Oedipus becomes aware of what he has done and puts out his own eyes, even after torturing the blind seer, Tireasas, in order to discover the truth – it is only when Oedipus can no longer see, that he truly sees. And in this way, *Oedipus Rex* follows Aristotle's "ideal" complex tragic plot – one in which a protagonist experiences a change of fortune, *peripeteia* from prosperity to misery, even they experience recognition, *anagnorisis*, as they progress from ignorance to knowledge. The dream circle is completed when the prediction comes true, and Oedipus is resigned to his fate. While using dreams to predict the future has unlikely success; the fact that we experience dreams as a way of experiencing a possible future makes perfect sense, since dreams are evolution's way of us preparing for every possible scenario that we may eventually face as mammals. The fact that we write stories in the same way, as tales of the probable possible, is only exemplified by the circle structure, a uniquely

Goddess-framed story-telling configuration tied to the Circle of Life, the Circle of Seasons, the lunar cycle, and many other Goddess-based circularities.

In the case of *How I Learned to Drive,* the circular structure allows the audience to "see," experiencing both *peripeteia* and *anagnorisis* after being blinded by their own prejudices. In the exercise that follows, Vogel's dream circle becomes our guiding structure, that of moving from ignorance into the knowledge, even as we recognize our own narrow-mindedness and preconceptions. In that sense the *peripeteia* that occurs comes with our realization that our privilege, our prosperity, has blinded us to the deep misery experienced by victims of pedophilia. Notably, throughout the play Vogel has suggested certain kinds of music from the late 1950s, early 1960s to provide a kind of soundtrack to the play, and this music ironically frames our understanding of our own complicity in Li'l Bits' fate. So, as part of this next exercise, we'll play with the use of musical progression to help shape our non-linear, dreamlike dramatic structure.

Exercise 3: Paula Vogel Exercise – Circles of Revelation

Step 1 – Creating the Circle Elements – To discover a circle of revelation within your script, build a *dream cache* that is tied only to the world of this play. Thus far we have created dream caches to come up with play ideas, explore characters, but in this dream cache we'll be working on the elements that will make up your play. You can work from the dream cache of your central character, but you might also want to create a dream cache that is solely tied to the construction of your play. In the process of creating this dream cache for your play, in addition to the prompts we have included in the dream cache in chapter one, add a few new sets of prompts – and keep these in a separate dream cache:

a. *Character scenarios*: Write down six to eight different simple scenarios that involve your central character's want, obstacle, and antagonist. These may or may not happen in the play, and they follow no chronological order. Tear each off as a separate element and add them to your dream cache.

b. *Music Progressions*: Write down six to eight different pieces of music that provide a background for those scenarios; there should be an emotional progression involved. How might the music you choose contribute to our understanding of the central conflict in your play? Again, these should each be on separate tabs of paper; add them to your dream cache.

c. *Instructional Placards*: Provide six to eight different placards that might accompany these scenes and music – tied to an organizational structure that might be tied to a PowerPoint lecture on some banal subject (perhaps guidelines on how to perform a medical procedure or how to handle a difficult guest at a theme park) – these can be totally invented, or feel free to draw upon received words of corporate wisdom. Add these to your dream cache.

Step 2 – Arranging the Circle – After you have created this separate dream cache/and assuming you had a first dream cache that you had created for your central character, lay out the six to eight scenarios in front of you – withdraw a piece of music, and a placard and start to arrange a circle – with one scenario relating to the next in an associative manner. This is not necessarily linear, with one scenario leading to the next or causing the next to happen, but simply inserting scenes which feel right together – one leading to the next. Bear in mind that we're arranging a Circle – meaning that the first scenario and the last scenario have a relationship – not necessarily a causal one, but one that feels related – whether through content, theme, dramatic action, character relationships, or even setting. These may be scenes that fall into your play – or not.

Step 3 – Filling the Circle – now using the dream cache for your play which includes the traditional elements from a dream cache: needs/desires, emotions, people, locations, objects, animals, plants, etc. Allow all these elements to flow into the scene you will write using each of your prompts from Step 1 of this exercise – the scenario, the music, and the placard – now look at what you have created and look at the linkage between these scenes. Is there a moment that takes you back to the beginning of the play, even as it ties to the ending?

Step 4 – Finding the Circle – for now you have a series of six to eight scenes, scenarios peopled by the characters you are interested in – look at the scenes you've created, and think about the order, think about the climax, the intense moment at the beginning of the play – and think about how the ending will lead to the beginning of the play – coming full circle. This is key – how does the circle get at the heart of what you want to say within the play? How does the circle fill out and bring a sense of completion to your audience? That place of recognition, of surprise, should be *real* – as you should not have decided what it will be, you should find your circle from the material you have already written. Write your dramatic work now, using your circles as a reference for its structure.

The ancient rhythm of *peripeteia* and *anagnorisis* provides a useful energy to your play, and in *How I Learned to Drive*, the non-linear circularity of the play's structure keeps its audience rounding around the same situation, again and again, seeing it from different angles, different times, gaining new insights, weighing Li'l Bit's options and choices, judging and re-judging Peck, so that in all the circling there is also a refocusing and re-examination of all the characters, until, with a final circling in and landing, we are left with a deeper understanding of a dark situation that has, too often, gone unexamined.

3   Lanford Wilson's *Book of Days* – The Lyric Chorus

Another author, Lanford Wilson, who worked with Paula Vogel at the famed Circle Repertory Company in New York City in the 1980s and 90s, and was one of Circle's founding members, also used both a chorus and a nonlinear technique borrowed from a classic modern drama in his play *Book of Days*. In *Book of Days* Wilson borrows his dramatic structure for the play from George Barnard Shaw's *St. Joan*, dramatizing the challenges of a small-town hero, Ruth, as she solves a dark crime perpetrated by one of the ruling elites of her hometown. Like Joan, Ruth comes up against a powerful, corrupt leadership, and despite her honesty and convictions, she is sacrificed, though not burnt at the stake; she is ultimately run out of the town along with her husband, Len.

Throughout the play, Wilson uses all the characters to create an effect that I like to call Choral Collage – using language to establish mood, location, season, and to set the pace of the play. In a play by Lanford Wilson, a simple traditional psychological realism is matched with a lyrical technique of choral collage, that amplifies and transforms the world of the play from the banal into the extraordinary. Like Tennessee Williams and William Inge before him, Wilson uses the magic of lyrical language to cause the banality and tedium of the Midwestern life to burst into flower like a grey prairie which, after a spring rainstorm, explodes into full bloom. For Wilson's characters, under the grim quotidian of daily life lies a deep churning sea of passion just waiting for the right moment to surge – and that moment is quite often blasted from the deeps by a shuddering gale of language.

In *Rimers of Eldritch* and in *Book of Days*, Wilson's technique is a choral one – taking full advantage of the Pentecostal ritual of speaking in tongues, also known as glossolalia, which is the normative proof, but not the only proof, of the baptism with the Holy Spirit. The rhythm of the Pentecostal service flows through Wilson's plays with praise choruses and an untethered vocal cacophony of inner expression. Read through Wilson's *Book of Days*, and experience some of these splashes of choral technique, then try the exercises below.

Exercise 4: Lanford Wilson – Choral Collage Technique – To Intensify Action

Using several of your characters from your play, establish a basic conflict scene with two or more. A character wants something desperately, must get it without overtly doing so, and the other character(s) present an obstacle to that need. As always, you should give the characters a real urgency, a difficult physical activity, and at no time should you allow any of the characters to discuss their real need directly.

At a moment of emotional intensity, allow the scene to freeze, and allow the other characters of the play to speak either in unison or separately, following a stream of consciousness approach to what is happening in the scene. Allow the scene to start up again and keep the interspersed comments flowing through the scene now, allowing them to flow in and around the conversation as it intensifies.

Exercise 5: Lanford Wilson – Choral Collage Technique – To Establish Place

Using all the characters in your play, allow a flow of language to begin with each character individually speaking a single word or words to describe the central setting of the play – and allow those words to occasionally join – with the characters speaking at first in unison, and then coming apart – perhaps joining with other characters, and finally coming together again (or not). Consider also allowing this unified choral effect to fall apart into single words, sounds, or even just breathing.

Exercise 6: Lanford Wilson – Lyric Realism Technique – The Repeated Scene

Another technique used by Lanford Wilson is the repeated scene, used in plays like *Balm in Gilead* and in *Book of Days*. This dream technique is simple but very interesting; simply write a conflict scene like the one described above, but then repeat it, with slight variation, perhaps fragmented, giving a different character more to say, or a slightly different attitude. This is not unlike the kind of enigma variations that happen when you daydream – or even when you have a recurring dream. All the same people are there, but perhaps the location is different. Or maybe a character changes or seems to flip back and forth in what Paul Castagno describes in his excellent book, *New Playwriting Strategies*, as an Equivocal Character – a kind of character which is iridescent as some other character, changing at a particular cue or with a certain talisman. See what you uncover in the scene – there's always an odd mystery in how these Wilson scenes change. It doesn't take much, a subtle switch of focus in the scene – a minor variation on the language – whatever it takes to give you a different insight into a scene you've already written. You may use it in your final script or not – but the twists that you uncover will linger in your mind and may affect a different moment in your drama.

4   Marcel Camus' *Black Orpheus* – The Liminality of Carnival

Switching to film mode, a classic example of a modern film taking on the structure of Ancient Greek myth is Marcel Camus' brilliant *Black Orpheus,* an adaptation of Orpheus and Eurydice, based on a stage play *Orfeu da Conceigao* by Brazilian poet Vinicius de Moraes. The film shifts the scene of the ancient story to Rio de Janeiro at the time of Carnival, and focuses on the intoxicating rhythms of the Samba, the quintessential dance of Brazil, as a thematic and structural tool. While Paula Vogel and Lanford Wilson make use of the ancient device of the chorus in their dramatic dream technique, here the power of the ancient structure is that of the Dionysian festival which permits a realm of liminality, what Mikhail Bakhtin termed "the carnivalesque" to open a field of strangeness that transforms the characters of the drama from one state into another.

In the ancient story, Eurydice is a nymph who, shortly after her marriage to the gifted musician Orpheus, a disciple of Apollo, wanders distractedly into a wondrous meadow. There Eurydice is pursued by minor, rustic god, Aristaeus, makes a terrible misstep and is fatally bitten by a snake, and her spirit descends to the underworld. Her young husband, distraught, seeks to bring her back from Hades, and because of the brilliance of his music, is permitted to do so. But as Orpheus leads Eurydice back to the world, and against the wishes of Hades, he looks back to make sure Eurydice is following him, and she is lost forever. What is key in the myth is the magical meadow that seems to have within it all the possibility of a lifetime. It is a place entered by Eurydice in the process of becoming a wife – and she never leaves it. She is caught between being a maiden and a matron, living in nether world, yet existing with the liminal possibility of each.

Another way to think about it is to borrow Mikhail Bakhtin's notion of the *carnivalesque*. Baktin was a Russian theorist and literary critic, who was analyzing a particular kind of literary work that had its basis in the grotesque, and as an example of this type, analyzed the work of medieval author, François Rabelais, and his novel *Gargantua and Pantagruel*. For Bakhtin, the *carnivalesque* was a state which has several primary aspects:

1. Freedom to connect: Unlikely people are brought together and interact freely in ways they wouldn't normally during real life
2. Bizarre behavior is encouraged: The uncanny is welcomed, and one's inner, truer self is beckoned.
3. Strange bedfellows occur: Abnormal misalliances take place, opposites attract, Heaven joins with Hell, Good with Bad, Old with Young.
4. Blasphemy rules: Debased behavior is encouraged, and all piety is thrown to the wind, the rulers are stripped of their power, all brought down to earth, to their baser natures.
5. A King is crowned: The Lord of Misrule becomes the King of the Carnival and is only uncrowned at the end of the festival, signifying a return to normality.

The Carnivalesque is, in other words, an opportunity to dream reality in new ways, unhindered by the traditional rules and mores of society. In *Black Orpheus*, Euridice is an innocent farm girl coming from her farm to escape a man who has threatened to kill her. She arrives at Rio de Janeiro at the time of Carnival on a ferry, looking for the home of her cousin, Serafina, and is guided by a blind vendor to the trolley car, Babylonia, where she is swept up into the frenzy. The driver of the trolley car is Orpheus, and he is not only taking Euridice to her destination – he *is* her destination. From the moment she arrives, she is confronted by threatening and erotic realm of aggressive male dance – and is only saved when the women of the realm, equally aggressive in their gyrations, somehow swath her in the costume of Carnival. When she arrives at the last stop, she is greeted by Hermes, the station master – and in ancient myth, Hermes accompanies the dead to their destination, the Underworld.

The film begins the day before competition of the Samba schools, and during that evening's rehearsal, Euridice is introduced to Orpheus formally, instantly falling in love with him, much to the displeasure of Mira, Orpheus's jealous fiancée. It becomes clear that Orpheus has many young women at his beck and call, because of his unnatural abilities in music, as is noted by the two young boys, Zeca and Benodito, who are enchanted by his ability to cause the sun to rise. Orpheus's ability to bring the world to life with his song is both the means to his uncanny rise to fame as the leader of a Samba School in Carnival, and the seed of his final misfortune, as he is so fiercely loved by his female followers, they kill him in their passion to possess him.

Deep into the night of Carnival we descend, with Euridice suddenly pursued by death, spirited down the cliffsides of Rio de Janeiro, and Orpheus racing to protect her from an inevitable fate. As Orpheus ascends his success at dance and song, he is thrust into a fatal and hopeless chase, and in his desperate desire to shed light on Euridice's pursuer, electrocutes his love instead. Accompanied by the figure of Death, Euridice's body is raced to the hospital in an ambulance, siren crying into the night. And Orpheus attempts to follow, to no avail; she cannot be found – and instead, he is lead to a Voodoo ceremony, where he sings again, and Euridice's spirit reaches out to him – only to be fetched back into darkness. When Orpheus attempts to see behind him during mystic rites of the Voodoo, he only encounters an elderly woman, who has been possessed by Euridice's spirit.

Hermes provides Orpheus with the papers he needs to retrieve Euridice's body from the morgue, which is a white refrigerated world, harshly lit in florescence against the wild darkness of Carnival night. Orpheus sings as he ascends the mountain trails, and is suddenly killed as Mira, his maddened fiancée, not unlike a maenad, hurls a rock at his head, and causing him to fall down the side of the cliff, along with the body of Eurydice, like two broken ragdolls. The film ends with Zeca, a young handsome boy, as he picks up Orpheus's guitar the next morning, and strums the sunrise into being. His friend Benodito and a little girl dance to Zeca's enchanted guitar music with Carnivalesque frenzy into the morning light.

In the screenwriting exercise below, you will create your own place of Carnival for your characters, drawing upon the same Baktinian and Dionysian principles of liminality that created some of the most powerful moments of dream dramaturgy in ancient play structures. This exercise is built on the basic idea of a character entering the realm of the carnivalesque and follows the anthropological pattern of Separation – Liminality – Incorporation as proposed by anthropologist Arnold van Gennep (Gennep was, incidentally, hugely influential on Victor Turner, whose anthropological theories in turn affected experimental theatre directors and theorists such as NYU's Richard Schechner and others). Each step grows out of the work you've already done using your dream cache, and you'll be drawing elements from your character cache. Bear in mind that the exercise might be a structure for the entire drama you are writing – or it may simply be another form of character exploration – or it might result in a film sequence that you are able to incorporate into the whole. For now, commit to nothing – let it be an exercise.

Exercise 7: Marcel Camus – Dream Carnival – Separation, Liminality, Incorporation

Step 1 – Creating the Carnival – using the elements of your central character's *dream cache* you'll be using four types of prompts to create the Carnival into which you'll be thrusting your character – these will include events, settings, plants, animals, and objects. As in all the exercises in this book, your *dream cache* will be the central well into which you dip in order to keep coming back to your character's wants, emotions, and experiences. Bear in mind that the Carnival you create may have no relationship with the Carnival of Brazil – any wild party situation – a night in the forest, the mosh pit on the dance floor, a melee at a bar, a strange rave weekend at a resort, may result in the carnivalesque. Your goal is to find a world where slippage may appear – as wildly and strangely as you desire. It might be quite subtle, or it may be utterly bizarre – but it is a time and place of the uncanny. As you pull these elements from your dream cache, associate upon the elements themselves and their opposites – and write down these opposites – so that you'll have several pairings of a physical world that borrows from the dreams of your character. The Carnival should be a place, an event, a ceremony that has these elements:

1. Freedom to connect.
2. Bizarre behavior is encouraged.
3. Strange bedfellows occur/Opposites attract
4. Blasphemy rules.
5. A King/Queen is crowned.

In the process of creating your Carnival, bear in mind that it a ceremony like others that we have established, so you might want to add these elements to it:

– Efficaciousness: What does it bring about?
– Physical element: Where does it take place?
– Shamans/Priests: Who is in charge?
– Dance/Music: How can you incorporate movement and aural spectacle?
– Talisman(s): What are the spiritual objects involved?
– Dream elements: How will you incorporate the following from your dream elements:
  – Event
  – Setting
  – Plants
  – Animals
  – Objects

Step 2 – Separation – Descent into the Beast

Now that you have created your Carnival, you must plunge your character into the realm you've created. How will you do that? It should involve a three-step process:

1. *Journey into the realm* – how will your character get to your Carnival? Where are they coming from? Where are they going? Why are they coming? What do they hope to achieve in their state of Carnival? What is the physical vehicle for their journey? What kind of journey have they had – have things happened along the way that have changed them?
2. *Gate Keepers to the realm* – who do they meet when they get there? How are they greeted? Who guides them and takes them around? Who is an initial threat? Who might be a boon? Do they meet the king/queen? Is this someone they already know? What are the attachments these characters have to their past?
3. *Rules of the game – the initiation* – What is expected of your character? What is their goal? Who shares the rules and why? What are the rules, and how are they explained? Where are they explained? What is involved in success? In failure? How dangerous is it? And what is at stake?

Step 2 – Liminality – In the Belly of Beast

The game has begun, the bell has run, your character is within Carnival, and anything can happen, but you should still consider mapping out what happens:

1. *Navigating the waters* – at this step, your central character must dip their toes in and get wet – how do they do this? Who do they meet? Who helps them, who hinders them? How do they start to engage with future King/Queen? Where are they and where will they be going?
2. *Challenge/Crisis 1 – Strangeness Occurs.* What first occurs to rock your central characters world? It may be subtle at first. How do they respond? Who do they meet – friend or foe? Are they successful or wounded in the attempt? Is it a good or bad experience? What new revelations do they discover; and how has the strangeness of this realm transformed their experience? What questions are raised? How does this begin the process of coronation? This challenge/crisis leads them to the next:
3. *Challenge/Crisis 2 – The Strangeness is Deepening.* What causes this challenge/crisis, and how does it relate to the first? Who is added/deleted as friend or foe? What has your character gained or lost? How does this change your character? The coronation now is underfoot – who is it and why? This challenge/crisis leads them to the next:
4. *Challenge/Crisis 3 – The Strangeness is Transformational.* What aspect of the first two challenges/crises occur here? What is gained? What is lost? What is the build here? And how is it pointing in a new direction? Which characters benefit, which lose? How does your central character begin

their transformation into their final self? The coronation of the King/Queen has occurred – how does this change the game. This challenge/crisis leads them to the Climax.

5. *Climax of Ritual – The Strangeness must Dissipate.* The ceremony or ritual tied to your Carnival comes to its climax in this scene – the King/Queen has been crowned, and now that crown must be removed so that normality occurs– how does that occur? How does the strangeness, the bizarre and the uncanny point to a new normal?

Step 2 – Incorporation – Bringing about the New Normal

Carnival is over, but your central characters story is just now beginning, and you must bring them to their final incorporation into the world.

1. *The Return* – How does your character return to the real world? Do they take another journey? What is that journey like? Who remains with them? How do they get there? What has been gained or lost?

2. *What Is the World Like Now?* – How does your character return – dead or alive? If alive, how have they changed – if at all? Where are they and what is that brave new world like? Has the world changed at all because of what they have been through? Have they achieved their goal? What is left undone?

3. *What Happens Next?* – Now that your character has returned – dead or alive – what does this bode for the future? Who will be involved? If your character has survived, where are they going now? What has changed or remains the same in their goals? Who will your character be now that they have lived through Carnival?

The ancient structures, particularly those that come to us from the Ancient Greeks, that provide a foundation for your non-linear, non-traditional dream dramaturgy will continue to feed your writing for years to come – as there are so many ancient tales to retell for your own age. While this isn't necessarily a book on adaptation of literature or history to the stage – the same techniques that feed into that kind of dramatic writing feed into what we call the ostensibly original. In the next chapter we'll look at the specific nature of African-American dream ritual structure in the writing of two unique voices, Adrienne Kennedy, the major non-realistic voice of a generation of playwrights, and Julie Dash, the first female African-American film maker, to get at the unique and powerful heritage in non-linear work, that transforms ritual into art, and art into ritual.

CHAPTER 4

African-American Dream Funhouse – Creating Ritual Liminality

Adrienne Kennedy's Funny House of a Negro *and Julie's Dash's* Daughters of the Dust

Adrienne Kennedy and Julie Dash occupy a primary presence in my mind not only as the iconic African-American dramatists of their generation, but also as trailblazers in the creation of dramatic ritual liminalities – free realms where dream plays grow and thrive. Kennedy presides over several generations of major voices which have been highly influenced by her including Ntozake Shange, Suzan-Lori Parks, Jackie Sibblies Drury, Jeremy O. Harris, Antoinette Nwandu and Jordan E. Cooper, among many others with her nightmarish cacophony of conflating, clashing white and black American cultural icons in her play *Funnyhouse of a Negro* (1964). Julie Dash is the pre-eminent voice of a generation of black female filmmakers and used a different kind of storytelling in her film *Daughters of the Dust* (1991), built on the narrative traditions of the African griot, unfolding stories which dissipate and come back, unfolding multiple times over the course of the film's day and a half in the lives of Dash's fictional Peazant family. With *Daughters of the Dust*, Dash became the first black female filmmaker to release a major commercial feature length film. Both black women explored techniques in their non-linear, dream-based technique that create fluid, liminal, structures that in their essence license an anti-racist, activist approach to drama that is particularly powerful because it is indirect, subliminal, and emotionally engaging. Before I provide specific essence exercises based on their work, I thought it would be helpful to explore Adrienne Kennedy's very specific connection to her dreams, as she has been crucial also to my own work as a dramatist, and I have corresponded with her for many years on this subject.

1   Adrienne Kennedy: Syncopated Mimesis of a Many-Faced Storyteller

In her plays, Kennedy seemed to mostly eschew an overt political focus in favor of a subliminal activism, and this makes sense in that dreams seem to do the same thing – the politics of our lives are revealed in the anxieties, inconsistencies, violence, and horror that lay within our own dream journey. Specifically, identity politics, such as those that may be found in Adrienne Kennedy's *Funnyhouse of a Negro, The Owl Answers,* and a *Movie Star Has to Star in Black and White* are described by Elin Diamond as the "mimesis of syncopation," in that Kennedy provides a subjective experience of culture that unmasks the unspoken racism inherent in American culture.[1] Even specific objects and identities within her plays contribute to this dream-like syncopated anti-racist mimesis, "including swarming ravens, floating skulls, ebony masks, a statue of Queen Victoria ..." and "various cultural icons, what Kennedy calls her other "selves": The Duchess of Hapsburg, Patrice Lamumba, a hunchback Jesus, Queen Victoria," all of which resonate "repressed racial and sexual tensions."[2] In the process, Kennedy offers specific non-linear strategies for opening up our own dramas in a uniquely subliminal yet effective form of social engagement.

In *Funnyhouse of a Negro*, the play that made her famous, the central character of Sarah is in a crises mode – and it is never clear whether we are seeing Sarah's reality or her nightmare. Alienated from others, living as a student in a white world where she has tried desperately to fit in, Sarah has a white boyfriend and white landlady. Sarah is haunted by her memories of her father in the play, who has both died and yet still is still coming to remind her of her deeper African roots. The other characters in the play include icons of white culture, including Jesus, the Duchess of Hapsburg, and Queen Victoria, as well as African voices, such as the murdered 1960s activist and politician, Patrice Lumumba. The play moves from one nightmarish crisis to another, and the framework that holds the play together is the mirrored funhouse, filled with distortions and illusions which threaten to subvert any attempt of Sarah's to break free. In the end, Sarah commits suicide, though within the context of a nightmare, is she simply shedding one version of herself in favor of another? It is impossible to know, and when her father finally does appear, he is a monstrous creation, a kind of Frankenstein monster, bloodied, unholy, and yet perhaps yet another version of herself.

In Adrienne Kennedy's early plays, the mimesis of dreaming (or the syncopated mimesis, per Diamond) is created primarily through constant character transformations, what Rosemary Curb calls "fragmental mental states" or "separate selves" which seem to be "alternate visions of the same divided

---

1   Elin Diamond, "Mimesis in Syncopated Time: Reading Adrienne Kennedy," *Intersecting Boundaries: The Theatre of Adrienne Kennedy*, eds. Paul K. Bryant-Jackson and Lois More Overbeck (Minneapolis, MN: University of Minnesota Press, 1992) 131–141.
2   Diamond 134.

consciousness."[3] The characters of Sarah in *Funnyhouse of a Negro* and Clara in *The Owl Answers* are both fragmented into several versions of themselves, and Curb argues that other characters in these plays are simply manifestations of these central characters. The fragmentation of the characters creates a dramatic crisis, a "what if" raising the question whether Sarah or Clara will ever become whole again or survive at all. Bert O. States, the theorist I discussed earlier, exploring the phenomenology of dreaming and fiction, would consider Kennedy's *Funnyhouse* as a dream of what he calls the "dramatic" genre:

> By dramatic I do not simply mean violent or shocking or a plot that involves a cliff-hanger crisis. Dramatic dreams are what we might call "What if?" dreams in the sense that they carry the dream situation to its furthest possible extreme[4]

Kennedy's *Funnyhouse* follows the spontaneity of dreams, in that it "thinks first and raise moral questions later," and exists "at the threshold of thought." Like a dream, Kennedy's relentless, instantaneous linkage of images, has "a way of making realities out of possibilities."[5] In addition, *Funnyhouse of a Negro* is driven by Sarah's dream desire to make a connection with her father – a very real, very palpable desire. By learning how to tap into their dream desires, Kennedy has special access to an extraordinarily complex yet visceral reality, one in which the trappings of the real world are transformed by dreaming into powerful and bizarre landscapes wherein the playwright's alter egos struggle with transformations of themselves and their families in a world plagued by systemic racism.

In her autobiographical scrapbook, *The People who Led To My Plays*, Adrienne Kennedy comes to a similar conclusion: her dreams are more interesting than her writing. At this time Kennedy was having "many recurrent dreams," and so began to write "tiny stories" incorporating them, without consciously editing them as fiction. In addition, reading and seeing Lorca's play *Blood Wedding*, and studying the work of Picasso and Jackson Pollack made it possible for her to "abandon the realistic set for a greater dream setting."[6] For Kennedy, dream structure and the goal of writing "without a linear narrative" went hand in hand. Kennedy began to sense that her dream diaries had "more

---

3   Rosemary Curb, "Fragmented Selves in Adrienne Kennedy's *Funnyhouse of a Negro* and *The Owl Answers*," *Theatre Journal* 32.2 (May 1980): 180–195.
4   States, *Dreaming and Storytelling* 141.
5   States, *Dreaming and Storytelling* 87.
6   Kennedy, *The People Who Led To My Plays* 100, 108.

life" than her fictional work. She simply allowed the images to "accumulate by themselves."[7] She then made a breakthrough discovery – those characters could have other personas, and in doing so, she made use of two dream strategies that Bert States describes (using the theories of Allan Rechtschaffen) as single- and double-mindedness.

States describes single-mindedness as "a strong tendency for a single train of related thoughts and images to persist over extended periods without disruption or competition from other simultaneous thoughts and images," and double-mindedness as "the replacement of one scene/character with another and the ability to hold the sense of several scenes or characters in simultaneous or oscillating suspension."[8] It is the combination of these two phenomena in dreaming that create what States calls the "Harrison Ford Syndrome," by which he means that within a dream a character may, or may not either look or sound like a person in real life, yet within the dream one is *certain* that it is in fact that person and is recognizable as that person, even though there is nothing there but an emotional recognition.[9] Each of these syndromes or phenomena create a kind of "bizarreness" which is endemic to dreams alone, yet States believes that "the bizarreness of dreams is a function of thinking an 'idea' through for the first (and only) time," or that dreams are "final drafts" rather than finished narratives.[10] In Kennedy's early plays this oneiric drafting structure translates into characters and settings which are constantly "finishing" themselves, moving from one transitional state to another, morphing visages in a "Harrison Ford Syndrome," thinking themselves into existence through multiple shocking revelations of self. These ideas will be key to our creation of multiple selves in our own dreamwrighting technique.

Time in Kennedy's dream-like plays is also distorted. Elinor Fuchs believes that "the very disappearance of linear time into spatial transformation" is tied to Strindberg's influence on Kennedy.[11] And it is this remolding and reformulating of time that adds yet another powerful dream strategy to the writing of nonlinear plays. Time repeatedly moves backward and forwards in Kennedy's work. But crucial to understanding Kennedy's technique is her connection to

---

7   Kathleen Betsko and Rachel Koenig, *Interviews with Contemporary Women Playwrights* (New York: Beech Tree Books, 1987) 253.
8   States, *Dreaming and Storytelling* 19, 22.
9   States *Seeing in the Dark*, 112.
10   States *Seeing in the Dark*, 122.
11   Elinor Fuchs, "Adrienne Kennedy and the First Avant-Garde," *Intersecting Boundaries: The Theatre of Adrienne Kennedy* eds. Paul K. Bryant-Jackson and Lois More Overbeck (Minneapolis: University of Minneapolis Press, 1992) 80.

the theory and practice of Antonin Artaud, who most theatre theorists consider the creator of the notion of "Theatre of Cruelty." Regardless of States' concerns with Strindberg's *A Dream Play,* reconciling Strindberg's symbolistic ideas of the bizarre with States' phenomenological insights is Artaud's theatrical concept of dreaming as a visceral oneiric healing that occurs when theatre itself becomes "cruel," a state which can be read, perhaps, as being nonrealistic, nonlinear, and nonintellectual.

Artaud describes his favored dramatic structure as "localized and precise as the ... apparently chaotic development of dream images in the brain."[12] For Artaud a connection with the dream world is the ultimate goal of theatre. By imitating the action of the oneiric, Artaud believes "this naked language of the theatre ... must permit ... a kind of total creation in which man must reassume his place between dream and events."[13] Additionally, humanity has somehow become lost in reality; people have lost their connection to the world of dreams. Theatre is how people can synthesize the two spheres, thus becoming whole again. Not only is theatre like a dream itself, but it weds dream to reality, which States might also consider the job of fiction. To this end, Artaud posits that "to believe that dreams themselves have only a substitute function, is to diminish the profound poetic bearings of dreams as well as of theatre."[14]

The theatre should be, "like dreams ... bloody and inhuman" with the added function of being rooted in "a perpetual conflict, a spasm in which life is continually lacerated."[15] This idea seems to be an extension of what States considers one of the most important dreamlike qualities, that the world of the dream should feel inescapable; no other world exists but the dream world when one is dreaming. What Artaud articulates is that not only should theatre imitate the quality of a dream, but that it should be as all-consuming and as terrifying as a nightmare. Thus, to write a dream play is to create a world that embraces the terror, power, and inescapability of a dream. In Kennedy's *Funnyhouse of a Negro* this spasm of dream laceration occurs when it is revealed that Sarah has hung herself. Kennedy uses the horror of dream landscapes to fascinate and thereby imprison the audience in the world of her plays. There is no escape, no release, no other world but the dream realm of their plays. Let us now experiment with this essence – the syncopated mimesis nightmare.

---

12   Antonin Artaud, "The Theatre of Cruelty," *The Theory of the Modern Stage*, ed. Eric Bentley (New York: Penguin, 1979) 57.
13   Artaud 58.
14   Artaud 58.
15   Artaud 58.

Exercise 1: Adrienne Kennedy – A Syncopated Mimesis Nightmare

The trope of this dream exercise is that of a Nightmare or Lyric Dream – A lyric dream, according to Bert O. States, is one of pure sensation, no plot, with moments moving from one point to another framed only by our five senses and the associative elements of the dream. A lyric dream can also be an erotic dream – it is deeply felt, it has fragments of people, places, objects, that are from our daily lives, from the deepest part of who we are. Worry less about what happens, worry more about specifically and emotionally evoking the world of the dream drama.

STEP 1: Read *A Lesson in a Dead Language* or *Funny House of a Negro* by Adrienne Kennedy. Allow those plays to resonate with you. They are deeply autobiographical – yet distanced by the "ostranenie," the strangeness of Kennedy's style. As you read them – contemplate the *nightmares* you have experienced – write these down or examine those you have already written about in your dream cache. Nightmares are almost always *lyric* dreams – dreams which have no plot, but an explosion of sensual detail.

STEP 2: Include in your play your protagonist who is a character in the play, but is also, already, always you. Include several *elements of truth* from your *dream cache* – these are people, places, objects that are *real* and that have *real emotional values for you.* Include a character or two from the world of the play you are creating. Write two to five pages of character study incorporating *elements of truth* (real people, places, objects, animals, plants) – these character studies work best as scenes or monologues.

STEP 3: Imagine four to five different evocative *settings* – they can be places that you have already found and added to your *dream cache* from dreams you have had; they can come from the play you are writing; or they can come from a play that your character might write or dream. These settings will flow in and out of the play; floating under the characters, and the characters will shift to deal with them. Write two to five pages of settings.

STEP 4: Imagine two to three real characters from history, celebrities, politicians, movie stars – they will fall into your play – and note your emotional reaction to them, and give them a brief, evocative physical and psychological description – you will incorporate one or more of them into the scenario.

STEP 5: Give yourself twenty minutes and no more to write this exercise. Play quiet music during this exercise that is gentle and trancelike, yet has dissonance integral to its composition – these disturbances are key. Bear in mind, you are writing a nightmare – a lyric dream that has little plot, but mountains of sensual description – and language that is lyrical, poetic, unreal and perhaps uncanny. Put all these various elements into a dream cache or receptacle – then, at intervals of 1 minute, extract them, and incorporate each into your play – do not worry if the play is abstract or seemingly meaningless. Allow each interval to shift the scene – as you incorporate dream elements, keep shifting the scene – allow it to flow. Write five pages.

STEP 6: If you cry while you are writing, it is okay. You are writing a nightmare, after all. If you laugh while writing this, it is okay. If you yell in anger, if you decide to sing, if you feel the need to dance or feel erotic pleasure while writing this exercise it is okay, if you bring it into the scene. Care for yourself as you work – this will not be easy, but it will be powerful. Now write another five pages.

STEP 7: Once you have written ten pages, find a place of completion – and rest. Adrienne Kennedy wrote short plays – because this process, her process, is emotionally exhausting. Make sure you take a moment and read the scene out loud. Note where you are spiritually at its completion.

2 Julie Dash and the Structure of the Griot's Song

Julie Dash's *Daughters of the Dust* takes a decidedly non-traditional, non-linear approach to storytelling, ignoring notions of a central character striving against a specific obstacle, and instead looks at an entire family dealing with a life-changing event. In this case, it is the Peazant family, a family rooted in the traditions of Gullah culture, as they move their lives from the islands where they have lived for centuries to the mainland, and to the north, joining the great migration. The film then is built around several narratives that grow out of various competing African rituals and myths – there is a simple linear action – the Peazant family arrives on the island (Yellow Mary, Trula, Viola) to be greeted by Eula, Nana, Haagar, Eli, Myown, Iona, among others – a picnic is had, a family get together – then everyone leaves.

Key to the structure of the film, and the exercise below is the Unborn Child, who operates as a narrator for the film, but who also lurks strangely as a kind of unborn ancestor. Ancestor worship and the construct of ancestors influence in one's daily life is key to African religion, as well as to the dramatic forces impelling the characters to pursue specific goals. There should be no difference of influence with whether the characters are living or dead – and the dead characters may either be physically present or not, but we should still have a sense that the dead characters are influencing the present moment, either directly through supernatural power or indirectly by an earthly representative who can feel their presence directly.

Also key to this film is its languid, gorgeous, pace which leaves plenty of time for the audience to experience the music, dance, and ritual of the Gullah culture in the film – so consider long stretches of meditative "rest" time, when the camera is allowed to simply take in the environment without dialogue – allow the landscape to offer its own contemplative power, and trust that you've written filmable images that help tell the story of the dramatic action without a lot of words. What is important here is that mix of music, dance, image, and physical action that tells the story framed by ritual, but not in a direct way. The ritual technique here is indirect; it creates a ceremony within the context of a liminal, life-changing event, that is tied to the dramatic action, involving the ancestors, but has real world implications. Liminality is a term used by anthropologists, and most famously by Arnold van Gennep (1873–1957), mentioned earlier, whose work *Les Rites de Passage* (1909) traditionally defined liminality as a place where someone is on the threshold of a new stage of one's life, and in the midst of a ceremony or ritual which facilitates that transition. There are three steps – one in which you are separated from the world, another in which you enter into a world which is neither your past or future world, and finally, you enter the world transformed into your final state of being. The key location is the one is the realm of possibility – where anything and everything is possible, and where the rules breakdown entirely, and the world comes apart, and you are tested in totally unexpected and unique ways that profoundly change you. What you are shooting for in this exercise is to create a dramatic action that seems somehow highly ritualized and consecrated, and yet ties directly into clear stakes and consequences that affect the characters powerfully and believably.

Exercise 2: Julie Dash – Daughters of the Dust – Creating the Ritualized Liminal Event

Method: In this exercise you will explore an event in one or more of your characters in which ritual and myth plays an important part.
1. The Liminal Event:
    a. Choose a life-changing event in your character(s)' lives that involves a ritual of some kind, tied to something in your own personal background which may be present in your daily life, or from your family's historic past:
        i. A death.
        ii. A birth.
        iii. A marriage.

    iv. A coming-of-age ceremony.
    v. A seasonal event.
    vi. A religious event.
    vii. A family event caused by history, the government, the environment:
        1. The family must move because of eminent domain.
        2. The family is being adversely affected because of war, climate change, politics.
        3. The family is being affected by local events, such as a drought, a hurricane, or a tornado.
b. Key to this event is a notion of liminality, that the rules of the regular world are no longer in force:
    i. People behave in contrary ways, ways that are unusual or unacceptable in daily life.
    ii. The rules of this world are broken, shifting, fluid, changing, growing.
    iii. The result is a maturation process, a process of growing, changing, improving, and possibly moving from child to adult, innocence to knowledge, outsider to insider, becoming a part of the whole, moving into leadership and responsibility from a place of apprenticeship.
c. Select several family characters who would be present at that event. These may be dead or living –
    i. Whether they are dead or living, they will still influence the action.
    ii. Some may be yet unborn, coming to the present moment from the future, with their own agenda.
    iii. The dead or the unborn may serve as a narrator in the film.
d. Select characters who are religious/organizing leaders or celebrants tied to the event.
    i. Consider these as the priests or shamans.
    ii. Is there an official storyteller or Griot?
    iii. Is a member of the family a chieftain or shaman?
e. Consider outsiders to the event:
    i. Choose characters who are friends with the major characters and tied to event for that reason.
    ii. Choose characters who are strangers to the event, and are participating for reasons that are tangential to the event.
    iii. Choose a few characters who have some kind of connection to your character in a significant way.

iv. Note that these characters must be "educated" about the event as outsiders, which is useful for the audience (who are also outsiders).
   f. Choose one or more characters who are dead or not yet living, but present at the event for mysterious reasons.
   g. Describe the characters with the following elements on slips of paper:
      i. Character name.
      ii. Physical Description.
      iii. Personality.
      iv. Relationship to your central character.
   h. Hide the character's descriptions – Turn over the first five of characters and add others as necessary. Follow the instructions below.
2. The Myth:
   a. Describe a myth that is tied to the event, it can be tied to the following:
      i. A family myth or story.
      ii. A religious myth.
      iii. A classical myth from Greek or Roman mythology.
      iv. A biblical myth or parable.
      v. A myth from a specific culture (native American, African, South American, Asian, etc.).
   b. Write out the myth and its relation to the family event.
   c. Assign certain roles from the myth to members of the family or friends present at the event.
3. The Ritual:
   a. Describe a specific ritual or rituals tied to the event – give it a name, and describe its nature.
      i. Is it a religious ritual?
      ii. Is it a ritual tied to family traditions?
      iii. Is it tied to the seasons?
      iv. Is it a ritual tied to some other kind of event – a sporting event, an occupation, a life event, etc.
   b. Break down the ritual in terms of the following:
      i. Progress in terms of steps, processes, activities to be completed.
      ii. Language involved in the ritual – prayers, incantations, chants, etc.
      iii. Religious figures tied to the ritual.
      iv. Objects and/or talisman tied to the ritual.

          v.   Specific outcome hoped to be achieved by the ritual.
- c. Assign the characters who are to be directly involved in the ritual, those who will be watching, those who are the lead the ritual.

4. The Story:
   a. Beginning with the event itself, allow the following to occur, starting with the five characters, and adding others as necessary, turning them over without knowing who will appear:
      i. The arrival of the characters.
      ii. The preparation for the event.
      iii. The description of the myth from one or several of the characters.
      iv. The ritual and its completion.
   b. Bear in mind that as you describe what happens, allow the elements of the event, the myth, and the ritual to overlap, think about the following story elements, using a new character at each moment (keeping that character unknown until used):
      i. The characters share or hide a secret.
      ii. The characters move with or against the event.
      iii. A character changes or remains the same.
      iv. A romantic love is shared; a love goes unrequited.
      v. A conflict begins, a conflict resolves.
      vi. A crime is perpetrated or prevented.
      vii. A crime is solved or made unclear.
      viii. The forces of good or evil prevail.

5. The Screenplay:
   a. Write your screenplay based upon these elements, event, myth, and ritual and story, allowing each to ebb and flow on the revelation of each character.
   b. Work through the levels of reality you've set up and pay attention emotionally to how they interact – the present, the past, and the future, and living, the dead, and the unborn.
   c. Allow the shape and structure of the screenplay to have a meditative, slow-moving quality, focusing on images, ritualized behaviors, and ceremonies, while allowing the desire of the dreamer's eye to drive the emotional reality of the film.

In this chapter, we've attempted to look at the powerful tools of an African American dramatic structure, tied to power of liminality, a powerful dream-like state where traditional rules of order fall apart to free your characters to become who they need to be to fight for themselves in a difficult, unfair world. In Adrienne Kennedy's plays, that place of liminality is a kind of funhouse of the mind, borrowing from her play *Funnyhouse of a Negro,* where the absolute worst of one's environment becomes a nightmarish hellscape, and the self is splintered into many competing selves.

Despite the horrific nature of Kennedy's plays, they offer, like most absurdist works, a parabolic story opportunity which allows its characters to learn a new way of thinking and believing.

From Julie Dash's perspective this liminal place to create non-linear dramatic action is an environment from the past, where, as in her film *Daughters of the Dust*, the past is evoked in a moment of family history, showing the transitional moment as a family moves from one side of the country to the other. Key to Dash's sense of liminality is the agency of ancestors and ancestor worship to affect the present moment. Because Dash was drawing upon her own Gullah family history, one might be tempted to consider the possibility of looking into your own heritage – please do! While we have been focusing on African and African American culture in this chapter, it is important to note that in every faith and every culture, there are elements of liminality that are useful to explore. It's important to note that the mystic, the supernatural, and the mysterious aspect of religion exists across many faiths, including the Kabbalah in Judaism, Gnosticism in Christianity, and Sufism in Islam. The sense that there is much more to the world than is able to be seen in empirical reality is an important tool in the dramatist's non-linear toolbox, and the use of the mystic and the supernatural to create a space of liminality where the rules fall apart, and anything might happen is key to magic and theatricality in one's writing.

In the next chapter of this book, I'll be concentrating on yet another kind of liminality, and that is gender fluidity and gender transformation. The ability of characters to transform and challenge traditional notions of gender, sexuality, and queerness is key to building non-linearity to non-traditional dramatic action. Two dramatists that get at that kind of transfiguration are Jean Genet, who was a kind of wide-eyed, gender criminal of the 1950s and 60s, and one of the major Absurdist playwrights who gleefully broke all the rules of gender and sexuality, and in the film world, Sally Potter, who is the screenwriter and director of *Orlando*, the gender transformation film based on the novel by Virginia Woolf, who is a multi-media artist who also creates performance art, rock, and choreographs dance. The next chapter explores how the nature of gender transformation provides a useful means to deepen one's ability to create equivocal characters, characters who are much more than who they are on the surface of things.

CHAPTER 5

Transfiguration of Gender and Identity – Transformations, Mutability, and Androgyny

Jean Genet's The Balcony *and Sally Potter's* Orlando

1   Jean Genet: Criminal Gender Illusionist

We start our exploration of the Absurdist playwrights with Jean Genet simply because there is no other Absurdist dramatist discussed in this volume who approaches Genet's cheerful willingness to subvert and twist reality to his own pleasure. For Genet, whose life was intimately intertwined with both his deep embrace of his homosexuality as well as his criminal history, there is no reality that moves beyond total illusion. Jean Genet, a French dramatist of the 1950s and 60s, was raised in foster homes, and served time in both juvenile and adult prisons because of his predilections for petty crime and the unfortunate criminality of his subversive notions of sexuality. Genet became the patron saint for outsiders and the disillusioned. He very nearly spent his entire life in prison and might have done so if it hadn't been for his supporters, which include Jean-Paul Sartre, who was so captivated by Genet's doings that he wrote *Saint Genet* which is neither biography or literary criticism but merely a subject for Sartre to apply his further explorations of existential philosophy through the lens of Jean Genet's rebellious life and work. Genet is our unlawful absurdist, inserting scandal, disgrace, and a pleasurably subversive sexual ambiguity to our dream-wrighting, drawing us into a wild, turbulent, yet cleansing world of androgynous hedonism and debauchery to reveal ourselves to ourselves.

Key to understanding Genet is his unadulterated magical queerness, and tied to that, the importance of the theatricality of cross-dressing, and his attachment to costumes and a child-like love of make-believe. In his plays, *The Maids*, *The Screens*, *The Blacks*, and *The Balcony*, Genet's essential project is to unmask his characters by putting them behind masks. In the very act of pretense, and in particular, sexually immersive pretense, which includes an erotic embrace of role-playing and the scenarios that grow out of role playing, Genet finds a queer ironic truth. The victor and the vanquished, the violator and the violated, and the criminal and his victim, are all happily playing the roles they must play – knowing full well that these pretenses give them agency. For without role-playing, at least in the world of Genet's dream-based realities, there is no reality at all. Pretense creates corporeality and materiality that is more real than the everyday, and in fact, the quotidian world is nothing but a canvas on which pretense must be written, to maintain the barest sense of what is the here and now. Without fantasy, the human being becomes nothing more than animal, but with each castle in the air comes the fully embraced truth of the moment – even if the characters themselves are not quite sure who or what they are.

In Jean Genet's *The Balcony*, we enter the world of the upscale bordello, a "house of illusions," which is the classic French euphemism for a brothel. This place of sexual pretense is run by Irma (played in the film version by a voluptuous, heavy-lidded Shelley Winter), and Irma is the star of her own world of fantasy, she casts, directs, and stars in a place of infinite mirrors and private theatres. There is a fake bishop in the process of seeking confession from a penitent woman; an austere sham judge imposing a criminal sentence on thief; and a mock general who mounts his trusty steed. Outside the house of ill repute however, there is a real revolution occurring, and the violence of the outside world begins to impinge upon the fantasy within the brothel. One of the prostitutes, Chantal, decides to join the revolution, and not long after, the Envoy from the Queen appears to reveal that the pillars of society, the real Chief Justice, Bishop, and General have all been murdered in the unrest. In a quick twist of fate, Madame Irma suggest that the fake Bishop, Judge, and General take on the real-life power of their assumed roles using the regalia and props from her "house of illusions" and so these ersatz figures do just that as a counter revolutionary measure to restore order with a kind of utter criminal pretense that is more truthful than what is real. The exercise below allows you the dramatist to experiment with this exploration of the cross-gendered mask, as a non-linear device to reveal what is true, rather than what is real. The essence of law-breaking and illicit artmaking is key to its success, as well as slippage of gender as a tool to tear down the walls of societal hypocrisy.

Exercise 1: Jean Genet – The Balcony – The Forbidden Mask of Gender-Fluidity

According to the theorist Erving Goffman, and his famous book, *The Presentation of Self in Everyday Life*, we are always playing a role. With that in mind, this is an exercise in gender criminality. In the exercise below, you can create a scene to add to a current dramatic work, either stage or film, or you can use this exercise to create an entire new world. Bear in mind that in dreams, the nature of disguise is tied to the Harrison Ford effect – in other words, a character may be transfigured to physically become several different people,

TRANSFIGURATION OF GENDER AND IDENTITY   101

but remain who they have always been. A character may behave in layers – a gas meter reader in real life can be playing a priest but may be much more than either role. A gum-smacking waitress may be a man who becomes a queen, a football quarterback may be a transitioning high society matron, who is also mustachioed villain. At any given moment a character may revert, switching back to who they once were, or become someone new in a new situation. Key to this is the instability of gender, its fluid nature is key to any dramatic conflict you create. All the elements involved come out of a dream cache created for this specific exercise – as you conceive of each prompt, add several elements to the cache from which to choose.

1. Characters: Start by creating two to three characters – playing a role; in disguise; made up – maybe playing a different gender; one character is from the underclass, an outsider, an immigrant. The others are from above – upper class, higher spirituality, but meeting the other somehow in a middle space, a place of liminality where the rules may be broken.
2. Situation: A crime; a criminal event, a crime runs underneath this – a crime that borders on a good deed. A crime that forces the two classes to meet and intertwine uncomfortably. The crime is one with national importance, and therefore implicates all major governmental figures.
3. Relationships: one of the characters is in love with another of the characters, and yet must maintain their formal role in society. The love is criminal, unacceptable in society, and a threat to peace in the community. The love puts the characters at risk of death, and at the same time is totally false and a kind of performance.
4. Physical activity: An illegal game of chance with very high stakes. The game is criminal – there are real, terrifying consequences tied to its outcome.
5. *Location*: The location is a place of change, instability, illusion, a liminal place where normal rules break down: a prison, a brothel, an asylum, or even government or business office overrun with revolutionaries or criminals; one is imprisoned or under duress – yet freed from traditional mores and morals.
6. *Sacred Object:* This is an item that has a strange, talismanic, and mystic quality to it – it can cause change, it can change itself. It is present whenever something magical happens – indeed, its presence may cause the change to happen. Tied to this is some kind of *mirror*, which provides a vehicle of change.
7. Moment of greatest tension: This is a stressful moment that causes a character to totally change into another character with the introduction of a *sacred object*. An uncanny transformation; it has aspects of criminality

tied to it – there should be a carnivorous quality or a quality of horror to it, aligned with mounting sexual pleasure.
8. Final event: A moment of unspeakable obscenity – violent, passionate, erotic, and awful – a shocking moment that is irresistible.
9. Include: Sacred Object. Mirror. Make-up/Disguise. Undergarments.

Leaving Genet and the theatre behind, we move into the realm of another dramatist, Sally Potter, who explores the shuddering shifts of gender as a wholly invented realm, where those who live lives under the LGTBTQ + rainbow find safe spaces for creation. Potter, who was as much a performance artist, musician, and dancer as she was a filmmaker, has made a career out of defying norms of gender and sexuality in order to get at a broader, deeper realm of highly theatrical gender behavior that exists in stunning simultaneity with heterogeneity.

2   *Orlando* – Sally Potter – a History of Gender Fluidity

In *Orlando*, Sally Potter has taken great liberties in her adaptation of Virginia Woolf's novel primarily to deal with the vast swath of 400 years of history that takes place over the course of a two-hour film. The technique of moving from one intense, imagistic dramatic action to the next with sudden cuts that juxtapose unlike situations connected by rhythmic editing creates the impression that Orlando, the central character whose gender transformation is not entirely complete – the male persona lives within the female body once the change has occurred, and in this sense, the depth of the change and its implications in society is all the more powerful.

A strangely beautiful moment that begins the film provides a metaphor for its entirety: a dead peasant woman frozen in clear ice in a lake. This horrific figure elicits a great burst of cruel laughter from a noble looking down at her lifeless body surrounded by small orbit of the fruit she was selling. It is horrific, but oddly crystalline moments like this throughout the film get at the inherent strangeness of Orlando's life. The violent explosion of laughter at this tragic image twists the moment into something terrible and grotesque and yet utterly fascinating. One cannot turn their head away, and yet this same image followed by Orlando's pursuit of a Cossack bride gets at the same weirdness of culture. We cannot see this arrangement ever working, and yet, it does, at least momentarily, for the Orlando, even as we sense, with the many scenes on the ice, with Orlando and his Cossack lover skating, that the ice is thin, and once it breaks so will the romance.

The film is filled with moments of filmed theatre, mini performance pieces which, like most fairground stages, provide a satiric insight into the very real conflicts occurring throughout the film. Another dreamwrighting technique is Potter's use of the breaking of the fourth wall, with Orlando turning to us, through the camera, and delivering brief non-sequiturs, in metatheatrical moments, akin to the techniques used in Epic Theatre by purveyors such as Bertolt Brecht. The same technique might also be considered a form of alienation or ostranenie, "making strange" in order to process the situation from the outside in, forcing the audience to engage personally with the subject of the film at hand. But there are other intriguing techniques used in the film to unsettle the audience, particularly in the realm of gender.

Throughout the film, the use of the countertenors creates an unbalancing act, the piercing, ultra-high, clear tone of male singers singing in the range of sopranos, has the unforgettable and perhaps unnerving quality of an ethereal angelic otherness. And still, in its translucent beauty, reminds one of the famous castrato singers, who were violently castrated to maintain their prepubescent voices. This somewhat unsettling experience is a perfect tool in the film to help startle its audience into a state of acceptance of the central transformation of Orlando – if this voice occurs in nature, perhaps it is possible that men may transform into women and vice versa in the world of the film. The moments of castrati singing occur several times in the film, particularly before important moments tied to Orlando's gender.

One of those major moments takes place as Orlando, now transformed into a female body, confronts a salon of major poets and writers, including Alexander Pope and Jonathan Swift. The poets smugly remind Orlando that women are like children and, without husbands and fathers, are lost. Shortly thereafter, Orlando discovers that because of her transformation to womanhood, she is considered to be dead and numerous lawsuits are filed against her. And yet, somehow, Orlando slips into contemporary times as her non-binary life has conferred upon her a kind of immortality that allows her to transcend gender. The film ends with a now independent and triumphant Orlando pointing out to her daughter an uncanny floating angel, metallic and somewhat alien, strangely singing in that primordially high-pitched castrato soprano, in a celebration of androgyny.

Exercise 2: Sally Potter's Orlando – Shifting Androgynies of History

In the film Orlando, the structure is built upon specific moments of history, slammed forward by simple intertitles that move us in time, 1600-death;

1610-love; 1650-poetry; 1700-politics; 1750-society; 1850-sex; birth. In addition, the film moves us using the sudden sliced juxtapositions of specific images and landscapes, which have a certain textural similarity and a huge phenomenological difference. The effect is very Brechtian; each change is a kind of slap to the face, or a splash of cold water, and it is enhanced by Tilda Swinton's uniquely gorgeous, androgynous, queer persona – her angelic unblinking presence which thrills because of its beautiful, uncanny, yet classical proportions.

In the exercise below, you'll be working with several androgynous characters, neither male or female, at times both and sometimes neither simultaneously. You'll also be exploring those characters in a play of history. We'll also be using intertitles to help shape the structure of the dramatic conflict, using the strategy of association to create them.

STEP 1: Assembling the characters – working with your dream cache, you'll work from a prompt – who are the men and women in your life who have engaged you specifically as men or women? The goal here is to use characters from your real life, from history, and from your imagination to create people who firmly fit into the gender binary. Try and create, tear-off, and insert into dream cache at least ten different characters; five men and five women. Again, focus on gender and how it has shaped your image of them.

STEP 2: Gender Mix – Of these characters, draw two of each gender out of your dream cache – and then pair them together, giving them one body each. You are creating "equivocal characters" – characters who possess the ability to flip between multiple selves. If you want to take this a bit further, choose four characters for each body, blending two male and two female characters into each physical body. Bear in mind that the same actor will play all these characters – they are the one body that will host these characters.

STEP 3: Creating the intertitle structure – In this step you are going to do what I call a condensation of experience. The condensation process is a kind of winnowing down to an essential aspect of a character's life experience, as you will be moving in rather gigantic leaps through time and space.

a. *Choose a Center* – Out of your four central characters, choose two that will be bound in one body/actor – this will be your central character. The other character that is also a bind of two characters will become an antagonist, a foil, a friend – but will also be quite significant. However, right now, to create the structure of your film, you'll be working with just this central character.

b. *Tab the Center* – Set a timer – you will have eight minutes to tab in, briefly, evocatively, at least thirty events of both central character's bound lives. Brevity here is the soul of wit – don't worry about these events' importance at this point, the trick is to create as many as you can, and thirty

events is ideal. After eight minutes stop – take a breather. Walk away from the list of events and take at least a 20-minute break.
c. *Winnowing the events* – Once you have taken your break, take a moment and find at least ten events of the thirty (five for each character) you have discovered that affect you emotionally. That is your meter of success – whether you find yourself crying, laughing, terrified, inspired by the events of your character's lives. Write these down – and step away for at least twenty minutes.
d. *Essence of events* – Creating your intertitles; once you have ten events, five for each of your characters' two genders – and now have the characters tell you about what happened. This would be a short monologue, using all five senses to describe what occurred to them. Focus on the sensual experience rather than the emotional experience – keep it specific. The emotions will come with the sensual experience – but what you want are specific phenomenal, sensual details of what happened. Step away for twenty minutes, one last time.
e. *Intertitle the events* – Once you have all ten events, you will create the intertitles – read what your characters have told you about each event. Let that description of the event feed your imagination – and subjectively allow yourself to respond to how that description made you feel. That response should be a *single word* that describes the event – and it may be a word that your character used in their description, or it may be your own word to get at the emotional essence of that event. By the end you should have ten words tied to ten events.

STEP 4: Writing the film sequence – of these intertitles you will be using a total of six, three of each that you've created, saving the rest in case you need them. These six intertitles, tied to the events from your character's past, will provide the structural form for your film, from which you can build your story. The sequence may be the entirety of the film or just a portion that you specifically desire to explore for this exercise. These may be tied to specific time periods like the broad swaths of history explored in *Orlando*, or they may be just tied to your central character's two lives. They may be intertwined – and they certainly don't have to be linear. Remember that you'll be exploring gender extensively in this sequence, and you should bear in mind that you have two additional characters (bound to one actor) that you'll be drawing into these events, so that will help substantially to transform this sequence into a much larger project if you choose. The goal here is the flow the gender possibilities, and allow gender confusion, surprise, and wonder to occur.

In this chapter we have allowed the flow of gender and desire to mutate and change, taking us into the lyric realms of sexuality and sensuality, which provide a profound backdrop for some of the major dramatic questions of our day tied to LGBTQ social justice issues. More importantly, with this last exercise, we tell the story of those whose gender flows in ways that defy and augment traditional roles in our society. Perhaps, at least through subliminal means, we can manifest a revolution using our abilities to create non-linear dream dramas, that profoundly revolutionize what it means to be a voluntarily gendered human being.

In the next chapter we'll look at another spin on powerful story-telling technique, one which we have touched upon briefly, which is both radical and yet very ancient – because if we mostly don't dream in a strictly causal, linear fashion, we might be writing backwards! Moving backwards in plot to move forwards in story is one of the most ancient non-linear storytelling techniques we have in our toolbox. Yet it can seem utterly radical and strange – and often it is tied to a deeper Noir mystery that lurks deep within us with an accompanying sense of horror. We'll explore that technique by looking at two uniquely contemporary award-winning writers who both continue to push the envelope on stage and in film – Martin McDonagh and Christopher Nolan.

CHAPTER 6

The Dreamer's Heart – Thinking Backwards First

Character Dreams and Storytelling – McDonagh's The Pillowman *and Christopher Nolan's:* Memento

In this chapter we're going to look deeply into what I call the Dreamer's heart – which is key to the realm of non-linear story-telling; the Dreamer's heart holds mystery, it holds the unknown, the uncanny click at the back of your skull that says dig deeper, go back further, there is something more there, and the quest to find it will not be easy, but in fact, because it is mysterious, it will be powerful, life-changing, and either wildly ecstatic or deeply horrific. In fact, digging deeper and further back is one of the keys to Film Noir, and both dramas we explore in this chapter, *The Pillowman* and *Memento* have deep roots in Noir culture. How do we define Film Noir? Well, it's in the name itself – noir, black – but really what we're thinking is black and white, like American detective films in the 1940s. The qualities we associate with Noir are tied to its dreamlike, dark, erotic, and yet crystalline cruelty – it has all the qualities we associate with the dramatic dream, a clear reality that unveils a glowing menace, and what I call the "uncanny click" as you get closer to the Dreamer's heart. It's like the painful snap that sometimes catches you at the base of skull when you turn your head the wrong way – and you suddenly see the world in a different, new way. And quite often the detective is the one who feels that click – and we feel it with them.

Of course, Noir's detective roots go all the way back to *Oedipus Rex*, the original detective story – Oedipus, the King, is driven to discover what has happened in the past to solve the current plague on Thebes, the city he rules, where the bodies are piling up, and it is his own relentless, merciless hunt for truth that becomes his undoing. To get at the truth, Oedipus must, like other detectives, work his way back from the current corpse, the body that is the result of many actions, by digging deeper and deeper into the past. Working backwards through time, he must root out what happened to cause all this mayhem – and in the end, of course in *Oedipus Rex* it is he, himself, at its dark root. It's this structure, which is distinctly non-linear, that has become a powerful storytelling formation – one which drives so many non-traditional, dream-like dramas.

Noir's roots may also be in German expressionism, and much of its shadowed, psychological, and brutal mood qualities can first be found there, but it also has deep American veins with the storytelling of Dashiell Hammett coursing blood-red through its enigmas. Think of films like *The Maltese Falcon* (1941) with Humphrey Bogart as the quintessential detective, Sam Spade, and *Murder, My Sweet* (1944), with Dick Powell as Philip Marlowe, or stepping into a more universal horror, *The Invisible Man*, as directed by James Whale. In these films we find the Dreamer's heart is an undiscoverable mystery, deadly and pure, the answer for which might only be found by a brutal unmasking of the hero, who is often undone done by stunning, irresistible femme fatales, such as Barbara Stanwyck in *Double Indemnity*, or Lana Turner in *The Postman Always Rings Twice* (1946), or Ava Gardner in *The Killers* (1946).

Both the dramatists we'll explore in this chapter have their own powerful roots in this style of drama, and in particular, Martin McDonagh, whose own stage plays have a unique Gothic blend of bloody violence and wildly funny characterization, brings a muscular twist to his characters' quest into the dreamers' heart. In his *Beauty Queen of Leenane*, the central character, Maureen, brutally murders her own mother, bashing Mag's head in, but only after pouring hot boiling oil on her mother's hand making dark quips along the way. Yet key to the play is the fact that Maureen's madness has us fooled throughout much of the play, and we find ourselves secretly or not so secretly rooting for her – until she and the audience learn simultaneously exactly how criminally insane she is. McDonagh's dramatic essence is really tied to revelation of character, and while the dark, disturbing violence of his plays may be deeply off-putting to most audiences, what becomes even more disquieting is the level of comedy woven through his plays, so that we find ourselves laughing, even as his characters commit heinous, bloody violent crimes. And director and film-maker Christopher Nolan, who has become known for his ability to create noirish, experimental, and deeply enigmatic films, crystalizes this process of working backward in his own detective film, *Memento*. This film has come to be one of the most important and seminal non-linear films along with *Citizen Kane*. The unreliable nature of his detective-narrator, Leonard Shelby, who has a memory deficit, and can't remember anything beyond the previous fifteen minutes, becomes key to Nolan's storytelling in the film. But as we'll learn, there are specific visualizing techniques to understanding and experiment with the structure of *Memento* and we'll examine those at the end of the chapter.

In both the case of cases of Martin McDonagh and Christopher Nolan, we will be playing with the reverse journey of the Dreamer's heart, using backwards framing to reveal clues that force the audience to work closely with the film, creating a kind of working thought experiment to make sense of what is happening. Key to both McDonagh's and Nolan's work as dramatic artists is a demand to deeply engage, as their audiences are forced to unravel an impossible mental knot which has led the protagonist of their dramatic works into a slippery world of dramatic action – and in both cases, we'll discover that there is a tenable, canny technique to get at a bizarre, uncanny result.

1   Story Structure in McDonagh's *The Pillowman*

In Martin McDonagh's brutally funny and moving play *The Pillowman*, the protagonist Katurian is a writer of stories about children. Katurian's stories are at times needlessly brutal and cruel, yet at other times tender and just a bit ridiculous, and the structure of sharing stories in the play is a framework that has been proven over time to be an intriguing associative dream-like structure that relentlessly triggers the audience's curiosity. Each story leads to another, and another, and the final story somehow embraces the whole while unveiling its own mystery. Katurian is driven to tell his stories, in the immediate moment of the play, by Topolsky and Ariel, in a good cop/bad cop interrogation, attempting to do so for two reasons, 1) to protect his brother, Michal, who seems to be slow-witted and innocent, and 2) to save his stories, which Ariel has threatened to burn. As the play progresses, Katurian becomes more and more desperate, trying to somehow protect his stories from destruction, while at the same time digging deeper into his storytelling abilities, pushing the envelope, forcing his audience to wrestle with the deeper horror of what it is Michal has really done – and how real Katurian's stories have turned out to be.

With each of Katurian's stories, "The Little Apple Men," "The Tale of the Three Gibbet Crossroads," or "The Tale of the Town on the River," Katurian is trying to get at a larger concern, and that is how the abandonment of children to their own resources creates deeply troubled adults. It's "The Pillowman" himself, this creature of Katurian's imagination, who seems most kind as he provides the key moment of hope as he ends of the lives of children before they have their most horrible experiences as adults. Even though Katurian and Michel will each have a violent end, in the final moments of the play, it becomes clear that Katurian's stories, by the grace of Ariel, the bad cop who, ironically, found the stories the most offensive, will survive into posterity.

But *The Pillowman* also raises moral questions about the kinds of stories we *should* tell – are there certain boundaries we should never cross? Perhaps the detectives Topolsky and Ariel are right about Katurian – he should die for telling horrible stories in which children are maimed and murdered and which inspired his brother to kill. What are the ethical standards we should hold as writers – are there limits to our imagination? What responsibility do we have if our stories encourage unethical, immoral behavior in others? Or are any restrictions on the writer's imagination a form of censorship that ultimately betrays the writer's ability to paint an unvarnished view of our society. Do we have a greater responsibility to protect the writer's imagination, so that truths may emerge – even if they are deeply uncomfortable truths? *The Pillowman* is ultimately about storytelling itself, about the importance and necessity of storytelling for our survival as a species, and because of that, hails to an even earlier, more basic, more ancient tale.

One Thousand and One Nights, otherwise known as the story of Scheherazade, the Persian daughter of a Vizier, who tells stories to Shahryar, Persian Sassanid King of kings, to save her own life, is an old one, and it has a similar structure to McDonagh's play. In that story, King Shahryar had an unfaithful queen who had betrayed him cruelly. In his rage, the King demanded that a virgin be sent to him each night, and at the dawn of that next day, he would have the young woman executed. Upon hearing of this terrible fate for the young women of the kingdom, the daughter of the Vizier, Scheherazade volunteers to be the next virgin – despite the pleas of her sister, Dunyazad. But Scheherazade is no ordinary girl. She is a genius and an autodidact, who has an insatiable curiosity and has read and absorbed the stories and histories of all the kingdoms that had preceded that of the present king. She has an enormous library, and has collected over a thousand books, that dealt with ancient races and defeated rulers. She has the wisdom of one much older than herself and is conversant in science, mathematics, music, and philosophy. She has a kind and polite demeanor, a gentle, witty, and self-deprecating humor, and has cultivated herself to be an attentive, pleasant conversational companion.

That evening, after introductions were made, Scheherazade proceeds to entertain the king, but first asks that she might have the audience of her sister, who loves her stories. The King, knowing of Scheherazade's special talents for storytelling through her father's ministrations, allows Dunyazad to appear. Having been previously coached by her sister, Dunyazad asks for a story that she knows would intrigue the King. Cleverly, Scheherazade times the telling of her story to the rhythm of the evening, so that by dawn, she is at one of its most captivating moments – and the King, unsurprisingly, allows Scheherazade to live another day. And so, the storytelling continues, day after day, for a one thousand and one nights, until Scheherazade's life is saved.

If a play is essentially a series of scenes, then understanding each scene as a separate story provides an intriguing way to build the structure of your play and one that is very different from the traditional notion of the Sonata structure with its set-up, struggle, and solution. One other element to think about – how much of the storyteller's own story are in the stories the storyteller tells? What is real and what is dream? Can the two flow in and out of each other, creating a somewhat unreliable, but thoroughly evocative narrative? And finally, in your own Dreamer's heart, there should be a real, tangible key to the mystery – it may never be wholly revealed, but it should always be there.

Exercise 1: Katurian/Scheherazade – The Structure of Stories-within-Stories

- Write down the name of your protagonist, who will be a storyteller of some sort.
- Provide a setting for your character, which is conducive to the telling of stories.
- Provide a desperate reason for why your character must tell stories right now and the dire consequences if the stories are not told.
- Provide an antagonist to whom the stories must be told, and why they would want to hear these stories. The antagonist may ask questions, which must be answered.
- Your character will now tell six fictional stories, that she or he has made up, framed by the brief details below. Consider that your protagonist and the characters listening to the stories, may themselves become characters within the stories that are being told – and that their roles in those stories may correspond and have meaning for who they are outside the realm of the stories – in the "real" world of the storyteller.
- Create a character dream cache for your protagonist – six elements from the dream cache become central images, symbols, animals, plants, characters or landscapes for the six stories.
- Each story can have a totally different heroine/hero – or they can be linked – as you write these mini-dramas – think about them as ten-minute plays that can stand on their own, but make sure they pull together with that of the storyteller. Contemplate also, how all these characters might be double-cast to additionally link the stories.
    1. The First Story – Call to Adventure
        a. In this story, the heroine/hero find her/himself drawn out of her ordinary world by perhaps supernatural means, and her/his life perhaps forever changed if they take this step – which may or may not be taken.
        b. There is an object from your central character's dreams (from their dream cache), which is a part of this story.
    2. The Second Story – Crossing the Threshold

  a. In this story, the heroine/hero has entered into a world which is strange, unknown, perhaps threatening, and is forced into a dilemma which is fairly terrifying.
  b. There is an animal from your central character's dreams (from their dream cache), which is a part of this story.
 3. The Third Story – The Meeting with the Goddess/God
  a. In this story, the heroine/hero meets the all-loving Goddess/God, who engages the hero in a romantic tryst that raises questions about the hero's deepest desire.
  b. The Goddess/God gives the hero a task, which has to do with the hero's mother or father.
  c. There is a person from your central character's dreams(from their dream cache), which is a part of this story.
 4. The Fourth Story – Atonement with the Father/Mother
  a. In this story, the heroine/hero faces the Father or Mother who they have wronged (or has wronged them), who stands in judgment of them, who requires reconciliation for them to move on.
  b. There is a person from your central character's dreams (from their dream cache), which is a part of this story.
 5. The Fifth Story – The Magic Flight
  a. In this story the heroine/hero must escape with a treasure, from a dangerous place, using magical and/or amazing powers, the gods have been jealously guarding.
  b. There is a place from your central character's dreams (from their dream cache), which is a part of this story.
 6. The Sixth Story – The Crossing of the Return Threshold
  a. In this story, the hero learns the secret to returning, how to retain the wisdom gained on the quest, and how to share the wisdom with the rest of the world.
  b. There is a question from your central character's dreams (from their dream cache), which is a part of this story.

As you complete this series of scenes, you might want to consider a few questions tied to its structure and allow these questions to further shape the drama that you're writing.

– How did this dramatic writing exercise get at the nature of storytelling and what questions did it raise about how we tell stories through dramatic action?
– What ethical questions did you raise about the behavior of the characters in your story? Key to *The Pillowman* is the ethics behind the choices made

- by the characters – what have your characters chosen to do (or not do) that gets at a fundamental truth that you believe about people.
- Given the fact that you're probably working on a larger project, how did these exercises fit into that project – and did you get at the Dreamer's heart in your project? Was there a key that you discovered to that mystery, and if so, how might you use it to develop deeper characterization, richer plot, and a more dynamic dramatic question for your drama?
- Finally, given the stakes involved in the storytelling in this exercise, how do those same stakes tie into why you tell your own stories? How has the telling of this story taught you something about the stories you like to tell?

2   Hairpin: The Structure of Christopher Nolan's *Memento*

Christopher Nolan's *Memento* is a neo-noir, revenge film – and revenge tragedy dates to plays like *Hamlet* and *The Spanish Tragedy* and uses several devices – an unreliable narrator following cues that may or may not lead to the killer, a structure that follows two threads – one leading *to* the revenge murder, and the other *leading* from the revenge murder. Here the mystery of the Dreamer's heart lies in why the detective, Leonard Shelby, does what he does – and even more important, does he even understand what he is doing? The story moves backwards in time – and there are two points of view – subjective (color) (backwards chronological order) and objective (black and white) (chronological order). The two strands meet by the end of the film. The film's structure is essentially a hairpin – and its structure is tied to where the two strands of story meet in the moment before Leonard Shelby kills Teddy. Bear in mind what a hairpin or a hairpin turn really is – it's an impossibility made possible – and it is life-threatening at high speeds. Keep that metaphor in mind – and yet a hairpin is also just that, a pin to hold down hair. It provides a structure to what would be otherwise a chaotic mess. As for the story structure in *Memento*, it is incredibly challenging for an audience to understand – especially as they are watching it. Do they understand the difference between the subjective/color world of Leonard Shelby, and the objective/black & white world of the film's narrative? And here's the kicker – does it matter if they totally understand what is happening? Leonard is covered with tattoos and other bits of memories that he follows to solve his mystery. But some of these leads are complete and utter lies. It's impossible to know, because of Leonard's inability to remember anything beyond the last 15 minutes, what is true or not in his world. And it might be that for some audiences, it is too mysterious for them to follow, and they drop out. However, for many others, the film, despite how confusing it might be – is utterly gripping because of the unusual storytelling. We are left at the end of the film wondering how much Leonard Shelby can ever possibly understand – given his level of anterograde amnesia. Larger mysteries linger. Leonard Shelby may be Sammy Jankis who inadvertently murdered his own wife through an insulin injection overdose, and/or Leonard and his wife may the victims of a horrible crime. In the end, we are left with more questions than we have answers – and ironically, if one views the scenes of the film in order, the story is actually very, very simple and clear. Again, it's the reverse storytelling that makes it so powerful – and that storytelling is made powerful by its unreliability – we are fascinated because we can't get ahead of it. And isn't that a wonderful place to be for an audience?

Exercise 2: Memento's Structure of Revenge – Creating your own Hairpin

In this five-page exercise, you will create five separate scenes that build toward a complete sequence. You're challenged to explore a simple plot built from the oneiric elements you have mined from your dream cache.

1. Bear in mind that your basic story is one of *revenge* – for a heinous crime has been previously committed by an antagonist whose essence you have drawn from your dream cache.
2. First, draw five elements from the dream cache with the idea of revenge connecting the dots. You can do this randomly, or just keep pulling dream elements that seem to work for you.
3. Examine them in relationship to each other, thinking about them literally or from an associative manner.
4. Set these elements up into a basic story – follow a linear/causal path – that is, a story in which this causes this causes this causes this – essentially a series of dominos that cause another domino to fall, until the end.
5. Now reexamine the story elements you have created – bearing in mind the original dream elements.
    a. Choose one of elements as the central axis of your sequence.
    b. Choose two of the elements that will now work backwards – or in some sequence that is non-linear – and perhaps based on a connection between the original dream elements.
    c. Choose two of the elements that following chronological – and therefore linear/causal – structure. Intersperse these between the other two.
    d. The axis story element will end the sequence.

      e.   Think of your linear sequence, 1-2-3-4-5, as actually being filmed and edited in this non-linear sequence as 5-1-4-2-3.
6. Write out the sequence with scene headings, action, and dialogue into a short screenplay.
7. Give the screenplay a title and consider – what would happen if you switched around the scenes? Could you rework it with the non-linear elements becoming linear and vice versa?

In this exercise, and in a few of the previous exercises in the book, we're playing with story elements – how to move past traditional linear structure and choose a structure that is closer to how our dreams work – in an associative rather than linear manner. But what does it mean to work in an associative manner? Well, it's tied to how we solve a knot or a problem – we keep tugging at strands to figure out how to unknot, untie, and straighten the string of narrative that has been tied up for us. And audiences faced with a knot have both a fascination and a frustration – if it's too easy to solve the knot, they'll quickly get ahead of our story and check out. If it's too difficult and or impossible to solve, audiences will also check out. What you need to create is a knot that adds progressive bits of solution and deeper mystery as the audience moves closer to payoff – but there must be some sense on the side of the audience that there is a payoff, even if that payoff leaves a few knots knotted at the end.

In the final exercise of this chapter, we'll look at the nature of how to create these knots, which are always built around that earlier concept we discussed in this chapter – the Dreamer's heart. In Scotland there is a population of travelling peoples known as the Scottish Travellers, who have some connection (though not always) to the Romani of Europe. Donald Braid, a scholar and folklorist, has written extensively on the Scottish Travelers in his book, *Scottish Traveller Tales: Lives Shaped through Stories* and has written about what he calls "dream stories," which are stories that are told in a manner that is intentionally confusing to the listener. In these stories, the teller incorporates a "knot" or a confusing element, so that the listener is thrown off the tale for a moment wondering, "did that happen ... or not?" In that moment, there is a slippage of reality, a moment that can only be accepted in the corporeality of dreams.

One of the more famous stories is "The Black Laird and the Cattleman," which follows a night of tall tales being told around the hearth of a local Scottish lord. The eponymous Laird [Lord] calls upon one of the local cattlemen to tell "the biggest lie" and if it is good enough, the Lord offers a "golden guinea" in reward. One cattleman is terribly embarrassed by the idea of being called out, and instead of telling a story, the Lord tells him to clean his boat down by the river instead.

The cattleman steps into the boat to clean it, and in the next moment is swept away down the river and arrives across it on the other shore. In the process the cattleman is transformed into a beautiful young woman, and is greeted by a handsome young man, who falls immediately in love with her. Years pass, and now the young couple return to the river with their baby in hand, and the young woman notices the boat that brought her there. Out of curiosity, she steps into the boat which immediately whisks her back across the river, and she is transformed once again into the cattleman. The cattleman, caught in the deep sadness of leaving his lover and child behind, returns, distraught to the hearth of the cattleman, and after sharing his sad tale, wins the golden guinea after all.

The knot in the story, and how it captures the attention of the listener, is the gender transformation that occurs in the middle. It is told from the point of view of the cattleman, who accepts the new reality without questioning it – much in the style of a dream. The magic of the moment is how subtly it occurs – almost without the listener noticing, with the effect of that listener wondering, did that happen for real – or not? Using this Scottish Traveller's dream story technique is a variation on the Scheherazade exercise, since it starts with the device of an evening of stories being told, and there is a step away from that fire of the imagination, and a return there at the ending.

Exercise 3: The Scottish Dream Story – The Dreamer's Hearth

In this exercise, the steps you take will be framed by a larger plot line – that of the story circle – and in this case, you'll be framing the stories around the dream caches of the various characters you are exploring in your drama.

Step 1 – The Dreamer's Circle – Conceiving a Creative Realm
In this first step, you'll gather five to six of the characters you want to explore in your drama; give them a dramatic situation where they are compelled to tell stories – perhaps to save their own lives! Your central character's job is to listen – and perhaps in the last moment, tell a final story. Make sure the stakes are high, and that each is egged on, so that each character feels that they must top the others in their story telling. Give the storytelling space a specific, evocative, emotional feel to it, as well as a season, a time of day, all of which add to the need to tell the stories. Decide the order of the story telling in advance, even if the characters themselves don't know what that order is – and as the stories are told, make sure they link back to *why* they are telling the stories. There should be a compelling reason, perhaps driven by a threat or a reward. Perhaps, for

example, they are telling their version of an event that happened that they all experienced – giving their own variation, their own spin, not unlike the storytelling in Akutagawa Ryunosuke's short story *Rashōmon* which was used as the basis for Akira Kurosawa's film *Rashomon* (1950).

Step 2 – The Dreamer's Circle – Telling the Stories

1. Each of the characters tell a story incorporating at least three of the elements from that character's dream cache – the story may have a larger connection to the situation at hand, but mostly it should serve to reveal who the character is and how they have come to be within the Dreamer's Circle.
2. Remember that each story should have a *knot*, that is, a story element that doesn't quite make sense or has a surreal or magical quality. Remember to submerge the magical moment, so that it happens in such a subtle way that the listener should have difficulty knowing whether it is within the reality of the story.
3. One story leads to the next story by means of something within the Dream circle reality – again, these stories may all link, share a common theme, be variations of some central event, or perhaps all share that same "knot" that creates the magic. By the end of the storytelling there should be a change and an inexorable movement out of the Dream circle moment.

Step 2 – The Dreamer's Circle – The Shift in the Universe – A Final Tale

1. At the end of the telling of the stories, there is a seismic shift in the landscape of the Dreamer's circle, and it precipitates a final story by your central character.
2. This final story ends the Dreamer's circle and incorporates all the stories in some manner – transforming the circle into a different realm – and providing some kind of solution to a problem in the major dramatic project you're exploring while experimenting with this dream work.
3. By the telling of these stories, revelations about each of the characters are now known, making it possible for your central character to move forward in the major plot of your drama – and whether you include this dreamer's circle in your drama is up to you.
4. What is important is that you now know things about each of the characters that you didn't know before – and that knowledge will transform your central character and the drama you are writing.

In this chapter we have explored the nature of the Dreamer's heart – looking first at Martin McDonagh's play *The Pillowman*, and then at Christopher Nolan's screenplay for *Memento*. We have also borrowed storytelling technique from the Scottish Traveller's stories and key to this chapter, dug into the past worlds of your characters working backwards to forwards, ignoring traditional notions of plot. The storyteller telling stories in competition with other storytellers and even themselves, is one of the most powerful and ancient structures in how we build narratives.

Moving ahead to Chapter 7, we'll look at a very powerful technique in non-realistic, non-linear technique that builds on this idea of the conscious storyteller – using another ancient dramatic technique – the metadramatic twist. We'll also be doing something that is key for all dramatists of major full-length scripts – we'll be creating a roadmap for our writing using *plot cards*. In this case, we'll be using *magic* plot cards that work on three levels, Mythos, Logos, and Performance. These three levels of plot exploration allow us to move in a 3-dimensional manner, not unlike the 3-D chess board on the Starship Enterprise in the old Star Trek Series – we'll be able to structure our non-linear dramatic technique in ways that may be utterly submerged and mysterious for our audiences, but completely apparent to ourselves and our collaborators.

We will be working with three different dramatic writers and their works for the theatre and film, Tony Kushner's *Angels in America,* Charlie Kaufman's *Eternal Sunshine of the Spotless Mind,* Guillermo Arriaga's *21 Grams.* In each case the writers' play with the lucid, self-conscious nature of telling stories – metatheatricality and metadrama – and using these techniques open a whole new sphere of the uncanny and bizarre in dramatic writing.

CHAPTER 7

Magic Plot Cards – The Dreamwright as Storyteller

Tony Kushner's Angels in America, *Charlie Kaufman's* Eternal Sunshine of the Spotless Mind, *Guillermo Arriaga's* 21 Grams

Until this point we've been working mostly in an exploratory mode – delving deeply into our dramatic characters and exploring the worlds of those characters in dream-like ways, using structures of ritual, myth, and ceremony – plumbing their dreamer's heart by accessing the deep well of ideas in their dream cache throughout this process. However, many of those who will read this book, will be needing a more formal method of finalizing the structure of their dramatic work, whether it is for the stage or screen, and this means working with a plot outline and formal dramatic treatment – something that a producer can read to decide whether to produce your film or play. In this chapter we're going to focus on how dramatic writers, working from alternative, non-linear, magic dream structures, create an organic organizing principle for their dramatic writing projects. To get at this somewhat weird yet orderly way of thinking about storytelling we'll begin from a very simple source, an index card. Working with paper index cards to build your scenario may seem a bit preschool for creating a mystic plot, but having a concrete method to access one's creative muse really helps move one's art from the abstract to the specific. And like our work with dream caches (which also involves simple items like construction paper, markers, and paper bags), it also adds an element of surprise, which forces you to think outside of the box.

Exercise 1: Magic Plot Cards – Finding Your Journey

Creating a plot for a non-linear, non-traditional play requires a bit more textured plot card process than writing a plot for a traditional, linear play. In addition to the traditional story event cards, and the cards that mark performance moments, you'll want to consider layering in cards that suggest a nonlinear structure. This adds the magic that lifts a traditional plot into new territory. You should work with three different color index cards – one color for the *Mythos* cards, another color for the *Logos* cards, and yet another color for the *Performance* cards.

1. First contemplate the story of your play: these are your MYTHOS cards:

What is the actual story of your play – following chronological order? What actually happens? Let's consider an old-fashioned detective story.
   a. The Detective Examines the Body.
   b. The Detective Gathers Clues.
   c. The Detective Makes Sense of the Clues and Decides Who May be Suspects.
   d. The Detective Interrogates the Suspects.
   e. The Detective Pulls together the Clues and the Suspects' Accounts
   f. The Detective Realizes to their Horror that They Themselves Committed the Murder.

This is the actual story of your play – and it has a beginning, middle, and end – it is linear, causal, and it takes the audience in a traditional arc. But in a non-linear play, these story cards may be scrambled to make the play more challenging to the reader.

2. Then contemplate the alternate structure of your play: these are your *LOGOS* cards:

Is your alternate structure a myth, a geometric design, a game, a ritual? Set up those cards in some relationship to your Mythos cards – to have as a parallel structure to your play.
   a. Each card should represent the basic "station" of your alternate structure. Create as many as would realistically work within your alternative structure from beginning to end.
   b. In the examples discussed in this chapter, Tony Kushner's *Angels in America*, Charle Kaufman's *Eternal Sunshine of the Spotless Mind*, and Guillermo Arriaga's *21 Grams*, there are very specific logos structures that each author is working with. You may not understand that they're there when you see the film for the first time, but after careful analysis, they reveal themselves.
   c. And the reality is that your audience may never see or understand your Logos structure, but it needs to be there for you the writer, so that you can create your alternative, magic structure that will beautiful complement the more traditional story running underneath that magic. Otherwise, your work may lack shape, form, art – and remember, this is not a book about creating a dramatic mess! This book is all about creating beautiful, organized, alternative structures that are crafted in such a manner as to organically complement the traditional, linear story you're wanting to tell, but get at it in an original, unsuspected, and dream-like manner.
   d. On each card, break down your myth, ritual, game, geometric design into different events: give each a title, a description, and an

emotional color. These are your LOGOS or Structure Cards – for example, if you were using the ancient myth of Oedipus – you would have these ritualized Logos cards which would be tied to the events of the myth:
   i. DOOMED CHILD: Oedipus is Born to Jocasta and Laius – The Oracle predicts he will murder his father and marry his mother.
   ii. HEELS BINDED: Baby Oedipus is left on a hillside, his heels bound, to die.
   iii. BABY RESCUED: A shepherd finds Oedipus, brings him to King Polybus and Queen Merope of Corinth.
   iv. MURDERER UNLEASHED: Oedipus Kills his Father.
   v. HERO REVEALED: Oedipus kills Sphinx.
   vi. ADULTERER UNPUNISHED: Oedipus Marries his Mother.
   vii. DEATH BY PLAGUE: Oedipus the King must solve the Mystery of the Plague of Phebes.
   viii. KING UNSEATED: Oedipus realizes he is the reason Phebes is Plagued, and Strikes out his eyes.
   ix. GODS INSERT THEMSELVES: Oedipus lives, but is condemned to contemplate his Hammartia [Error] and his Hubris [Pride].
   x. DOOMED WANDERER: Oedipus discovers at Delphi he is to murder his father and marry his mother, leaves Corinth to seek his fortune.
   e. With these LOGOS (Structure) Cards in mind, now you can move onto the PERFORMANCE Cards bearing in mind basic performance structure and the MYTHOS of your play.
3. Now contemplate your play within the Emotional and Temporal Cycle of a Performance: These are your *PERFORMANCE* Cards.
   a. The final set of cards you create are your PERFORMANCE cards – these are the building blocks of your play in performance, and these will affect LOGOS and the MYTHOS Cards. While these cards are seemingly crafted within traditional drama structure, they are tied to emotional temporal rhythm of performance.
   b. Within the time frame of an evening of *any kind of* performance that is approximately 2–3 hours long, an audience experiences physical waves of emotional involvement that any dramatist should be aware of – and should take advantage of – regardless of the structure of the LOGOS and MYTHOS Cards. In other words,

you need to ride these waves based on the very real temporal experience of an audience watching a performance.
c. The structure below has a basic logic to it. An audience needs to be *hooked* into the action at the start of the evening, then as it starts to get restless after the first hour of performance, it needs to *emotionally engaged* to stay past the intermission, so a series of *problems* or *complications* must occur to make the protagonist's job harder, and a major question needs to be raised just before the intermission (the *Turning Point*), so that they are willing to come back after the break. After the break, the audience has to been hooked again with the Major Complication, so that they settle in for the second act, then it needs to build to a Final Emotional Climax, not long before the end, with a *resolution* of some kind in the end.
d. Bernard Beckerman, in his wonderful book, *The Dynamics of Drama*, discusses performance using the example of the tightrope performer, who has a basic project to complete – going from one point to another traversing a thin rope or wire that is tightly bound between them. That project, walking the tightrope, must be performed facing some resistance, for example, the thinness of the rope or wire, the length of the distance point to point, and the immense height from which the walker might fall. The greater the resistance, the more interesting the performance. That is why a tightrope performer might add to their act, to make it more interesting, as they move across the wire, walking at first, then riding a unicycle, then juggle fruit, then knives, then, perhaps, torches of fire! Or they might choose to walk the tightrope between two sides of a canyon, with the wind, rain, and other challenges facing them. The goal is to build to a terrifying moment, right before the end, just before the tightrope walker gets to the other side – the moment when there might be a slight slip or waiver, and we have the sense that the performer might fall – possibly to their death!
e. For writers who are really trying to avoid traditional dramatic structure, consider that this last set of cards is just a reminder of that performance cycle – with timings on the cards marked out to give the dramatist a sense of when things might need to happen – even if the mythos and logos cards are working from a totally different structure. Things will still take place during the real time of performance – this fundamental temporal aspect of an evening's performance lasting 2–3 hours doesn't change, even if what happens is non-traditional, non-linear, and just a bit strange. Below

are five basic, traditional performance moments, and you can add these five basic cards to help shape that performance timing without being a slave to the structure.
- i. THE HOOK: Beginning of play needs something to grab the audience – INTRUSION – INCITING INCIDENT.
- ii. THE TURNING POINT: Before Intermission – needs HIGH MOMENT – 1st Act Crisis.
- iii. THE MAJOR COMPLICATION: After Intermission – Second Act Hook/Major Complication.
- iv. THE CLIMAX: The moment right before the end of the play when your central character is faced with her/his most trying moment – the moment when their PROJECT or OBJECTIVE faces the most RESISTANCE from their OBSTACLE – and it could go either way.
- v. RESOLUTION: How does your play end? What major question is raised?

4. Layering in Three Tiers of Cards: This is your Plot in Motion.
Remember that plot is the part of the story that you decide you want to tell *during* the performance of your play – it's not the whole story, nor should it be. It doesn't have fall into the chronology of events in your story – that's entirely up to you, and the alternative structure you've created:
   a. LOGOS and PERFORMANCE Cards first: Lay down your LOGOS and PERFORMANCE Cards in a parallel structure – and see where you can find linkage. Remember the LOGOS Cards provide the alternative structure to help you "make strange" your MYTHOS cards which are your traditional story cards.
   b. MYTHOS cards next: Now lay down your MYTHOS cards – these are the cards that represent the actual story of your dramatic work – again see where the linkage exists with the previous sets of cards. Let the MYTHOS cards tug at the LOGOS cards and vice versa. Be aware that you may not need ALL your mythos cards – or you may need to create more. At times this might be a bit strange – but let the process be improvisational and associational – allow the Logos Cards to interact with the Performance Cards and then for both to talk to the Mythos Cards (and vice versa, by the way). Let this sit awhile. Walk away. Breathe. Take a walk. Do something else for a while. Maybe even take a few days.
   c. Once you are satisfied – write EVERYTHING down: Come back with a fresh breath. Look at what you have. Fuss with it a bit more.

d. Then get it all down on paper. You might want to take a picture of everything first – then even draw a colorful chart of what you have. Whatever stimulates your creativity but include ALL THREE SETS OF CARDS. The result is that you have a structure that gets at the actual story, a method you will use to tell the story, and a sense of the effect it will have on your audience in real time.

d. Now write JUST your plot outline, hiding everything, but your MYTHOS Cards: Write down the basic titles of each Mythos card and make sure you document the organization that you've come up with. Embrace the structure of your Logos and Performance Cards but remember what you actually see on the stage – will be just the events of the Mythos cards – this outline will help you write your Plot Treatment.

e. GO I-CHING WITH IT: Now that you've got it all written down – fling your cards in the air, turn them all over, reshuffle them, cut them, and then lay them out and document the random order they have taken. I-Ching is a technique of foretelling the future that allows a chance and random order to prevail. Any revelations that you'd like to explore? You'd be surprised to see what happens when you go I-Ching with it!

Once you have a working plot outline, which details the actual events that will occur in your drama, you can start working toward a treatment or scenario.

Exercise 2: The Dramatic Treatment – A Trail Guide to the Journey

Bear in mind that the treatment is not set in stone but is only a trail guide to what you see on the stage. It provides the basic route to the story, but still leaves room for you to take a side trail, get lost a bit – but it's also there to bring you back to your story. The treatment exists so that even if you choose to meander a bit, you won't lose the whole picture.

Method:
– Based upon the plot outline from your work with Magic Plot Cards, write the Treatment in paragraph form, not as an outline or a scene-by-scene breakdown. Treat it like a novella or long short story. It is a narrative of the drama unfolding before your eyes with you in the orchestra seats. Imagine you're sitting in the ideal theatre with the ideal cast, watching the play or the film, scene by scene, frame by frame.
– It should be 5–10 pages long. No more than 10 pages.

MAGIC PLOT CARDS – THE DREAMWRIGHT AS STORYTELLER

- Avoid writing interior thoughts of the characters – especially if you are writing a screenplay, you are writing a *story in pictures*. If you can *see it,* you can *film it.* If you can't see an action, because it's primarily an interior thought, neither will the audience. This even more the case for a stage play. Cut those interior thoughts from your treatment.
- Make sure you describe each character in her/his initial appearance in the film or play.
- Don't write down much dialogue, instead briefly describe what is said, and what is running underneath it. If you must use dialogue, use only snippets.
- The treatment is to grab the visual eye of a producer, so it should appeal to the five senses. The treatment should sparkle. This is not about making it flashy and Hollywood, but suggestive, crisp, and interesting. Sometimes this is the only thing that will make it past the initial readers – make it snap!
- The Treatment should use active not passive verbs, colorful adjectives, and tell the story of the dramatic action, involve us in the characters, not just the physical actions, locations where they happen, or which character is entering and exiting.

Weak version:

> Jack enters. He sees Jill. He walks over to her and talks. They fetch a pail of water. They exit.

Better version:

> Jack, a lanky country curmudgeon of sixteen saunters in from offstage right. He stares at Jill, dumbstruck. She leans against the well, a Kansas redhead with a big bucket and an axe to grind. With a smarmy smile, he oozes over to her as they exchange off-color barbs and innuendo. He abruptly pushes the pail out of her hands and into the well. They struggle over who will pull it up, then, somehow, find themselves pulling it up together, caught in the rhythm of motion. After feeding each other a refreshing drink, they exit, bumping hips, with the bucket swinging dangerously between them.

- Do your best to connect with each scene and event you've created, describing the dramatic action of the scene, describing what each character wants and how they get it from each other.
- Remember you're doing this to tie everything together and keep the action flowing.

- Keep going back to your magic plot cards, an outline, and even play with some storyboarding to make sure you're telling a story in pictures if this is a film rather than a stage drama.

Now that you finished your work on your plot cards, you have a plot outline, and draft of your treatment, we'll spend some time exploring the work of three dramatic writers who used alternative story structures to build the journey of their dramatic works.

1 Tony Kushner's *Angels in America* – *A Reluctant Prophet and a Reformed Sinner*

Tony Kushner built the play structure of his Pulitzer prize-winning play, *Angels in America*, using an extra-biblical religious source, the Book of Mormon. This important religious document was allegedly translated from an ancient language, "Reformed Egyptian" by Joseph Smith, a modern-day American prophet, and told of a resurrected Jesus in America. Whether you are religious or not, the Book of Mormon is a significant religious text that grows out of a powerful American myth – that of a poverty-stricken, uneducated, rural, everyman who is visited by an angel, given access to a great revelation written on golden metal plates, and called upon to be a prophet and spread the word of his vision to all men.

Kushner's *Angels in America, Parts I & II*, takes this evocative story and applies it to a young gay man, Prior Walter, sick with AIDS (yet a part of him unblemished) and gives him the journey of a prophet to somehow bring a new peace to Heaven and earth by somehow staying the same, keeping to the same script. It is a clearly reactionary Heaven, and Prior, despite being changed profoundly by the experience of becoming a prophet, rejects the call, rejects the vision, and comes back to earth, recovering but deeply damaged by AIDS. It is the story of a profoundly reluctant prophet, who is deeply unenthusiastic about his call, disinclined to follow his vision, and who rejects it in favor of a far more earthly and progressive call.

The other major structural technique that Kushner employs in *Angels in America* is the use of the split scene – which allows him to create a very separate journey for Prior's lover in *Angels*. This is the journey of Louis Ironson, whose major dramatic act in the play is to leave his dying lover in a supreme act of unfaithfulness, and journey to a much darker realm. Louis's journey takes him into the arms of Joe Pitt, a conservative, Mormon lawyer who works for Roy Cohn, a right-wing operative, doing the dirty work of the Republican party. Joe, a closeted hatchet man for Cohn, struggles with his homosexuality, even as he tries to remain a good husband to his troubled wife, Harper, whose madness increasingly revolves around her coming to terms with her husband's closeted sexuality.

Louis's journey is that of the biblical sinner – and he follows that road down into depths of depravity and separation from God, even as he learns more about more about himself, and manages to somehow use this self-knowledge to raise himself out of ashes, and into the possibility of reclaiming his good name. Like Cain, the murderer of his brother Abel, Louis is forced to wander, and enters the dark world of the closeted, conservative, hatchet man, Joe Pitt, whose own troubled life provides fodder for Louis's redemption. As Cain entered the Land of Nod, a metaphor for a wandering life, and a place outside the realm of God, Louis enters an amoral no-man's land, doomed to continue sinning with his reactionary lover. Cain is promised by God to be permitted to live, and a mark is put upon his brow that reminds men that anyone who murders him will themselves "suffer sevenfold vengeance." And Louis notes the same feeling that he has been similarly marked, and is called out by the black transvestite character, Belize, in the play. Yet Cain is a builder of cities, and even though he is damned, he fathers a son, Enoch, and has a history and populates the world (though his people's legacy is to be wiped out by the Great Flood!). However, Cain's downward journey isn't the only sinner's legacy in the bible – there are many, and their stories are not simple descents – most are actually a descent down in order to rise above themselves. A more typical Sinner's Journey is that of Samson, the strongman whose God-given gifts are initially the source of a hero's ascent, then as Samson forgets God, and sins against him, they are taken away. When Samson is imprisoned, blinded, and now cognizant of his sins, he has his strength returned; he acts against evil, tearing down the walls of the temple where he has sinned, destroying his enemies and himself. But there are many others, Jonah who refused the call of God and is swallowed into the belly of a great fish, Peter who denies knowing Jesus, and Paul, who initially was a Pharisee and sought to persecute Jesus and his followers, eventually has his moment of revelation on the Road to Damascus and becomes a faithful follower and both become Apostles of Jesus.

If Prior is a modern-day Elijah, then Louis is a contemporary Cain – and here the dynamic of the play is built with a double-plot which turns in on itself as these two characters journey away from each other, and then return back, transformed by their experiences. Like the double helix structure of DNA, Prior's and Louis's powerful, intertwined dramatic action gets at Kushner's broad political message in a profoundly human process – and at the same time, similar to the magic plot cards technique, one can experiment with Kushner's technique by playing two journeys against each other to come up with a structural whole. The exercise that we can explore which gets at the essence of *Angels in America* is one that is built on these intertwining journeys – that of a reluctant Prophet and rectified Sinner.

Exercise 3: Angels in America–The Prophet/Sinner Split Scene Mobius Strip

What we'll be creating here is a series of scenes that will twist and intertwine like that of the sides of a mobius strip. You'll want to explore your central character and a character who is perhaps your central character's antagonist – but whoever you choose, that character will have as strong a storyline as your central character. If it's your antagonist, this is a great exercise to explore all the nuances of that dark character – and even though you are going to put that character on a trajectory of a great sin, there will also be the opportunity for that character to rectify their sin – or at least mitigate it. You'll want to have created dream caches for the two characters and borrow an additional two to three characters each from those two different dream caches.

SCENE STRUCTURE SUGGESTION – *Wrighting Behavior*: In each scene there should be at least one character who *wants something desperately* with the other either indifferent or openly antagonistic. The characters should have a physical activity, and their conversation should focus on *the physical activity* and the characters should *avoid* discussing the characters want directly. Instead, the characters must make their needs known totally indirectly, focusing on the physical activity at hand – otherwise your characters may be prone to *spoken subtext* – which happens when characters are a bit too quick to say directly what is on their minds. This is what I call *wrighting behavior* rather than writing dialogue – again if you can see it, you can film it – dialogue – language – should be sparse. We are focused on physical action here – and this is true of either a stage play or a screenplay. In each scene there should be a magic *knot* – a bit of something dreamlike that may be real or not but has *a real effect* on the characters – and it should be connected the physical activity in some way.

Step 1 – The Events of the Prophet and the Sinner

Keeping in mind the scene suggestion above, the first step is to brainstorm a series of events that your central character, who you will write as a kind of secular prophet, will experience in their vision quest. The overall arch and progression of these scenes will ultimately depend on you but think about the journey as a series of tests of faith – each one building on the next and testing the Prophet's willingness to accept their vision, act upon it, and defend it. Because we are dealing with a reluctant Prophet, we'll be helping your Prophet come to terms with a renouncing of their original vision, leading them to a greater if perhaps more quotidian truth. Here are the Prophet's Junctures of Crisis, and they have moments of cross over with the Sinner – and all of this takes place in a dreamscape – a place which drips of daily life, but rises into the abstract of the unconscious, the Noumenal World, the ideal yet unreal world in the clouds above.

Prophet's Junctures of Crisis

- *The Nesting Moment* – The Prophet and Sinner are caught together with an approaching Storm on the horizon – they are in a familiar comforting place. They are perhaps more than friends – lovers? Both sense the storm, but the Prophet has a deeper darker sense of it – the Sinner denies its presence (both inwardly and outwardly) but despite this, is only too aware of it. They separate for now after this nesting moment.
- *The Breaking Moment* – The Prophet is swept into the storm, confronted with its horror, shown its depth and breadth – the location is a crossroads where the Prophet can lean into the future, or retreat back into the past. Both are available, tempting, and the Prophet can go either way. It is either a Fail for the next moment, or a Step into the Abyss.
- *The First Fail* – This is a retreat into the past – a place of comfort that becomes somehow rotted and decaying during this event – there is slippage here and no safe harbor for the Prophet – and yet, so many temptations here, each of which offers a dark sin. If the Prophet takes this route, it will only reinforce their decision to step into the Abyss. This First Fail may lead to other fails – other sad moments of retreat, until the Prophet finally realizes it is time to step into the Abyss.
- *The Abyss* – This is the moment the Prophet succumbs to their darkest place, their personal horror, and yet even as their worst fears are realized in this place of despair, they find that the damage done to them in this terrible place has somehow opened their eyes, rendered them vulnerable enough to receive their vision. But it should be a place of horror and loathing, a place filled with real evil and the sense that this could be their end. What saves the Prophet is that at this moment of sheer terror and loss, they are ready for their first vision.
- *The First Vision* – This is their introduction to the supernatural – However, only the most minimal physical revelation of an Angel or Supernatural Messenger can be permitted. In *Angels in America, Part* One, just a feather from the Angel's wing descends. But this first vision must include some

minimal communication, it must extend out of and include terror of the Abyss, but it must also provide a hint of wonder. It should be just enough to whet the appetite of the Prophet, but not enough to engage the Prophet in their Task. That will come. At this point the Prophet must touch back into the real world – and allow the first vision to resonate there.

- *Real World Scene 1* – Back in the Real World, the Prophet is an ordinary person again, and this scene occurs at their home or their place of work or their school – some place where they must encounter the people in their daily life. Suffering from the trauma of the Abyss and their First Vision, the real-life repercussions of both must be visible in the Prophet's physical and emotional reality. The hint of the supernatural being is woven into the tapestry of their quotidian life. In this Real-World Scene there can be some interaction with the Sinner – and depending upon the relationship of the Prophet and the Sinner this can be quite intimate, but it should only be a minimal part of the scene.
- *Real World Scene 2 – The Test* – Before returning to the Noumenal World the Prophet will have a real-world testing of their belief. Something tied to their vision has affected their real-world experience, and the repercussions are severe and profound. This *Test of Faith* involves those people with whom the Prophet feels closest and the decision the Prophet makes in this scene affects them profoundly. The repercussions lead to the second major Vision.
- *The Second Vision* – In this scene the Prophet encounters a full-bodied supernatural messenger who spells out the Prophet's task in full. The supernatural messenger who provides the vision must test the Prophet's viability before tasking them. Think of Jacob wrestling with the Archangel Samael or Joseph Smith's encounter with the Angel Moroni – and consider a physical test of your Prophet. In the process, the Prophet prevails, but is physically changed, diminished in some ways, enhanced in others. In the biblical story, Jacob's hip is damaged by wrestling with the Angel. Also in the second vision, the remnants of the supernatural messenger enter into the daily life of the Prophet, so now it's not possible to relegate the Visioning to just the noumenal world – the supernatural being has moved into the Prophet's real world, and at this point the Sinner's re-entrance is at hand.
- *Real World Scene 3* – In this scene, the Prophet now encounters a remnant of the Supernatural Messenger in the real world. With this appearance, the details of the Prophet's Task are unveiled and at nearly the same moment, the Prophet encounters the Sinner. Their interaction takes place in a setting near and dear to the Prophet, and one that is uncomfortable for the Sinner. The encounter goes badly, driving the Sinner into the deepest depths

of their sinning, and sending the Prophet, reluctant as they may be, directly onto the path of the Task. There is no turning back at this point.
- Trial and Tribulations – This is a series of six short traveling split scenes, wherein the Prophet and the Sinner go on physical journeys in opposite directions, taking them deeper into their prospective realms – the Prophet executes a series of actions, mostly tied to unmasking their task, revealing the nature of its revelation; and the Sinner descends through several layers of sins, damaging themselves in the process. Both the Prophet and the Sinner are put on trial by their friends and relationships in their respective real worlds, linking them in ways both good and bad, with the caveat that hints of the supernatural and magic occur to both.
- A Final Assay – for both the Prophet and the Sinner, there is a final, major test or trial, and this is the Final Assay – the moment when they will be judged as worthy or unworthy of their respective tasks. In this scene they may switch roles temporarily with the Prophet becoming a Sinner and the Sinner becoming a Prophet – and both are linked in this moment of transformation. The Final Assay leads to one last transformation for both of them as they return to their original Prophet/Sinner roles – even though both are heartily aware of the other's transformations, and welcome it.

Sinner's Dimensions of Descent

Looking back at the arc of Louis Ironson's journey in *Angels in America*, it consists of a series of self-inflicted, clownish failures combined with uplifting conflations of self-fulfilling prophesy and diminishing returns. Whatever has happened to Louis is the product of his own malfunctions as a compassionate human being, and so there is no supernatural intervention; his is a journey among darker, if more pedestrian figures. Instead of a series of tests, Louis is confronted with deeper levels of his own weaknesses and inclinations. He is allowed to dig his own grave, as it were, and as he does so, his realization of what he has done resonates farther and more profoundly within, until having hit ashes, he must claw his way out – this is linked to the Greek term, Katabasis – meaning to "go down" and is a term tied to the work of Robert Bly, whose *Iron John: A Book About Men* examines the phenomenon of men descending from prosperity to misery in order rise again from the ashes of their failure. In ancient stories, this meant a trip to the supernatural underworld, encountering the horrors of a world gone mad – but in more modern times, this has often been the journey of a soldier into war – another kind of Hell. In Louis's case, it is a journey into powerful and tempting lust with a beautiful man whose deeper darkness is slowly revealed to be toxic and horrifying. The Sinner's scenes in this sequence, which will eventually be intertwined with the

Prophet's, create an interlocking funhouse of events that circle in on themselves to a powerful conclusion:
- *The Nesting Moment* – This remains the same for both The Prophet and Sinner, who are caught together with an approaching Storm on the horizon – they are in a familiar comforting place. Both sense the storm, but the Prophet has a deeper darker sense of it – the Sinner denies its presence (both inwardly and outwardly) but is aware of it. They separate for now after it occurs.
- *The Breaking Moment* – The Sinner separates from the Prophet during the Storm, seeking instead the Easy Choice. The Easy Choice seems to be a seductive alternative to the Storm, but in fact it is a much more treacherous situation. The location is an unfamiliar, but enjoyable, and perhaps erotic realm, where the Sinner, not realizing it, is seduced into his own portion of the Storm. The Breaking Moment is the door to the First Fall.
- *The First Fall* – Like the Prophet's First Fail, the Sinner's first fall is the beginning of the descent – it is the moment that the Sinner meets the Facilitator of their deeper sin, a beautiful Demon, in human form, who does not necessarily realize they are a demon, and could plausibly deny their true nature. Yet the First Fall provides an exact opposite experience to Prophet's First Fail, mirroring that moment, but in darkness instead of light. Like the Prophet's decision to step into the Abyss, the Sinner's decision is to give into desire, temptation, and move up – into False Heaven.
- *False Heaven* – If the Prophet's next step is into the Abyss, the Sinner's journey, which is primarily a descent into darkness, ascends into a False Heaven, where whatever bliss is discovered here quickly sours. False Heaven is neon bright, carnal, beautiful in a cheap but splendorous way – There the beautiful Demon is the host in a place of great decadence and charm – and surrounded by those who are also charming, carnal, and attractive. Yet, the Demon has a Boss – and the Boss is none of those things – the Boss is a crass, impersonal, hell-raiser, and while the Boss has their attractions, the Boss is clearly not good. It is the beautiful Demon's job to get the Sinner to work for the Boss.
- *Real World Scene 1* – As the Prophet goes, so goes the Sinner – back to the ordinary, quotidian world of real life. The Sinner goes back to their job, back to their home or apartment, and attends to the realities that face them – and there are several that are somehow tainted, twisted, by the Sinner's new friend, the Beautiful Demon, who has a place in the ordinary world. The Sinner could also be engaged with the Prophet, and the Prophet, having had their first encounter with the Noumenal World, now senses the Sinner's new role and their status as a Fallen One. The Prophet may also encounter the

Beautiful Demon, and without knowing exactly what is happening, understands that the Sinner may be significant danger without knowing it. The Friction between Prophet and Sinner is at its greatest here – at the Onset of their separate journeys. What happens in this scene, which involves the Beautiful Demon and a whiff of the Boss, propels the Prophet into their ascent and the Sinner into their descent.

- *Real Hell* – The Sinner is blown into their Fall now, accelerated by the clash with the Prophet, and now the Sinner begins the process of their indenture with the Boss. The setting is the same False Heaven, and the bright lights and music remain, but the real-life dinginess appears, and with it hints of the darkness and cruelty become more real to the Sinner. Yet the Sinner, buffeted by the rejection by the Prophet digs in their heels in their frustration and failure, and accepts the Boss's terms of indenture, becoming a permanent fixture with the other Beautiful Demons. The Sinner adopts the pose and physicality of the others, transforming into a fiendish version of themselves, and in the process burning brighter and more beautiful in persona.

- *Real World 2* – The Sinner, now transformed, begins their new life as a Beautiful Demon in the Real World – a pose, mostly, because the Sinner is only playing a part. The inhabitants of the real world of the Sinner's fellow employees, friends, family, all notice the change, and the Sinner's new behaviors, which though outwardly making the Sinner more attractive and charming, belie a much darker, violent, and cruel aspect – which slowly but surely oozes forward. The Sinner commits several sins – at first minor, then becoming increasingly disturbing, accompanied by their new friend, the Beautiful Demon, and the Sinner begins to reveal their true self. As the self appears, the Sinner begins a decline in appearance and behavior that chips away at their beautiful exterior, revealing the rot within. The Sinner is confronted with a choice in the real world – one that has fatal overtones, that will forever condemn the Sinner to the Dark Underworld – and the scene ends before the Sinner can decide what to do.

- *Return to False Heaven* – The Beautiful Demon, despondent at the Sinner's indecision and hesitancy, insists that the Sinner return to False Heaven – a place that once again exudes brightness and light, and great promise of wealth and power. Confronted once again by the Boss, the Sinner must confront their decision and their resolve – and the Boss, now determined to break the Sinner's will, threatens the life of someone in the Sinner's real world – possibly the Prophet, unless the Sinner makes the dark choice that will forever seal their fate. To protect this last connection to decency, the Sinner must commit an act of horror and treachery that will forever condemn the Sinner to a life of darkness.

- *Real World 3* – The Sinner digs in and commits to the act of crime, knowing that it means the death of someone they love in the Real World – possibly the Prophet themselves. With the Beautiful Demon by their side, the Sinner cleverly outwits the Prophet, gathers their victim(s), which may or may not include the Prophet, sets up the moment of horror, and at the moment of committing the deepest and darkest sin is stopped by some deeper place of decency within them, and abandons the murderous act, and then becomes the object of the Beautiful Demon's fury – who now led by the Boss, seeks terrible vengeance for the Sinner's Betrayal. The Prophet while not able to assist the Sinner, is somehow involved in making it possible for the Sinner to escape – though there is no escape from the Boss.
- *Hunter and Prey* – Like the Trials and Tribulations of the Prophet, the Sinner becomes a hunted figure, and this series of scenes explores the contradictions of Sinner's situation. They are hunted by both those who represent good and those who are called to evil – as the Sinner is caught between both worlds. The scenes here are also traveling scenes – as the Sinner attempts to shake off the Boss and the Beautiful Demon, the Sinner draws them closer to those who the Sinner loves and holds close (possibly including the Prophet). The Sinner is caught and confronted with their own conflicted conscience and the Boss forces them to either commit the act, and thereby be condemned to Hell (False Heaven) or be destroyed themselves. The Sinner choses self-annihilation instead, and thereby denying the Boss satisfaction on any level, sending the Sinner, dying, into the arms of the Prophet.
- *The Final Assay* – for the Sinner, who is rapidly declining, the Final Assay ties directly into the challenge confronting the Prophet, and again there is the possibility for complete transformation for both. The Prophet can fully condemn or exonerate the Sinner, and the Sinner's absolution is key to the Prophet's ascension. Still there must not be an easy choice here, and the choice can go either way. Bearing in mind that this structure, tied as it is to the more traditional Hero's Journey as enunciated by Joseph Campbell and others, is much more open to interpretation. What you, the dramatist has to say, what your dreams ask you to explore, is much more important than this structure – and so it ends as you choose, failure or fulfillment for the Prophet and the Sinner.

Step 2 – *The Mingling Mobius Strip of the Prophet and the Sinner*

At this point, after having written these two sets of scenes and/or sequences for Prophet and Sinner, there are several ways to approaching pulling these two sets of scenes together – I will give you three major possibilities, but there are many more. For this part of the project, you will identify each scene with a titled index card with the numbering and basic scene information on it, so you can manipulate it, before you start to pull the scenes together.

Alternating Structure – Moving Forward
The simplest and most obvious structure moves these two storylines forward moving from the Nesting Scene to the Final Assay, switching back and forth, slipping from one to the other as they meet at the Final Assay. While this might seem somewhat predictable – you might want to use this for a project in a popular medium where the audiences may not have as adventurous tastes as you do. You'll still have a very powerful structure in place, not unlike the Heroes Journey, but you'll be keeping things accessible for a broader audience.

Alternating Structure – Moving Backward
More interesting is to work backward, starting with the Final Assay and moving into the past, allowing the story to be more of a detective tale, getting at the deep powerful connection between the Prophet and the Sinner, as we uncover what happened to them to bring them to the beginning.

Submerged Structure – Moving Backwards and Forwards
I would be lying if I told you that I didn't have a preference – I do – and that is to totally submerge the structure with the two stories slipping in and out of past and present – and let the audience figure out what is happening – in this case you could still have those scenes of Prophet and Sinner and fit them within kind of structure of the Performance Cards I have suggested above, but now things are much less predictable.

Mingled Mobius Strip Structure – Time No Longer Matters – I Ching
Finally, the last structure you might consider is one where you not only submerge the structure, but you disregard the nature of time and progression entirely – in this case the drama (film or play) becomes abstract, and you can pull the entire set of scenes – after placing the titles and numbers on the index cards and pulling them from a Dream Cache in a random manner. Remember that even if you choose this chance/random "I Ching" method, you should still bear in mind the kind of structure of the Performance Cards – only because they will provide a measure of where audiences need emotional breaks.

Step 3 – Considering the Ancients – Other Prophets, Other Sinners
As you complete your drama, bear in mind that it is worth looking deeply at the story structure of ancient prophets and religious figures and great sinners,

whether they are biblical or coming from other cultures and histories. Using the actual events of historical religious figures such as Mohammed, the Buddha, Joseph Smith, Edgar Cayce, Moses, or considering the events in the lives of historical sinners such as Adolf Hitler, Saddam Hussein, Genghis Khan, Pol Pot, Osama Bin Laden, Adolf Eichmann, Josef Stalin, or Vlad the Impaler, you can twist, invert, and subvert your own mobius strip structure of a Prophet/ Sinner drama.

2   The Persistence (and Absence) of Memory: Lucid Dreaming in Charlie Kaufman's *Eternal Sunshine of the Spotless Mind*

If Tony Kushner's *Angels in America* is built on what we might term the Prophet's dream/vision, Charlie Kaufman's *Eternal Sunshine of the Spotless Mind* is a romantic dream of a lucid dreamer trapped in a cycle of memories and their erasure into lacunas/absences. Being lucid in a dream means you are aware you are dreaming – it's not unlike a central precept of Epic Theatre, which is the notion of metatheatre or metadrama – that is, theatre that is aware that it is theatre (which we'll discuss more in Chapter 11, exploring Bertolt Brecht). In lucid dreaming, the dream is aware it is a dream, and the dreamer then seeks to control that dream landscape. And yet in *Eternal Sunshine*, that control only goes so far – Joel can't escape Dr. Mierzwiak's advancing lacunas/erasures, but in attempting to do so, the structure of romance, of the memory play, is subverted and turned on its end. Lucid dreaming is taken to other extremes in Christopher Nolan's wonderful film *Inception* which deals with espionage and controlled dreaming, but in Kaufman's *Eternal Sunshine*, lucid dreaming is a strategy against memory erasure, dodging absence with an unstable presence – and it's a powerful structure to explore.

Exercise 4: Romancing the Lucid Dreamer

In this five-page exercise, you'll create a dream that grows out of character milestones – that is, profound events in a character's life that have changed that character forever. This exercise is a character study exercise, built on the structure of the romance.

1. Keep in mind that this is a brief romance – the structure of a love story – two people who find each other, fall in love, are somehow thwarted in

their love (by others or by themselves), and find love again is one of the oldest and most powerful structures in drama.
2. First, work on a Milestone character exercise so that you explore the character milestones for at least two characters that will interact in the film. The Milestone exercise is a wonderful journaling technique to help get at character, based on the work of Ira Progroff in his amazing book, *At a Journal Workshop* (TarcherPerigee, 1992).
   a. First take a moment to give birth to your character – what was their birthdate? What was their birth like? Have the character describe their birth with all five senses, and in their own voice as a monologue – but keep it brief and evocative.
   b. Then write as many important events from that character's life as you can in 30 minutes – give each a brief title and description – shoot for about 20 events (some can be wholly unimportant and pedestrian) and leave it there. Take a walk for at least an hour – better, consider coming back to the exercise the next day.
   c. Come back to the events you have written down and select eight of those events as the most important in your character's life. Take another break for at least an hour, and preferably another day.
   d. Come back to the eight events you have selected and whittle those down to about 3–5 events that are the absolutely most important in your character's life. Have the character describe each event with all five senses in their own voice, with any dialect, idiosyncrasy, jargon that they might normally use. Some of these memories will be *with* the other major character of your drama. It should be as if they are experiencing that event for the first time, even as they describe it – this is what would be called a phenomenological description. These are your Character Milestones.
3. After you have established Milestones for each character individually, establish at least five major/significant events in the couples' romantic life – good, bad, and perhaps iconic of their relationship.
4. Write each of these events – establishing a single scene that gets at the essence of each of these memories.
5. Now, bearing in mind that only of the characters is the dreamer – write a dream sequence, using these scenes – ignore chronology, write them using the following sequence, built on lucid dreaming.

a. The dreamer is caught in the pivotal scene of their relationship facing the conflict – the dreamer then realizes she/he is dreaming and can change elements of the dream.
b. The dreamer is amid a happy moment in the dream, and within the milestone event, the dreamer's lover also becomes aware of the lucid nature of the dream. Knowing where the relationship will end, the dreamer's love encourages them to change the events of their relationship.
c. The dream couple find themselves in a threatening, darker part of their relationship – a milestone that is at the heart of their eventual problems. They change things to make things go better. But there is a problem.
d. The dream couple find themselves in a new landscape – an event that never happened, that they have created because of their ability to change the dream. In this part of the dream things happen that they seem to have no ability to change – things become very dark.
e. The penultimate sequence finds the dreamer and the dream lover once again in a familiar happier event – but rumblings of the dark changes appear – yet somehow the couple finds a way out – there is just a touch of the dream lucidity left, and they can change things just enough. What is it that they change?
f. The dreamer awakes – where are they? Who are they with? Are they actually awake? At this moment the film can continue within the dream – or the characters actually experience waking reality.
6. Write out the sequence with scene headings, action, and dialogue into a short screenplay.
7. Give the drama (stage play or screenplay) a title and consider – what would happen if you switched around the scenes? Could you rework it with the non-linear elements becoming linear and vice versa?

3 Guillermo Arriaga's *21 Grams* – Daily Dreams and Time Jumps

The night after stopping to view the victim of a car accident, where a man was run over and left to die by a hit and run driver, Guillermo Arriaga, the brilliant Mexican screenwriter, was stricken by an intense dream:

> A guy runs over a father and his young daughters. Another man, terminally ill, receives the heart of the father and goes to look for the widow.

The man who killed this family feels so guilty he runs away from everything. That was what I dreamt, and I trusted my instinct.[1]

This became the essence of his screenplay for *21 Grams*, a story built on the idea of the weight of a human soul, and the love left behind by the person who has died. The structure of the film deals with three different character storylines in three different times, past, present, and future – each linked to the central story of the sudden death of a man taken in the prime of his life in a hit and run car accident. The film looks at the driver of the car, the wife of the dead man, and the doctor who receives the dead man's heart. The film moves the way one tells a story in real life, not in chronological order, but in drips and drabs, out of order, but in tune with emotions, with color, and with light.

There is also something very important going on in the film – the structure Arriaga is working with is built on contrasts – if one scene gives answers, another scene questions those answers. There might be passive scenes that are answered with active scenes, and vice versa in what Arriaga calls a "narrative yin-yang" a balancing act all directed to play with the audience's emotions and raise questions that beg to be answered. It is a structure that has a dialectic to it – it is confrontational and questioning, and forces the audience to participate, engage, and create their own response to the narrative to make sense of it. There are also contrasts and dialectics of light and darkness, day or night, morning, noon, afternoon, evening, which? These all affect lighting and these two must be contrasted and tied to the story. Finally for *21 Grams* the major question was, how deep into one's personal hell can one go and still have hope? If there is a continuum, it is between hell and hope – and a bit closer to hope, but with all the trappings of hell.

Exercise 5: Guillermo Arriaga 21 Grams – Getting Unstuck and Create Conflict

The Question Arriaga asks himself to get unstuck and create conflict is built on his basic go to technique, get close, get dialectical. When he's writing a story or scene and it's not working, he imagines, "how would Shakespeare solve this?" In his film *Amores Perros,* the story was not working, and he asked how it could work and then thought of Shakespeare. In Shakespeare, the way of doing

---

1 Guillermo Arriaga, "Writers On Writing: How I Wrote '21 Grams,'" *Script Magazine,* Jan 1, 2015, https://scriptmag.com/columns/writers-writing-wrote-21-grams.

things is – the closer the characters are, the greater the conflict. Since Arriaga grew up in the Marxist tradition, there is the fundamental Hegelian notion of structure – thesis, antithesis, synthesis. Keeping this in mind, your characters should go into a scene with a dramatic objective – and the other characters should have their own dramatic objectives, completely different, perhaps totally antagonistic, and ready to clash. When in doubt, explore the dialectic, the opposing view, and where your drama will go will be synthesized into a new view, one that neither of the opposing characters thought was possible.

Step One – The Central Incident – The Clash that brings All into Being

If stars are created out of the result of a huge explosion, dramas are built that way as well – You will write a scene that ends in the death of a character. Build these characters using your dream cache – if one is already the central character of your drama, establish how they are linked to this central incident. This will be a scene that takes place at a certain time of the day, in a certain location, and it is the incident that is key to the story of your drama. Events move forward and backward from this event, but this is the present moment. Wright that scene – and bear in mind that one of those characters will be in your drama, and the others will not. Your central character is tied to either the one who does the killing, or the one who dies. At heart of this work is a catastrophe – something awful that has cost a human life.

Step Three – The Parallel Moments – The ones tied to the Catastrophe

Write two to three scenes taking place *at the moment* of the Catastrophe for each of two different characters who are somehow tied to the character who died – in addition to your central character.

Step Four – The Aftermath – The ones who are affected by the Catastrophe

Now write two to three scenes taking place *after* the incident for each of two different characters who are somehow tied to the character who died – in addition to your central character.

Step Five – The Antecedents – The ones who effect the Catastrophe

Now go back and write two to three scenes taking place *before* the incident for each of two different characters who are somehow tied to the character who died – in addition to your central character.

Step Six – *Distant Shores – Where the dust settles*
Now go back and write two to three scenes taking long *after* the incident, far in the future, for each of two different characters who are somehow tied to the character who died – in addition to your central character. These may be the first scenes we ever see.

Step Seven – *Weaving Process – Dialectics, Emotions, Light*
After you write these scenes, give each scene a name, a time, a number, and a description, and using *different colored index cards*, a temporal location in either the present, the immediate past, the immediate future, or the far future.
- *Emotions*: Note on each card where they feel on an emotional scale – perhaps give each a color – red for hot emotions, blue for cool, purple for a blend. Consider this as you lay out the cards.
- *Dialectics*: Pair the cards on either side of a question – which scenes raise questions, which provide answers to questions, which refuse to do either?
- *Light*: Note on each card the time of day, the lighting, the season – is this a dark scene with questions, is this light scene full of hope, is this a grey scene full of mystery?

The Interweave Process
Arriaga didn't have a set pattern to his interweaving process, and neither should you – the goal is to avoid patterns, avoid anything predictable, but do keep in mind how these scenes play against each other. Throwing out the chronological order, pair the scenes, keeping in mind the flow of emotions, the clash of dialectics, and the arrays of light that seem to correspond to the scenes. Can the scenes, even if they are not flowing in a linear manner have a conversation with each other? Can one scene answer another, thwart another, raise or lower the emotional temperature on the other. Bear in mind that audiences need breaks after being ratcheted up emotionally, and they'll start twiddling their thumbs if a series of scenes feels flat and unresponsive.

As you lay out the cards, keep in mind the overall flow, and how much or how little you want to tie things up in the end. And it doesn't hurt to keep in mind Arriaga's final message of hope; though stay true to the message of your own resolution; sometimes the message is that life is hard. If hope is a thing with feathers, it shouldn't become a hammer that crushes your message. With these three writers, Tony Kushner, Charlie Kaufman, and Guillermo Arriaga, we've encountered truly inventive story tellers who are not afraid to invest some confusion and conflation into their dramas, so that audiences must work a bit to understand exactly what is happening. The joy in the viewer's experience is that not everything will be explained or clarified, that some aspects of the story remain a mystery, and probably remain that way for the writers as well. The structures can remain hidden for the audiences, but for those of us who are invested in storytelling, some of these formations may help us generate our own powerful dramatic experiences.

After stretching the non-linear technique quite far, using an uncanny skeleton of story structure, there are far more subtle, haunting, and tingling techniques of storytelling that grow out of the artistic movements of romanticism and symbolism, and we'll next experiment with how these techniques work exploring three dramatic works for stage and film, Anton Chekhov's *The Cherry Orchard*, José Rivera's *Cloud Tectonics,* Marguerite Duras, *Hiroshima Mon Amour*. Prepare yourself for the subtle throb of the noumenal in daily life, as these three dramatic writers get at the weirdness of the quotidian in quite a subterranean, indirect manner. At times their restraint becomes unbearable, and yet the power of this approach lies in roaring violence of the lava flows of human desire yawning beneath the hum of our workaday lives.

CHAPTER 8

The Snap of the Heartstring – Symbolism and Romanticism

Chekhov's The Cherry *Orchard, José Rivera's* Cloud Tectonics, *Marguerite Duras'* Hiroshima Mon Amour

We have been working in somewhat radical ways with our dream-based non-linear dramatic technique. Sometimes a gentler magic is needed in telling of a story, and the spell it casts is built on simple homey mysteries that grow out of a life lived quietly, harmoniously with nature, and yet with deep, penetrating sadness and, occasionally, a horrific twist deep within. In the telling of these stories, we encounter banalities which trip our dream energies, reveal secrets roiling at subterranean depths, and provide complexities of understanding appearing only within proximity to the hearth. Both romanticism, which has its roots in its reaction to the mechanics of the well-made play, and symbolism, which has its origins in its response to the excesses of Ibsenian social realism give us tools to access the noumenal world in ways that are both enigmatic yet quite subtle. The two are related and provide a needed counterbalance to realism and classicism, which have linked and somewhat repressive heritages (though both can be incredibly useful techniques, socialist realism was enforced in communist countries like the former Soviet Union and in China).

In this chapter we'll look at exercises which grow from the essence of three dramatists and their major works – Anton Chekhov's *The Cherry Orchard*, José Rivera's *Cloud Tectonics*, and Marguerite Dura's *Hiroshima Mon Amour*. All three work their magic through restraint and nuance, as well as a gentle, ironic comedy, and a deeper melancholy. Despite the frequently somber style and mood of their work, the comedy inherent in their drama is key. And this is an important point to remember – no matter how gloomy the work of romantic and symbolic writers, their quirky if somewhat cynical humor is what adds the magic and lift.

We start here with the acclaimed master of naturalism, Anton Chekhov, though he rejected that label and many others. Frequently cited by such esteemed dramatists as Edward Albee, Tennessee Williams, and Lanford Wilson as their inspiration for the writing of drama, Chekhov was also one of the world's first naturalists, whose early environmentalism included his writings about his encounter with the *Taiga* – the enormous tracts of coniferous trees that he found in his travels across Siberia to Sakhalin Island where the

Russian government had an offshore penal settlement. His stories are full of regret over the destruction of ancient hardwoods, and his desire for the preservation of forests – and *The Cherry Orchard* itself is filled with this sadness and longing, even as the cherry trees in the play are themselves chopped down in the name of progress.

Chekhov's connection to nature ties deeply with Romanticism, as one of the key aspects to this movement is an organic bond with nature. But there are other ways Chekhov's work, despite its traditional association to naturalism and realism, is deeply tied to the inherent magic of Romanticism. Romanticism itself is tied to the greater mysteries inherent in life experience, and it rebels against the rules of science, art, and society. As a movement it is tied to the notion of genius, that is, it reifies inspiration, subjectivity, and the individual over the importance of empiricism and the greater good.

During the 19th century, there was a growing excitement about the possibilities of science, accompanied by a great distrust of those same sensibilities in favor of new kind of mysticism. Romanticism reflected its roots in Neo-Platonism, a suggestion that there was another reality at play that could only be understood through an arcadian spirituality, a connection with the natural, mystic world of ideals. Chekhov's plays reject industrialization, urbanization, organized religion, and the rational rules of the contemporary world. Instead, Chekhov and other writers celebrated nature, beauty, the imagination, and idealized women, children, and rural existence.

There is often something uncanny or supernatural in Chekhov's plays, and the past is admired to a fault. There is above all else, a sense that there is much more to the world than is imagined by the petty bourgeoise – and it unveils itself in odd moments of lucidity in the face of ridiculous or idiotic behavior. In these moments, Chekhov's romantic technique ties into what is clearly symbolic technique. Symbolism is linked to romanticism, and it is a more refined, purified version of romanticism. The greatest and most well-known dramatist of symbolist technique was the Belgian playwright and essayist, Maurice Maeterlinck, who is perhaps most well-known for his symbolist dramas, *Pelleas and Melisande* and *The Bluebird*. Reacting to the overblown melodramas and grand guignol spectacles of the 19th Century stage, Maeterlinck famously declared in his essay, "The Tragical in Daily Life," that "There is a tragic element in the life of every day that is far more real, far more penetrating, far more akin to the true self that is in us than the tragedy that lies in great adventure." For Maeterlinck, most contemporary drama in his time was far too preoccupied with the wild adventures of melodrama, and that the real insights came far closer to home:

> I have grown to believe that an old man, seated in his armchair, waiting patiently, with his lamp beside him ; giving unconscious ear to all the eternal laws that reign about his house, interpreting, without comprehending, the silence of doors and windows and the quivering voice of the light, submitting with bent head to the presence of his soul and his destiny, – an old man, who conceives not that all the powers of this world, like so many heedful servants, are mingling and keeping vigil in his room, who suspects not that the very sun itself is supporting in space the little table against which he leans, or that every star in heaven and every fibre of the soul are directly concerned in the movement of an eyelid that closes, or a thought that springs to birth I have grown to believe that he, motionless as he is, does yet live in reality a deeper, more human and more universal life than the lover who strangles his mistress, the captain who conquers in battle, or the husband who avenges his honour.[1]

The notion of the noumenal world is tied to Kant, and rather than go into detail, just imagine that beyond this world, there is another more ideal world – and that we can only see the shadows of that world. If this sounds a bit like Plato's idea of the Cave, then you are getting the idea. Symbolism takes this notion further than Romanticism which exists within the trappings of the real world. In other words, Romanticism attempts to get at flashes of the noumenal world, while Symbolism places us directly in that strange, idealized realm.

1 Snapping of a String – The Essence of Chekhov's Symbolism

The argument of whether Anton Pavlovich Chekhov's *The Cherry Orchard* is a comedy, as the author suggested himself, or a tragedy, as proposed by his first director, Konstantin Stanislavsky, turns on a single sound, the snap of a string breaking.[2] This sound serves, towards the end of the second act of the play, as a contrapuntal note to the humor of Gaev's nonsensical elegy to nature, and in the last act, to distance the audience from the pathos of the imminent death of Firs, the elderly family servant.[3] Understanding it is key to our

---

1 Maurice Maeterlinck, *The treasure of the humble*. Translated by Alfred Sutro. With introd. by A.D. Walkley, (London: G. Allen, 1905), 95–121.
2 Maurice Valency, *The Breaking String: The Plays of Anton Chekhov* (New York: Oxford University Press, 1966), 264–265.
3 Anton Chekhov, *The Cherry Orchard*, trans. Robert W. Corrigan, in *Four Modern Plays*, ed. Robert W. Corrigan (New York: Holt Rienhart and Winston, Inc. 1962), 265, 292.

work here, exploring Chekhov's non-linear playwriting essence. The sound of a broken string prevents *The Cherry Orchard* from being either a tragedy or a comedy, but rather changes the play into a wry and dispassionate dramedy of dying and change. This sound of a broken string in *The Cherry Orchard* seems to be nothing less than Chekhov's purposely unsettling harbinger of death – and yet it is not. In the dreamworld symbolism of the play, the snapping of string is a strange, even bizarre event, which seems to be meaningless, but suggests the human pain of change, of the unknown just beyond our knowing. Let us consider the scene when it occurs in *The Cherry Orchard*: Gaev, the senile, elderly uncle goes off on one of his tangents, attempting to make a strange and quite lame benediction of nature. This embarrasses his nieces Varya and Anya, and he's made fun of by the leftist eternal student, Trofimov.

The String Snapping Scene from The Cherry Orchard:

GAEV. The sun's set, ladies and gentlemen.
TROFIMOV. Yes.
GAEV [Not loudly, as if declaiming] O Nature, thou art wonderful, thou shinest with eternal radiance! Oh, beautiful and indifferent one, thou whom we call mother, thou containest in thyself existence and death, thou livest and destroyest.
VARYA. [Entreatingly] Uncle, dear!
ANYA. Uncle, you're doing it again!
TROFIMOV. You'd better double the red into the middle.[4]
GAEV. I'll be quiet, I'll be quiet.

They all sit thoughtfully. It is quiet. Only the mumbling of FIERS is heard. Suddenly a distant sound is heard as if from the sky, the sound of a breaking string, which dies away sadly.

LUBOV. What's that?
LOPAKHIN. I don't know. It may be a bucket fallen down a well somewhere. But it's some way off.
GAEV. Or perhaps it's some bird … like a heron.
TROFIMOV. Or an owl.
LUBOV. [Shudders] It's unpleasant, somehow. [A pause.]

---

4 Ibid.

FIERS.   Before the misfortune the same thing happened. An owl screamed and the samovar hummed without stopping.
GAEV.   Before what misfortune?
FIERS.   Before the Emancipation. [A pause.]
LUBOV.   You know, my friends, let's go in; it's evening now. [To ANYA] You've tears in your eyes ... What is it, little girl? [Embraces her.]
ANYA.   It's nothing, mother.[5]

The snapping of the string is that sudden test of what it means to be "home" in a Chekhov play – that there is ultimately no "home" that one can depend upon in the end. Peter Brook writes:

> The real tone of "The Cherry Orchard" is that of a breaking string – that mysterious unidentifiable off-stage sound that twice interrupts the action, unnerving the characters and audience alike with the sensation that unfathomable life is inexorably rushing by .... We feel that strange tingle, an exquisite pang of joy and suffering, again and again.[6]

It is a sound that has come to be a key element of the script – and yet in terms of nonrealistic playwriting technique – the sound is at once a symbol and a very real element, however bizarre, of the world of the play. J. L. Styan, in his book *Chekhov in Performance, A Commentary on the Major Plays*, makes perhaps the most elegant case for its importance in the play:

> The accumulated mixture of all the thousand and one ambivalent details of the play is in that sound. But it adds a strange element of cosmic mystery. It suggests time in its most inscrutable mood; it is the passing of one order of life, with what seems its irreparable loss; but it is also the mark of change, ushering in the new order, both hopeful and frightening because it is unimaginable. To interpret that sound is to interpret the play.[7]

Styan's statement interjects the biographical basis for the sound, which is the sound of a falling bucket Chekhov heard in his youth. Lopatkin, the pragmatic businessman in *The Cherry Orchard*, immediately describes the sound as being

---

5   Ibid.
6   Frank Rich, Review of *The Cherry Orchard*, by Anton Chekov (Brooklyn Academy of Music, New York), New York Times, 25 January 1988, C15.
7   Styan, 337.

cable breaking in one of the mines.[8] The bucket is that of a coal miner, and the sound is that of a cable bursting, sending the miner to his death. Many of Chekov's biographers corroborate this description of the sound.[9] The brevity and the almost comical nature of the sound belies its deadly overtone – it is, in fact, the final moment of the final play of a playwright who, at the time of its writing, suffering from tuberculosis, certainly suspected it may be his last.[10] Chekhov, at the moment of his death, drank a single glass of champagne, uttered the words "Iche Sterbe" (I'm dying), and died shortly thereafter.[11] This director's replacement of the snapped string sound with a symbol of Chekhov's own passing is a bold and unequivocal statement of mortality. Here is another moment from the end of *The Cherry Orchard* when the snapping of the string is heard again – and notice here the timing of the snap.

> THE FINAL SCENE OF THE SNAPPING OF THE STRING IN THE CHERRY ORCHARD
> LUBOV ANDREYEVNA and GAEV are left alone. They might almost have been waiting for that. They fall into each other's arms and sob restrainedly and quietly, fearing that somebody might hear them.
> GAEV. [In despair] My sister, my sister
> LUBOV. My dead, my gentle, beautiful orchard! My life, my youth, my happiness, good-bye! Good-bye!
> ANYA'S VOICE. [Gaily] Mother!
> TROFIMOV'S VOICE. [Gaily, excited] Coo-ee!
> LUBOV. To look at the walls and the windows for the last time … My dead mother used to like to walk about this room
> GAEV. My sister, my sister!
> ANYA'S VOICE. Mother!
> TROFIMOV'S VOICE. Coo-ee!
> LUBOV. We're coming! [They go out.]

The stage is empty. The sound of keys being turned in the locks is heard, and then the noise of the carriages going away. It is quiet. Then the sound of an axe against the trees is heard in the silence, sadly and by itself. Steps are heard. FIERS comes in from the door on the right. He is dressed as

---

8   Anton Chekhov, The Cherry Orchard, 265.
9   See n. 7 above.
10 Valency, 301.
11 Valency, 287–288.

usual, in a short jacket and white waistcoat; slippers on his feet. He is ill. He goes to the door and tries the handle.

FIERS. It's locked. They've gone away. [Sits on a sofa] They've forgotten about me ... Never mind, I'll sit here ... And Leonid Andreyevitch will have gone in a light overcoat instead of putting on his fur coat ... [Sighs anxiously] I didn't see ... Oh, these young people! [Mumbles something that cannot be understood] Life's gone on as if I'd never lived. [Lying down] I'll lie down ... You've no strength left in you, nothing left at all ... Oh, you ... bungler!

He lies without moving. The distant sound is heard, as if from the sky, of a breaking string, dying away sadly. Silence follows it, and only the sound is heard, some way away in the orchard, of the axe falling on the trees. Curtain.[12]

This sound, like all the sounds in Chekhov's plays, came from his interest in recording the details of life with an almost journalistic manner – and yet the sound itself is a huge mystery. It is clear from the reminiscences of Stanislavski and other colleagues that sounds were important tools for the playwright. Chekhov was certainly involved with how they were performed in production.[13] The significance of research into this single sound should not be underestimated; it is, as many of his critics have stated, the final brushstroke of his dramatic oeuvre. Chekhov's intent came not from an overt desire to provoke a particular mood or evince a symbolic gesture, although he was certainly well-read in the work of Maeterlinck, but rather from his desire to depict the magic of arbitrary acts of nature paired with the crisis events in his character's lives.[14] For the critical reader of *The Cherry Orchard,* as well as those who perform his plays, to understand the snap of a single string is to perceive the inherent darkness of the play, and perhaps in all of Chekhov's work.

2   Exercises in Chekhov's Symbolist Technique

One of the best ways to experiment in working the way that Chekhov worked in his plays is to explore natural sounds, smells, images, landscapes, animals,

---

12   Anton Chekhov, *The Cherry Orchard*, 265, 292.
13   Hingley, 311–13.
14   Senelick, Laurence, "Chekhov's Drama, Maeterlinck, And the Russian Symbolists," in *Chekhov's Great Plays: A Critical Anthology*, ed., Jean-Pierre Barricelli (New York: New York University Press, 1981), 161–177.

plants, aspects of the weather as they are experienced by the characters in your play.

Exercise 1: *Anton Chekhov* – The Cherry Orchard – *Repeated Elements*

- Place your characters in a setting in your play where they are forced to be outdoors – have them describe the world they see to each other – make sure they have a concrete need to do so.
- Your characters need to be in a point in the world of the play where they are confronted by a choice they must make, or a change in their situation that must be addressed. The stakes are high; the consequences of their decision are profound. They may *not* speak about the decision directly – they may only speak about the physical, natural world.
- Allow a sound, an image, or a smell to interrupt their description of the world of the play. Allow the characters to react to this interruption. They find interruption disturbing, some, profoundly so.
- The characters begin again to speak about the world they are living in – in terms of what they see, what they physically feel, what they smell, etc. Allow the decision they are facing to percolate up in their sensual description of the world. Don't worry if your audience understands this at all.
- Allow the interrupting element to begin again. And again, the characters react, but this time perhaps they take an exactly opposing response. But still, it rattles them.
- The scene takes a turn for the worse or better – and a major decision of the play occurs. Find an *indirect* way to let us know the decision is being made.
- A final moment of the interrupting element – the characters don't respond this time; they don't acknowledge the event. They struggle to go back to what they were saying but cannot. The scene ends.

Exercise 2: *Anton Chekhov* – The Cherry Orchard – *The Bizarre at Home*

- This time your characters are indoors in a very specific, homey space that has a meaningful importance to all in the room. Your characters lovingly engage with specific elements of the space vocally or with their behavior. Characters from your play engage in a conversation that deals with a very specific, detailed incident from their past – which has significance today, at

this moment. Allow the characters to recall that incident with all their five senses.
- A natural element (an animal, a tree, a plant, weather element, etc.) from the outdoors is observed in a window – allow the characters to notice it – and use it to tie into the incident in the past.
- An incident from within the house occurs – a sound, an interruption by a servant, an unseen family member, an object in the house topples. Something occurs in the house. It affects the characters. The house, the home, the family is suddenly the focus of a very specific discussion.
- The characters react, contemplate the situation, reflect on how it ties into the present and into the past. They specifically articulate how this current indoor space interacts with the incidents going on within the house – there is a history to this meaningful room that pulls at your characters *emotionally*.
- There is a repetition of the outdoor event – simultaneous with the indoor event – the characters are changed in the process; a connection is made between the indoors and the outdoors – and something important has happened in the world of the play.

What is key in this exercise is the linkage between what is happening in outside world with what is happening indoors. How does this connection with the natural world resonate with the central, key decision of your characters? This isn't a logical, linear connection – it is mysterious, disturbing, fraught, and yet there is the sense that what is happening in the natural world somehow suggests an answer or a solution to the problems that your characters have in their domestic doings. It is this very specific universe – the world of home and hearth – where Chekhov's plays have their greatest power, and he shares that expertise with a more recent writer, José Rivera, who brings a different kind of natural world magic to the table.

3   José Rivera – *Cloud Tectonics* – Latinx Realism Time Shift

When the magic dream structure of a drama is less abstract, less pronounced, perhaps even soothingly elusive, critics quite often term that technique as "magic realism." Not unlike the romantic non-realistic, non-linear technique we just explored in Chekhov's work, it is more nuanced approach to dream structure, and perhaps a better term would be "ordinary magic." In plays where instances of the miraculous seamlessly occur in settings that are otherwise realistic, this is the realm of magic realism. It has been a term most closely associated with Latin American writers such as Columbian author Gabriel García Márquez whose novel *100 Years of Solitude* is considered to the major influential work in the genre. José Rivera, a Latinx playwright of Puerto Rican roots, has long been considered to be a protégé of García Márquez, having worked with him at the Sundance Institute in 1989. Though there is much that happens in Rivera's plays that could be called magic realism, in recent years, Rivera has rejected the term because it somehow diminishes the work of Latinx writers and puts them into stylistic box – and from his point of view, any magic that works in his plays, works because it grows directly out of the specific, and sometimes harsh realities his Latinx characters experience in their lives. For Rivera this magic is deeper and blooms from ancient Afro-Caribbean religion Santería, which is a syncretic faith that grew out of the traditions of Yoruba in West Africa, Spiritism and ancestor worship, and Roman Catholicism culture as it has come up against the realities of Latinx immigration in America.

Rivera is also a literary descendent of the Spanish dramatist, Pedro Calderón de la Barca, who wrote during the Golden Age of Spanish Drama (1590–1691) and is most known for one of the most quintessential dream plays ever written – *La vida es sueño*, (*Life is a Dream*) written in 1681. The play is about Prince Segismundo who, because of a dark prophecy, is kept imprisoned by his father, King Basilio. When Basilio frees him Segismundo and allows him to rule, the prince realizing the injustice of it, goes quite mad and embarks on a villainous spree, which then leads to his second imprisonment. Once again imprisoned, Basilio attempts to convince Segismundo it was all a dream, but in the end Segismundo once again becomes free, but then realizes his fate is in his own hands and becomes a generous and wise ruler. Intriguingly, Rivera successfully adapted this Golden Age drama into a play of his own, *Sueño,* and so has taken on the mantle of becoming, at least to my mind, the Calderon of our own contemporary American Theatre.

Rivera is also the first Puerto Rican screenwriter to be nominated for an Oscar and is perhaps most well-known for his screenplay for *The Motorcycle Diaries* based on Che Guevara's diary about a motorcycle trip across Latin America with Alberto Granado Jiménez. However, in the theater he is most renowned for his spectacular and uncanny stage drama *Marisol* featuring the eponymous young Latinx woman who becomes caught up in a war in Heaven, with her guardian angel at the heart of fighting. Marisol suffers catastrophically in a twisted post-apocalyptic Manhattan where angels are street fighters and subways are inhabited by murderous madmen swinging golf clubs. Rivera's skills at combining this shadowy, bizarre world with an equally dark sense of humor, create a challenging landscape for his heroine, which combines her profound faith and generosity of spirit to combat the forces of evil.

However, the play we're going to explore here is his play *Cloud Tectonics*, which takes a tender and quixotic approach to the world's injustices. The magic involved in *Cloud Tectonics* is tied to a temporally unbound romance involving lovers Aníbal de la Luna and Celestina del Sol whose affair changes the dynamics of time. The play is a bit of a spin on Washington Irving's "Rip Van Winkle," as Aníbal discovers Celestina, a pregnant woman during a Los Angeles deluge, after she has hitched a ride with a truck driver in a cross-country attempt to find her baby's father, Rodrigo Cruz. Strangely, the moment Celestina enters Aníbal's home, his clocks stop, and their evening together turns into a love affair that transcends time itself. They are visited twice by Nelson, Aníbal's brother, who has returned home from war, after six years of service. Though the visits by clock time are only 20 minutes apart, in reality, two years pass between these interruptions, making it clear that time has come unstuck.

Rivera's unique and understated approach allows for Celestina to be much older than would be believable for a pregnant mother – she is 54 years old and has been pregnant for two years. The uncanny ending to the play, with a much older Aníbal living in a transformed Los Angeles, provides a powerful exploration of the poignancy of time and love, and how the world can change in a single evening. The exercise we'll explore is based upon Rivera's own work teaching playwriting, and the influence of his teachers, the previously mentioned Gabriel García Márquez and Maria Irene Fornes, who'll we'll be discussing later in the book. The Rivera essence exercise, borrowing from the Rip Van Winkle effect, is mostly an exercise in stretching your creative muscles in a uniquely temporal manner.

Exercise 3: José Rivera – *Cloud Tectonics* – *Dream Time Variations*

In this exercise, two characters engaged in an activity, and they only discuss that activity as it relates to their powerful desires (they may not directly discuss their actual desires). The reasons for doing the activity have been lost to the vicissitudes of time – their project changes as the time goes by, which they only understand as it is brought to them by other characters who then transform them in subtle fashion and transform the scene. The feeling should be of flow and fluidity, and their conversation never entirely stops. This is an exercise that should grow out of their character dream caches, using elements first developed there. Intriguingly, you can gather some of the elements within this exercise and re-deposit them into your character caches when you have completed the exercise. Note that this exercise, like all the exercises in this book, provide a leaping off place – and are meant to stimulate your technique – and help you find your own magic. Feel free to experiment with the steps and use what is useful to you, and discard what is not!

Step One – The Abandonment to the Activity – Loss of Self
Characters A & B are in a very specific location with simple symbolic, but very real elements, which suggest that location – it could be a bedroom, but it also could be the interrogation room of the police station, maybe both simultaneously – in other words, the location is equivocal, shifting, slippery. And yet everything feels unnervingly normal, perhaps even a bit boring.
- Some fundamental aspects of reality seem to be a bit off – not much, just a slant or a curve in places where they don't belong. Maybe gravity doesn't work correctly here, or time, or perhaps the sun hasn't set in days, or is always at mid-day.
- These aspects are noticeable, and yet ignored by the characters. There is a feeling of the ordinary even as the world becomes strange.
- Character A wants something desperately from Character B, and Character B has equal and opposed, desperate needs to Character A.
- They work on a physical activity together, and all they can discuss is that activity. The activity itself has strange elements – it seems very real, perhaps a tad boring, and yet, it has an otherworldly quality. The activity changes as Character C affects it with elements that they bring in with them.
- They continue this conversation for at least eight to 12 lines back and forth.

Step Two – Time Shift – Character c Entrance – Transference/Temporal Bleed
Character C enters, bringing an element which they add or detract to the space and/or the activity, changing it slightly. What has felt off before, becomes more disconcerting. Yet a sense of the quotidian remains.
- Character c notes an element of the world outside which has changed, significantly in terms of *time*.
- Characters A & B are somewhat shocked at the passage of time – but it's within reality at least on some level. Again, elements of pedestrian ordinariness prevail.
- Character c changes some element of Character A which changes their behavior – an addition or a subtraction, based on the passage of time (but Character A only changes subtly).

Step Three – Time Shift – Character B Exit/Re-entrance – Shaman Manifesting
During their conversation with Character c, Character B exits, and Character A gains a deeper understanding of what has happened in the outside world from Character c, who will shortly leave.

THE SNAP OF THE HEARTSTRING – SYMBOLISM AND ROMANTICISM   155

- Part of the revelation is that Character B is not who Character A thought they were, and therefore there is a growing tension. The uncanny effect of this world deepens noticeably, and yet its banal ordinariness prevails.
- Character C participates in the physical activity which continues.
- Character C now must leave, leaving Character A working solo on the activity. Momentarily, Character B returns, having transformed.
- It is now clear Character B is a *shaman* (a religious figure) of some sort – there is a threat or an opportunity for Character A in this transformation, though there is distinct sense of menace in the change. Still things lean to the ordinary – things are accepted as they might be in the real world.
- That Character B is a shaman affects the physical activity, as it is given a larger, spiritual context, and the stakes become much higher in the hopes that it is completed.

Step Four – Time Shift – Character A Exit/C Re-entrance – Collapse of Outer World

In this last sequence, Character A, given the intensity of the revelations shared by Character B, must leave, and Character A confronts the harsh reality of the world outside the door.

- Character B is left alone and thus continues to change the physical activity, which is now fully spiritual and transformative.
- Character B can somehow transform *time* and *space* with a much larger implication for the world, and for the universe. The ordinary world is now clearly and definitely changing to weirdness.
- Character C re-enters, fully transformed into the messenger deity that they actually are and interacts with Character B in a spiritual fashion tied to the larger religious mission that involves both.
- Characters B & C interact with the activity, commenting on it, but also somehow acknowledging their own special relationship and taking into consideration Character A and their relationship with each other.
- Character A re-enters, transformed profoundly by time and space – the protective bubble of the space within is now shattered with Character A's entrance, and all three come to the completion of the physical activity and its far larger implications. Still the trappings of the real, ordinary, pedestrian world remain – if a bit shattered by the seismic rumblings of an uncanny universe at work.

Living within the magic realist world of José Rivera's *Cloud Tectonics* allows for a gentle unraveling of reality, and at the same time, a reconnection with that same reality at the end of the experience. Key to all of this is to attempt to keep flowing toward normality, the ubiquitous quotidian, the banal, and the pedestrian even as things become deeply strange. The moments of the uncanny may leave the protagonist sadder and wiser at the end, or not aware that anything has taken place at all, even though the audience notices this change (perhaps this is the better choice). This exercise could be the building block for a new play or could simply be a means to character study, or a plot exercise to get at a Rip Van Winkle twist for your drama.

4 Unending Conversations: The Voice-Over Romance of Marguerite Duras's *Hiroshima, Mon Amour*

The next dramatist we'll explore is Marguerite Duras, who was a French novelist, playwright, screenwriter, and essayist whose experience of being born and raised in French-controlled Vietnam affected her unique sensibilities of having a Eurasian background, growing up in poverty in Indochina. Her work is profoundly symbolic and *Hiroshima, Mon Amour* has the uncanny brilliant crystalline quality of Dalí painting with its weirdness manifest in minute detail. Her writings are powerfully connected to her political sensibilities, and her screenplay for the film *Hiroshima, Mon Amour* won her an academy award nomination. In her work we take the notion of romanticism and explore both in its literary sense but also with its contemporary meaning in mind – Duras explores the nature of romance considering the human catastrophe and loss with the dropping of the atom bomb in Hiroshima, Japan.

5 Marguerite Duras – *Hiroshima Mon Amour* – Love in a Time of Nuclear Holocaust

Hiroshima mon amour is a 1959 French Left Bank romantic drama film directed by French film director Alain Resnais, with a screenplay by Marguerite Duras. It is the documentation of an intensely personal conversation between a French-Japanese couple about memory and forgetfulness. It was a major catalyst for the Left Bank Cinema, making use of miniature flashbacks to create a nonlinear storyline. It is a hauntingly romantic film – and here the romanticism refers to not only the unlikely love affair that takes place in the film, but how the mystery of this romance occurs – despite the horrors of World War II and the Bomb.

Hiroshima mon amour moves through a series of conversations (basically one enormous conversation) over a 36-hour long period between a French actress (Emmanuelle Riva), referred to as Her, and a Japanese architect (Eiji Okada), referred to as Him. They have had a brief relationship and are now separating. The couple debates memory and forgetfulness as she prepares to depart, comparing failed relationships (she is ostracized because of her affair with a German soldier during WWII) with the bombing of Hiroshima and the perspectives of people inside and outside the incidents. Resnais started to make a documentary about the effects of the Hiroshima bomb on August 6, 1945, focusing on the loss of hair and the complete anonymity of the remains of some victims. However, Resnais felt it was impossible to document that event on film and chose instead to shoot the film written by Duras, which takes a single long conversation by a couple linked to the event and explores trauma and memory from that point of view. It is the power of this wondrous and mysterious conversation, taking place within the context of a dream, that motivates the next exercise.

EXERCISE 3: Marguerite Duras – *Hiroshima Mon Amour* – The Long Conversation

In this exercise, you will build the entire exercise around a single conversation between a couple in love. Give the couple a specific timeframe for their affair and allow that time frame to be exact to the hour (for example, 48 hours in the case of *Hiroshima mon amour*).

A. The overall location of the film must be a place where horror has taken place – genocide, horrific disaster, mass suicide, or other human catastrophe which has permanently left a dark otherworldly aura to the location. The event is long in the past, but not so long as to be forgotten, and in fact we see historical placards, explanations, and even passing guides leading tours that make it impossible not to notice the particularly horrific and grotesque elements of what happened.

B. Your couple's romance is problematic for any number of reasons, and it cannot be consummated in marriage. They cannot ever meet again, though they will want to – desperately. And – this is important – how they have come together in romance must be very slowly revealed, even as their relationship is deteriorating.

C. Their desperation to be together must compel them to reveal themselves to each other and their linkage to the specific traumatic event in their lives. For one of them, the trauma is tied to location where they are. For the other, the trauma is in the past in another place.

D. Over the course of the conversation, images and flashbacks from past slip into their language – and you'll allow the film to drift into the past eight times. Those eight times are specifically tied to incidents and locations in the film:
   1. THE QUIET CONVERSATION THE NEXT MORNING AFTER INTIMACY (HIS STORY – 1)
   2. THE WALK AROUND A PLEASURABLE PLACE (HER STORY – 1)
   3. LUNCH OR A MIDDAY SNACK AT A RESTAURANT (HIS STORY – 2)
   4. A MOMENT WHEN THEY ARE APART (HER STORY – 2)
   5. DINNER AND A DRINK (HIS STORY – 3)
   6. WHEN THE EVENING GROWS PASSIONATE (HER STORY – 3)
   7. MORNING AFTER ANOTHER TRYST (HIS STORY – 4)
   8. JUST BEFORE PARTING (HER STORY – 4)
E. Both Character A and B have 4 sections of a past traumatizing event tied to a previous romantic relationship (though the two past relationships are wildly different from each other) that gets explored during these scenes in flashbacks – their stories follow a sequence of scenes, but not necessarily in chronological order:
   1. Character A – Past Event – Scene 1 (innocence), Scene 2 (attachment), Scene 3 (passion), Scene 4 (pain)
   2. Character B – Past Event – Scene 1 (knowledge), Scene 2 (encouragement), Scene 3 (sin), Scene 4 (horror)
F. Even as they live, love, and engage in their current location, a location of human catastrophe, they move through their past stories – though again, not necessarily in chronological order (consider, for example, exploring them in reverse). Note that their previous relationships take a terrible toll on their current one with each other. They both have some kind of deep tie to their current location (one has that relationship at the beginning of their current relationship, the other develops it because of their current relationship).
G. These past experiences, as they are related, have a devastating effect on their current romantic relationship, and they reveal their stories, it should be clear there is no escape for them from this past.
H. At these moments of past revelations, your film moves to fill out what has happened to the two of them in the past, even as we learn the mystery of how they came together – there should be both a leisurely quality to the film, and moments when it's clear the time has come for them to part forever, and the time they have is quickly ending.

However, ironically, it should always feel leisurely, as every moment they have right now, at least initially, is wonderful, and we feel them wanting it to last forever. Still at these same moments there is a feeling of desperation, as the time to leave is not far away. What is key is that we never stop noticing that there is a memory of horror present in the present location of the film – and that both of these people have some link, however tangential, to this horror, and they can never entirely escape it. The grotesque, awful reality of radiation poisoning and awful consequences of the dropping of the bomb – the sheer instant incineration of human beings – is key to this exercise (though any reverberating horror you create will suffice). The Hibakusha (survivors of the bombings of Hiroshima and Nagasaki) continue to advocate for the ending of any kind of nuclear devices on the planet. If you have never written a romance before, this romantic/symbolist exercise from Marguerite Duras' *Hiroshima Mon Amour* is a perfect place to start, as it advocates never forgetting, never ending the protest against the horrors of nuclear war.

We end this chapter linking three writers whose experiments in non-linear, non-traditional technique are much more gentle and subtle than some in this book. The influence of romanticism and symbolism in the writers is quite powerful, and sense of the real is profound, especially when laced with elements of the uncanny. The next two writers that we're going to explore, Thornton Wilder and David Lynch, have influenced generations of writers who have followed in their non-linear footsteps and their work grows out of a homespun, humorous, oddball sensibility that has sometime led their critics to dismiss their brilliant experimentations as a kind of eccentricity. But in fact, their uniquely American style of dreamwrighting gets at deeper elements of drama than most of their contemporaries have achieved – and in so doing, they embrace the history of their own medium in uniquely informative ways. It is not surprising that both have become such powerful influences on the dramatists who have followed them. so now let's borrow from the essence of Wilder's and Lynch's dreamwrighting techniques and see how they can help us enrich our characters, stories, and dramatic imagination.

CHAPTER 9

Realms of Theatricality – Surrealism and Waking Dreams

Thornton Wilder's Pullman Car Hiawatha *and David Lynch's* Mulholland Drive

Thornton Wilder (1897–1975) was one of America's most theatrical and experimental writers – writing plays that employed the simplest of sets – a few chairs, a table, a ladder – to tell the largest and most magic of tales. His plays had a disarmingly *Saturday Evening Post*, homespun quality to them, yet revealed a dark, heartbreaking dose of reality. Wilder's work was tied to an even more wildly experimental writer, Gertrude Stein, whose own tiny, abstract dramas had a large influence on Wilder. Wilder was "America's professor" in his time, and considered himself a teacher first, a writer second. He was an academic at heart, with sisters who were poets, and a sensibility that was pure Connecticut blueblood. His influence on American playwrights such as Tennessee Williams, Edward Albee, and Lanford Wilson was profound and like them he was gay and had gay sensibilities – though deeply closeted – tied to a deep appreciation for the power of artifice and technique. He shared with Oscar Wilde a profound sense of style and form – and though his plays could be as hard-hitting on the side of the poor and working class as any other writer of the 1930s, he was far piece from leftist, socialist-leaning writers like Clifford Odets and Arthur Miller. If anything, his experimental spirit hearkened back to Eugène O'Neill's own rough-hewn dramatic investigations, and his realm of theatricality might be termed the surrealist experience of the waking dream.

Later in this chapter, we'll be adding David Lynch to the discussion, another uniquely American dramatist and film director whose screenplays flirt with dream and reality. While when thinking of Wilder's work, Lynch's name probably isn't the first to come to mind, the two writers have worlds in common – beginning with like-minded powerful interest in experimentation and their deep connection to the American zeitgeist. Lynch's deeply creepy and bizarre *Eraserhead* (1977) a horror film that builds its terror on the increasingly strange yet humorously banal world of its titular character. For both writers, it is this powerful connection to ordinary human beings caught in a surreal world not of their own making, that connects them powerfully as dream dramatists. While Wilder leans toward a kind of urbane homespun if heartbreaking comedy and Lynch bends toward a quotidian horror, they share an enthusiastic sense of weirdness, an unreliable, shifting realm of theatricality, and a dry, somewhat quizzical sense of humor. It is not too far a stretch from Wilder's peculiar second act of *Our Town* to David Lynch's curious sojourn in American television with *Twin Peaks*; both can take the everyday normality of Main Street, USA and transform it into a slippery realm of an all-too-perfect veneered reality, always all too ready to burst into a deep void of revulsion.

Wilder and Lynch are often considered surrealists, writers who succumb to their dream visions, allow their writing to flow automatically without the censorship of their editing brain, allowing their unconscious desires and the chaotic influence of chance to help create their art. Heavily influenced by Freud's *The Interpretation of Dreams*, Surrealism as an artistic movement is most associated with André Breton and his *Surrealist Manifesto* (1924) which insisted that art must pour forth unencumbered by rational thought and society pressures. The goal was to become more aware of oneself, freer in technique and subject, and to ignore outside influence and follow the inner workings of the subconscious. Visual artists like Salvador Dalí and René Magritte with their oddly grotesque, detailed, and crystalline revelations of inner dreamscapes are the best examples of this movement in visual art, and writers such as Apollinaire and Jean Cocteau are dramatists most associated with the surrealist theatrical vision.

1 *Pullman Car Hiawatha*: The Debut of Thornton Wilder's Shaman Stage Manager

A brilliant and prolific author, Thornton Wilder won both the Pulitzer Prize in drama (for his plays *Our Town* and *The Skin of Our Teeth*) and in fiction (*The Bridge of San Luis Rey*), one of the only American writers to do so. His most famous play is *Our Town* which used just a few pieces of furniture and a stage manager, a figure normally never seen onstage, as a kind of shamanistic puppeteer who brings the stage to life. Wilder used the stage manager as a character in his one-act plays *The Happy Journey to Trenton and Camden* and *Pullman Car Hiawatha* and most notably in *Our Town*, as well as in *The Skin of Our Teeth* and *The Alcestiad*, though not as directly. The stage manager served as an onstage director, communal commentator, magician, sage, and shaman, providing deeper truths for the audience to glean from the sometimes disarmingly simple staging. If anything, Wilder's stage managers are avant-garde, eastern performance artists, borrowing from Kabuki, Noh, and Peking Opera in their simple, evocative control of time, setting, and situation on stage.

Wilder was a scholar and was profoundly affected by the Greeks – his notions of theatricality were tied to the Greeks' open acceptance of pretense – and so Wilder was uninterested in naturalism. Key then to Wilder's work was his deep sense of conventionally unconventional theater, with the Greeks' use of supernatural characters, chorus, keen sense of fate, and the Gods above as a huge influence. Yet theoretically he also insisted that every theatrical moment on stage happened right now, in the perpetual present. And despite his theatricality, a powerful blood and guts realism peeks through all his work, sometimes betraying itself in its simple revelation of the everyday moment. In other words, his plays are a combination of the real moment now, and the imagined magic of theatrical ritual – and therefore are of their own dream reality.

As much as Wilder is tied to a homey, American honesty in his content, there is a subtle modernist sensibility in his technique which he borrowed deeply from Gertrude Stein. For those who aren't familiar with Stein's own writing, and in particular her dramas, they are largely amorphous prose-poems broken out into acts. The language itself becomes the drama without characters, plot, or action, and Stein's short surrealist plays, such as *What Happened, Do Let Us Go Away*, and *Please Do Not Suffer* are open texts for those who want to stage her work, as they must essentially create it anew with each production, inventing their own world within language. Most famously, Al Carmines, the lay minister and artistic director of Judson Poets Theatre in New York's Greenwich Village of the 1960s created playful, evocative musicals from Stein's plays, including *In Circles* and *What Happened,* and Stein's plays not only influenced Wilder, but she was also his close friend and colleague in the last twelve years of her life. Wilder's *Pullman Car Hiawatha*, the play we'll be discussing here, was profoundly affected by Stein's freewheeling dramatic technique, and Stein's focus on language as drama is also influential on more recent "language" playwrights such as Mac Wellman, Len Jenkins, Constance Congdon, and Jeffrey Jones, as documented in Paul Castagno's important book *New Playwriting Strategies*.

However, as noted above, Thornton Wilder's style also borrowed broadly from classical Greek and Roman theatre and the ancient audiences who came to give homage to their Gods while they allowed their minds, souls, and bodies to be pierced and purged by the drama in front of them. Thornton Wilder's embrace of the chorus, deux ex machina, the simplicity of the Greek stage, its artfulness and artifice are clearly demonstrated in the play we'll examine here, his madly theatrical one-act play, *Pullman Car Hiawatha*. It is an early precursor to his famous *Our Town*, and one which encapsulates Wilder's incredibly inventive, yet oddly simple techniques in one short splash of stage magic. In *Pullman Car Hiawatha* we follow the deliberations of a passenger, Harriet, a middle-aged woman who is unaware that she is dying, in the Pullman sleeping car of a train traveling from New York to Chicago on December 21, 1930. In the process of her life's ebbing, we briefly connect with the ordinary lives of the other passengers, the conductor, and other train workers as the train crosses the country. The magic of the play is how simply it is done – the stage manager creates the train car using chalk on the floor and a few chairs and within moments populates it with the cast.

Over the course of the play, we not only hear from the passengers, we visit with ghosts, tramps, mechanics, entire towns, hours, planets, and archangels, all through the dream logic of the comings and goings of a train car making its way through the mysteries of the night as one of its passengers dies. Key to all this magic is the stage manager – a character who in the real life of a professional theatre, you would never see – but is in fact the person who is calling all the cues. The sound, lighting, entrances by actors, and all the other trappings of the theatre happen only with the command of this mysterious figure, the stage manager. In your drama, the one you will create below, your "stage manager" can be any authoritative figure – but someone who has a priest-like, shamanistic power in the world of the play. Digging deeply into the nature of the *chorodidaskalos*, or the Greek Chorus Master, your "stage manager" will control the action of the play, how the action is physically staged, and will remain as a kind of choral figure, engaged and disengaged with the characters and the action of the play. Your "stage manager" can completely transform the scene to a different time or place with a flick of the finger and a whisper – and may interact with the actors or with the audience and break the fourth wall. They are profoundly affected by what happens on stage, and can be a character within the story, or can be a totally disaffected narrator in their own world entirely.

Exercise 1: Thornton Wilder – *Classically Surreal with Shaman Stage Manager*

In the exercise below you must embrace Wilder's own fundamental rules of theatre, tied to both Aristotle and Gertrude Stein:

1. The theatre is an art which reposes upon the work of many collaborators;
2. It is addressed to the group-mind;
3. It is based upon a pretense and its very nature calls out a multiplication of pretenses;
4. Its action takes place in a perpetual present time.
   THORNTON WILDER, "Some Thoughts on Playwriting," 1941.

This exercise takes full advantage of Wilder's basic rules for theatre and theatricality – and is useful for a new play or for your experiments on a work-in-progress.

1. Consider using elements from your *central character's dream cache*, and perhaps create dream caches for the other characters in this drama.
2. Add more items to your *central character's dream cache*. Invent elements that tie closely with your central character's own personal predilections: large philosophical questions, flora and fauna, animals, historical events, important people, settings, and the larger cosmos (akin to what happens in *Pullman Car Hiawatha*), such as stars, planets, moons, galaxies, or even more esoteric cosmic phenomena such as quasars, black holes, rogue planets, or nuclear pasta.
3. Your drama takes place on moving object, a train, a car, a plane, a bus, a boat, a submarine, a blimp, something in motion, with a journey moving from a specific place to another specific place. Select the vehicle from your central character's dream cache.
4. You may only use chairs, tables, benches, and other pieces of furniture for your setting of your vehicle. Otherwise, the stage, the screen if you're writing a screen play, is blank.
5. You have a shaman/stage manager/production assistant who narrates, controls the action. They may engage with the actors and the audience as much or as little as you would like.
    a. The Shaman has unique ordinary, pedestrian quality. In Murray Schisgal's comedy, *Steambath*, God is a Puerto Rican steam room attendant.
    b. The Shaman has a metatheatrical quality – they can talk directly to the audience and reminds the audience of the artificiality of the theatre setting.
    c. The Shaman can transport us through time and space.
    d. The Shaman can transform individuals.
    e. The Shaman can temporarily take a role within the drama itself, and often does.
    f. The Shaman can narrate, but hides important facts, and is quite a shifty, slippery, unreliable narrator.
6. The play takes place over titanic periods time – but time can move forward and back as you prefer and can speed up or slow down. Yet we always return to the present moment.
7. The play includes characters who are not human beings; instead, they may be anthropomorphized places, things, inanimate objects, embodied symbols, philosophers, planets, angels, galaxies, cities, and time itself

(consider using your character's dream cache to create these unique characters).
8. There are 7 movements-conducted by the Shaman with sounds, lights, and spectacle:
   a. Ritual of the stage: Journey's Beginning.
   b. The dramatic situation occurs: An Uncanny Crack in the Cosmic Egg.
   c. Stage manager intercedes: Inner Revelation of Characters.
   d. Stage Manager Intercedes: Geography.
   e. Stage Manager Intercedes: Philosophy.
   f. Stage Manager Intercedes: Theology.
   g. Stage Manager Intercedes: Political Action.
   h. Dramatic scene with a major question of life and death: Your Protagonist Transformed.
   i. Closing Ritual tied to the Dramatic Scene: Ending of Journey.
9. Consider using three classical elements, Greek or Roman, or from some other ancient civilization, Hindu, Kingdom of Benin, Mayan, etc. – consider food, music, place, people, mythology, history, and theatre structure and professional theatre jargon.

I find it difficult not to cry at the end of *Pullman Car Hiawatha* as Harriet, not feeling worthy of going to Heaven, leaves behind a husband who she loved and who loved her. Her desire to take a moment with the Archangels, a pause to make sense of her life as she is caught off guard when she dies, strikes me as particularly heartbreaking and lovely. And the sudden rush of the cleaning women onto the train car at the end of the play, to do their simple task of ritually cleaning what is essentially Charon's Ferry, somehow takes my breath away. I imagine the play, as a director, taking place in a kind of black and white greyscale of 1930s film noir, making Harriet's lonely death a moment of Americana – romantic, sad, vast, and silent as a Midwestern prairie.

Pairing a filmmaker/dramatist as dark and menacing as David Lynch with someone like Thornton Wilder who seemed to be as classic as a Norman Rockwell painting may make no sense at all to some, but for me, both writers are classically Americanist, yet willfully experimental, and transformative for their contributions to the dramatic form. Lynch's *Eraserhead*, which has a nightmarish dream logic that makes sense only within the context of its vaguely science fiction camp everyman story, doesn't seem to be anywhere near stylistically to Wilder's *Our Town*, which recalls Frank Capra films like *It's a Wonderful Life* and *You Can't Take It With You*. But to see only the veneer of Wilder's parody of Americana in his plays is misunderstanding the deep darkness of Wilder's work. In the same sense it is easy to miss the wildly funny sensibility of David Lynch's irrepressible satire of Hollywood and entertainment culture in his sinister, yet comic films such as *Lost Highway*, *Blue Velvet*, and *Mulholland Drive*.

2　　Twisted Noir: The Mobius Detective in David Lynch's *Mulholland Drive*

To understand David Lynch's films, it's important to first understand David Lynch the visual artist – the two are inextricably intertwined. Lynch's early years painting and creating visual work at the Corcoran School of the Arts and Design, School of the Museum of Fine Arts in Boston, and the Pennsylvania Academy of Fine Arts had a major influence in his filmmaking. Lynch's fascination with animation and creating dark, violent, primitive effects are a fixture in his films and filmmaking, which spring directly out of his work as a visual artist. A multi-talented auteur, Lynch often created the music for his films, and because of this his films feel almost like a kind of performance art.

The screenplay and film we'll examine here, Lynch's *Mulholland Drive* is a twisted film noir story, with its mentally shattered protagonist as a sort of stream of consciousness detective. *Mulholland Drive* synthesizes the seemingly unmediated and free-flowing thoughts and impressions of one or more fictional characters following the whims and wanderings of a restless, rootless young actress in Hollywood, Diane Selwyn. Well known stream of consciousness works includes the novels *Ulysses* by James Joyce, *To the Lighthouse* by Virginia Woolf, and *The Sound and the Fury* by William Faulkner, and in each case the narrative follows the associative logic of a dream, flowing as river does around the rocks and boulders of daily life, creating meaning in the cracks and crevices of imagination. *Mulholland Drive* depicts Diane Selwyn's consciousness as it transitions among four states:

1. Her *real life*, or consciousness while awake. Diane's real life in the film takes place entirely in her apartment.
2. Her *memories* from her own life. Diane's flashbacks at the end of the movie are critical to understanding the film.
3. Her *dreams*, or consciousness while sleeping. Diane's dreams are constructed in her twisted mind from real life memories and populated the double-lives of her characters: their real selves conflate with their dream selves.
    1. In Diane's dream, Camilla appears as Rita, Diane appears as Betty and the Winkie's waitress is named Diane.

2. In *Mulholland Drive* the dream characters are introduced *before* they are seen in Diane's real life or memories.
3. Think of this like an inversion of the classic film version of *The Wizard of Oz*, a similar but more accessible film, the viewer sees those dream characters – the Cowardly Lion, the Tin Man, the Scarecrow, and the Wicked Witch of the West – *after* they are seen as real characters, namely the three farmhands and Miss Gulch.

Diane's *hallucinations*, which are constructed with real and imagined characters, including characters remembered from her dream. Like the *Wizard of Oz*, there is a high element of camp to *Mulholland Drive*. Lynch's work always has an element of Hollywood parody, and so don't be afraid to allow your funny bone to tingle when you're writing these scenes.

In the exercise below, we'll play a similar game with your own drama, shifting between states of consciousness, to create a kind of holistic living experience of your character, adapting and transforming to these different worlds, like an amphibian of multiverses. In the process, we'll play with whole notion of Hollywood Noir, subverting it, playing with pop and camp, to inject irony, twisting bad taste into comic genius.

3 *Muholland Drive* – Twisting the Noir – Arouse Your Nocturnal Detective

In this five-page exercise, you will use your protagonist as a kind of detective, in search of the clues within the context of an epic or journey dream. Like *Muholland Drive*, the chronological story is only the starting place for what really happens – there is both that chronological story and there is a competing dream story, and they will be intertwined.

1. DREAM: *The Death*. The dream begins with a murder – perhaps the murder of the protagonist her/himself. Or it's a suicide masked as a murder. Think of the murder both as the visual result, with a corpse reveal, and the physical action of murder, without revealing the suspect, but providing uncanny or unnatural clues.
2. REALITY: *The Apartment*. The real world has a very simple reality, your protagonist has moved to a new place, is a newcomer, and must find a job, a place to live, and friends to help navigate the new world. We start with them moving into their apartment.
3. DREAM: *The Investigation*. Your protagonist is the sleuth for what may be their own murder and/or they may be the murderer themselves. And of course, they are probably not a real detective. They will have both a real

life, and an imagined life as a detective. Consider giving them some peccadillos and idiosyncrasies when they are the detective that don't exist in the character's real life.

4. REALITY: The First Friend. Your central character befriends someone who begins to help them navigate this new world. This first friend makes a unique emotional impression on your central character.

5. DREAM: *The Confidant.* Choose another character, close to your protagonist in real life, to be your character's "Watson" or confidant. This person may be totally unreliable, and what they have to say may be totally inaccurate and/or crazy, but your protagonist must take them seriously. And, if we use one of the central theories about *Muholland Drive,* this confidant is the one who is murdered.

6. REALITY: Your protagonist begins their very ordinary and quotidian job, but the job has aspects to it where there is access to a higher class of famous people either in business, entertainment, sports religion, or government. At the job, something goes south for your central character; that something becomes very bad.

7. DREAM: *The Murder.* Working from a *dream cache* that you've created for your character, you will create a wild version of the upper-class world – with each dream element being a "clue" for how the murder victim was killed. This is when the murder happens.

8. REALITY: *Catastrophe.* This is really the final moment of your character's quotidian reality – their very ordinary business of moving to a new play, getting a job, securing a friend has become a nightmare because of one specific incident which involves all three elements.

Building your film noir dream, consider these elements:

a. Choose one of your central character's dream elements as the central axis of your sequence – bear in mind that you'll need a criminal – who is someone from your central character's real life.

b. ALL the significant characters in your screenplay will appear in the dream, as another version of themselves, intriguingly related to who they really are – perhaps their character's underbelly.

c. Choose several of the characters in your central character's dream cache to be the suspects. Bear in mind that, once again, these characters will have two selves – real and dream.

All the clues should come from the dream cache and must be openly available to the reader. Fair is fair (even in dreams), though those clues may be total nonsense, and bear in mind the pop art/camp quality of these clues.

i. Bear in mind that bits of *reality* must flow through the *dream.* And vice versa. The sense is that reality and the dream are *aware* of each other.

ii. Red Herrings and MacGuffins are of course permitted, and the weirder the better!
iii. Write out the sequence with scene headings, action, and dialogue into a short screenplay, and bear in mind the associative logic, noir quality of this sequence.
   - Consider physicalizing the interiority of the characters by dissolving in and out of specific symbols or visual elements key to inner psyche of your central character – and having that lead to another scene or world. The use of a symbol or visual cue is what is known as a "call" – a device that provides an entry into a different world and is something that David Lynch uses frequently in his films, taking us into places we'd sometimes rather not go!
   - Consider where these interior/symbolic moments might fit within your film to work as a revelation of character – a magical moment of self-revelation perhaps, that leads to your character to make a decision in the film. This is an entirely dream-like, non-linear process – working by association rather than by a causal response.
iv. Finally, working within the meta-cinematic style of David Lynch (film that knows it's film), don't be afraid to parody or satirize the film industry in your sequence; this is a technique that is conscious of its Hollywood roots; camp here is a form of subversion. And of course, you can certainly satirize any industry you feel works within your reality/dream.

working with the surrealist techniques of Thornton Wilder and David Lynch gives you a free reign over the rules of the universe you create, so don't be afraid to bend reality. Whether you work with the strange magic of a powerful shaman-like stage manager or play with the weird logic of an amateur sleuth, you'll tease out a different kind of meaning using these writer's essential technique. Both writers, whether you're working in the vein of Wilder's comfortably cosmic clowning or Lynch's more taut, ironic self-winking horror, will lead you toward a kind of everyday magic in your writing that tweak characterization and plot-making in unique and slightly terrifying ways.

CHAPTER 10

Inside out – a Feminist Expressionism of Dreaming
Sarah Ruhl's Eurydice *and Karen Moncrieff's* The Dead Girl

In this chapter, we'll be looking at two writers who explore two very different takes on expressionist technique – playwright Sarah Ruhl, and screenwriter and director, Karen Moncrieff. The scripts we'll explore written by these two talented writers, Sarah Ruhl's *Eurydice* and Karen Moncrieff's *The Dead Girl*, focus primarily on a feminist expressionism. In other words, using the classic definition of expressionism we'll see the world of these dramas *through the eyes of a female protagonist who has been twisted or damaged* by a sexist, unforgiving world. While they are two very different women writing in dissimilar art forms, they are linked by their unique magic take on some of the mundane realities of day-to-day living.

    Sarah Ruhl's *Eurydice* uses a theatricality of language, style, and technique and more specifically, a wild, dark, and ironic comedy, to get at the ancient Greek myth of Orpheus and Eurydice from Eurydice's point of view. Karen Moncrieff's *The Dead Girl* attempts to fill out the story of a young woman's corpse found in a field, and how that young woman's life connected with so many others – a mother, a sister, the wife of her killer, slowly making its way through the lives and experiences of each of those people until we experience the world through the eyes of the dead girl herself. We'll start with Ruhl, as of the two, she's a bit better known, but we'll end with Moncrieff, whose beginnings as a child star frame the narrative she creates in the film universe which she has so carefully crafted from her own life.

1 Sarah Ruhl's *Eurydice*: Genteel Subversion through Cosmic Feminism

Sarah Ruhl has been one of the most commercially successful experimental playwrights on the American Stage, taking up the mantle, at least to my mind, of a modern-day Thornton Wilder. Her plays share Wilder's gentle, genteel comic subversion of traditional drama through magic realistic technique, paired with a darker comic/cosmic response to the world. She shares with Wilder a healthy connection to the Greek stage as she's interested in the notion of reinvigorating ancient stories through the repossession of those narratives revitalized though a progressive, engaged technique. Sarah Ruhl also shares Wilder's love of the academy and has written several remarkable essays on dramatic writing in academy journals such as *Theatre Topics, Theater, Performing Arts Journal,* and *American Theatre.* Trained by Paula Vogel at Brown University, Ruhl was clearly shaped by Vogel's own interest in Russian formalism, plasticity of setting, sense of humor, and bizarre stage directions that are all but impossible to stage.

A MacArthur "genius" grant recipient, Ruhl shares Vogel's powerful populist vision for social change to her writing and a very human, gently ironic approach to comedy. Her plays such as *Dead Man's Cellphone, Stage Kiss, In the Next Room (or the Vibrator Play), The Clean House,* and *Passion Play* all demonstrate a wildly funny, but calmly comedic style that puts pressure upon some of the larger injustices done to women in our culture. Ruhl's real gifts lie in taking familiar objects and transforming them on the stage into talisman and charms, and working with those strangely familiar, yet distinctly odd realities, and wringing comedy out of them. With that in mind, the exercise that we'll start with here is a Dog Play. It is built on the simple fact that dogs don't talk, they don't respond to things as people do, even though we respond to dogs as if they were people!

Exercise 1: Sarah Ruhl/Paula Vogel – The Dog Play – Wresting Comedy from Tragic Circumstances

- *Step one – World of the Dog –* Choose a setting, time, location of the scene. The characters caught up in the tragedy do not directly speak about the odd, perhaps supernatural nature of the dog – they accept the dog as a dog, and yet the situation will be *very weird.* Consider borrowing from the dream cache of a central character you are working on; the world of the dog play will be tied to that character. Consider right away that this will be a comedy, but perhaps not laugh-out-loud comedy.
- *Step two – Invite Your Dog to the Table –* Create the character of the Dog – bear in mind the *specific type of dog* (Dachshund, Chihuahua, Poodle, Dalmatian, etc.) – Choose one of the other characters in the dream cache of your play or your central character – reimagine that play from the viewpoint of a dog (or cat, or another domestic pet if so inclined – but be specific in terms of both animal appearance and behaviors). Since this is magic play, your dog can talk, write, float in the air, etc. The dog should be created in such a manner, that its personality is a clear foil to that of your protagonist, redefining them by the dog's deep difference from them. And there should be an aspect of the dog that is *uncanny.*

- *Step three – A Dog's Tragedy* – Give the dog some desperate domestic emotional goal, tied to the characters involved touching, heart-rending family tragedy – yet not involved in the actual tragedy itself (unless the pet inadvertently caused the tragedy). Be aware that this goal has *desperate implications* and a *heart-breaking reality* for all involved, but also has a dog-framed reality that deals with the dog's current domestic situation. The dog can never directly talk about the real want or need they have, instead they might talk about the activity at hand.
- *Step four – Grooming Activity – Fun with Fido* – Have the dog involved with some *activity* that would be normal for the dog to be doing at that time of day, location, season of the year. The dog should be mystically engaged with your central character by doing this dog-like activity – and your central character should be dealing with a much larger issue outside of the dog's very real, lived desire or goal, but is somehow tied to the dog's very dog-like *activity*. Bear in mind that the dog may not talk about their goal or desire directly, but only about the activity at hand.
- *Step five – Between Dog and Owner* – create dialogue between the dog and its owner; is it real dialogue? Is it imagined? Is it a typical interaction dealing with feeding, grooming, walking, or playing with the dog? What might make it different today? Give the dog a specific and desperate *request* that it needs from its owner – and vice versa. Create a voice and personality for the dog that is uniquely human, and just a bit magical.
- *Step six – Issues within Issues* – Find a way to end the scene, bringing to bear the resolution of the dog's situation in tandem with the owner's larger challenge. Consider framing all of this within a dog-like event – a grooming, a dog show, a walk in the park, etc. Consider how this short play ties into larger issues in the major play you are developing – and if this dog play can fit within that other work or could become a larger work within itself. Bear in mind that the closer you stick to the beginning, middle, and end of a real dog activity, even while bending that event in some bizarre manner, the truer and more interesting this dog play will be!

The other major aspect of Ruhl's work is her ability to seamlessly blend the phenomenal (real) and noumenal (supernatural) world in her plays. In *Eurydice*, the title character arrives to the underworld in an elevator that is pouring rain within. In the world of the play, rocks can speak and are in fact an entire family; Hades is a spoiled brat on the tricycle, not the imposing, frightening Lord of the underworld; rooms can be fashioned out of string; messages can be sent by earthworms and sipping straws. What brings all these techniques together is a kind of theatrical synesthesia, a crossing over of the senses to create something uncanny and magical, scarily unreal, and yet totally ordinary.

In the next exercise, we'll explore a bit of this synesthetic dream technique, exploring simple properties in a scene.

Exercise 2: Sarah Ruhl – Eurydice – The Synesthesia Exercise

In this exercise you will work on a short drama or film of approximately ten pages – it is purposely brief so that you can find the essence of the strangeness of synesthesia – synesthesia occurs when you hear music, but you imagine shapes. Or when you hear a word or a name and instantly see a color. Or you see a color and you can smell or taste it. Synesthesia is basically the feeling that one sense is suddenly experienced by another sense, and the two are inexplicably and inextricably linked. Quite often this linkage of senses is also tied to a powerful emotion, and here, the notion of synesthesia is extended so that objects that work with one sense, suddenly seem to work with a different sense.

- *Step one – The Call – An Everyday Object in a Weird, Weird World:* Place your character in an otherworldly place – a place that grows out of an element in your character's dream cache. In this scene, your character will encounter an everyday object that seems to have an odd, entirely different use or sensual quality than its use in the real world, and this strangeness tied to something your character desperately needs.
- *Step two – Swallowing Genre: Drama, Essay, Poem, Rant, Or Short Story:* Your character will slip into the realm of a literary form in the world of the scene – the structure will follow the mini-version of a famous fable, essay, poem, rant, or short story – key to this is that you borrow a character from that world, and that you follow the structure of famous piece of literature, using for example the structure of a Greek myth like that of Arachne, a poem like "Lady Lazarus" by *Sylvia Plath*, or a short story like *The Lottery* by Shirley Jackson. Bear in mind you will be bending this bit of narrative to your own devices.
- *Step Three – Scenic Realm: Mutations and Transformation:* The scenic realm of the playlet you are writing must have one transformation, but as many as three – these may be all part of the world you initially created, or entirely new worlds which slip past the characters in your playlet, who disregard the change with a kind of insouciance and ennui.
- *Step Four – Character: Sense and Insensitivity:* Still, the characters themselves are subtlety transformed as well, gaining a super-ability, and yet have a part of themselves broken in the process. Again, these changes are tied to synesthesia – their senses have become supercharged. In this weirdly powerful,

but hobbled state, they are wrestling with a larger issue which stems from their first encounter with the object in Step One.
- *Step Five – Baader-Meinhof Phenomenon:* The Baader-Meinhof phenomenon is one where your character inadvertently encounters some obscure piece of information, a song, a phrase, something totally unknown to your character – and in this scene, encounters it again and again. There is a weird frequency to this experience, and it builds until there is a kind of existential explosion. The Baader-Meinhof phenomenon is the finale to this scene, and engenders a final transformation of setting, character, or situation. Write it out as a short play or film.

Finally, in the last exercise as we think about Sarah Ruhl's *Eurydice*, is another one that stems from the classic structure of German Expressionism, the movement that gave rise in the theatre to such modern classics as *Man and the Masses* by Ernst Toller and *From Morn to Midnight* by Georg Kaiser. In both classic plays an every-person character is caught in a bind between an oppressive, capitalistic society, and the personal, individual ideals of a world where people have dignity and spiritual value. The ecologies of the plays are twisted and abstract and are filled archetypal figures to contrast with the fully rounded human beings at the drama's center. Sarah Ruhl creates a similar world in *Eurydice*, and we experience her characters from the inside-out, and so we see the world of the play from the view of the protagonist twisted by the oddly discomforting world that has seems to work in ways that it should not.

In practice, most expressionist drama took on a rather ancient, non-realistic, non-linear structure, the medieval station play – where individual scenes were performed in small structures called mansions or stations (vignettes like the Stations of the Cross) either inside of the nave of cathedrals or outdoors in the abutting town squares in pageant wagons. Audiences could move from station to station to experience the play in any order they cared to go, with the final and most spectacular station or pageant wagon always being the Hell-mouth, where the sinners were dragged down into hell by costumed devils (possibly the best part in the play!). In the exercise below, we'll experiment with this classic form, inspired by the church-based theatre of the Middle Ages.

Exercise 4: Expressionist Station Drama Exercise – The Quest

Taking a step into the classic realm of Expressionism, in this exercise you will write a series of short dreamlike scenes (built on the episodic dream mode of The Quest), dreamed by your protagonist-who is an anti-hero (a person of low economic means and questionable morals, yet has an uncanny ability to seek and meet out justice). The strangeness of the world they experience will shape the physicality of the play – and that will be shaped by the trauma they have received in the real world. Use the material you collect for your central character's Dream Cache – using similar prompts that you used for your own Dream Cache.

At each station, allow the world of your play to flow through these specific scene titles – later, they will morph through your art into realities that will become part of the world of your play – you'll *retitle* the stations, after you finish each, with titles that come from your character's dreams. These new station titles may suggest an entirely new structure, one quite different from the order below. Each station requires about five minutes of writing time.

Station 1: – The Portal Challenge
- At this station your character will struggle to enter the world of the play – she/he will be challenged by your antagonist/gatekeeper and not permitted entry until the completion of a task or ritual.
- The Portal Challenge questions whether your central character is even worthy of the opportunity to go on the quest.
- Somehow your character will say the right thing, do the right thing, complete the task, and move onto through the Portal. The Antagonist/Gatekeeper remains always in the world of the Quest.

Station 2: – The Oracle/Soothsayer/Liar
- At this station your character will receive a confusing message, which is tied to the resolution of your play. It will be both positive and threatening and suggest a possible direction. The Oracle/Soothsayer/Liar is someone your character both knows and does not know, meaning that they have a physicality of someone your character knows – but a persona and perhaps even a costume that suggests someone else.
- There will be three challenges posed by the message of the Oracle/Soothsayer/Liar, and these challenges must be met before your character may end the play.
- Your character reacts and responds to this confusing message, and this causes her or him to do something, which leads them to the next station.

Station 3: – The Beast/Lover
- At this station your character will encounter a monstrous person, a Beast, who is a tormentor though eventually, through transformation, a lover of some kind.

- The challenge here will be both physical and mental. It involves a threat that evolves into seduction. The challenge transforms the beast into a lover.
- The scene slips into the next scene and a new landscape in which the transformation occurs.

Station 4: – The Lover/Beast
- At this station, which seamlessly flows from the last, your character will discover her/his lover is not all they believed.
- A transformation/discovery challenge will take place. It involves a natural event that forces your character to make a difficult and emotionally painful choice.
- This discovery will reveal the lover to be the Beast, who then threatens your character, providing a gateway into the Physical Challenge.

Station 5: – The Physical Challenge
- At this station, your character must wrestle in a physical sense with a situation, person, dilemma which is genuinely difficult and unpleasant. This is the Physical Challenge.
- This Physical Challenge will go well or poorly with your character and regardless of how it goes, your character will receive a Terrible Wound.
- This Terrible Wound will allow them entry into the final Station.

Station 6: – The Treasure, the Death, and Life
- At this final station, the Terrible Wound will unlock a magic secret or a magic ability which will open a final door into a place of either Wonder or Terror.
- Your central character will either survive and be Changed or Die and be Changed.
- The final event of this vignette in your character's dreams will represent the Circle of Life, the Seasons of the Earth, the Wholeness of Humanity, and the Inevitable.
- Whether the Outcome is terrible or wonderful, it will be true and have deep meaning for your character.

Working through the station drama above, you should contemplate how the narrative structure that you followed might be totally subverted by changing the order of the events, and one of the major strategies of dream-like, non-linear dramatic writing is simply to move from the end to the beginning, as we saw in Christopher Nolan's *Memento*. And as I mentioned earlier, another way to explore this exercise is vary the structure based upon how you *retitle* the stations – these new titles may suggest an entirely new reordering of the stations to get at an emotional state or a political message that makes a connection to your writing as you move from station to station. And of course, the retitling can also borrow from myth, folklore, or an alchemical formula of your own mystic construction.

2   Karen Moncrieff – *The Dead Girl* – Unpeeling the Onion of Grief

The next expressionist writer we're exploring is writer/director Karen Moncreiff, who began her career as an actress, and after years of unsatisfying experiences in nighttime television, and a career in soap operas, began directing in 2002 with her film *Blue Car*. Moncrieff has struggled against the patriarchal Hollywood culture to bring her feature films to mainstream audiences, but has consistently crafted tight, brutally honest scripts and directed them with powerful emotional focus and mesmerizing performances. In her film *Blue Car*, a young gifted teenage writer, Megan, is subtly groomed and seduced by her high school English teacher, Mr. Auster, a failed novelist. The film while traditional in structure, insistently digs into the deeply uncomfortable uneasiness of the experience, as Auster gently and soothingly mentors Megan, a troubled young woman living with her divorced mother and suicidal younger sister, as she develops her voice as a poet. In a moment of horror, her sister Lily is forced to be hospitalized after a breakdown, and later throws herself out of a window.

Making her way to a poetry conference, Auster later moves to bed Megan in a conference hotel where she is about to present her poetry. In one of the most awkward sad moments in American film, Auster realizes during his lovemaking, that Megan is repulsed by him, and humiliated, makes his discomforted exit. Megan simultaneously discovers that his novel is a sham, and the entire process of his mentoring has been a pathetic excuse to seduce her. The next day Megan recites her poem, powerful, beautiful, and haunting, revealing his abuse of her trust. Her sister dead, and her trust in her mentor broken, Megan leaves her mother's home, and finds solace in the embrace of her father's blue car.

Moncrieff mines similar deeply distressing emotional territory in her film *The Dead Girl* which explores the repercussions of the discovery of the body of a young woman – Krista. Facing the same gender challenges in the film industry, when Moncreiff directed the film in 2006, there were fewer women directors of feature films than there are women in high positions in the government of Afghanistan. *The Dead Girl* was written based on her experiences as a juror at a murder trial, watching witnesses recreate the life and death of a person, discovering that person, testimony by testimony, working back from the young woman's death – starting from place of anonymity to an almost uncomfortable proximity to victim. The structure of the film follows five vignettes, all which tie into the body of the girl. The film's structure is essentially an exercise in five degrees of separation from Krista in terms of character study. There is "The Stranger" – Arden, the woman who finds the body; "The Sister" – Leah, the young female forensic scientist who examines the body; "The Wife" – Ruth, the wife of the murderer; "The Mother" – Melora, the mother of the dead girl; and "The Dead Girl" –Krista, the victim of the murderer. In each case there is a segue taking the story one step closer – the segue is essentially built on the nature of "a call" – a sign, symbol, or scene, which provides an exit from one story and an entrance into the next.

Exercise 4: Karen Moncrieff's The Dead Girl – Five Degrees of Separation

In this expressionist exercise, you will explore several characters who are connected to your central character, and the deeper you go into that character's past, the more corners with cobwebs that you disturb, the more effective this exercise will be. The expressionist stations here are tied to five specific characters themselves linked powerfully to the broken and twisted world of your central character. Key to the exercise is your willingness to find as many characters linked to your central character as you can – you will be digging profoundly into your character's past, present, and future as you do so. Treat this exercise as a kind of dream cache for your central character.

1. *Characters*:
    a. You will write a series of brief character descriptions, for a total of ten descriptions, on separate slips of paper (you will not necessarily use all of them as *major* characters, but you'll use all of them eventually)– starting with the central character of your film. For each character description use the following elements:
        i. Character name
        ii. Physical Description
        iii. Personality
        iv. Relationship to your central character
    b. Choose two characters who are in the immediate family of your character with whom the character has a close personal relationship.
    c. Choose two characters who are within the character's work-day world, tied to their daily occupation.

- d. Choose two characters who are friends of the character of varying degrees of closeness.
- e. Choose two characters who have a connection to your character that is tangential but significant in some way.
- f. Choose two characters who have a connection to your character that is tangential but not in a significant way.
- g. Once you have written character descriptions for all these characters on slips of paper, turn them over and mix them up.
- h. Turn over five of the descriptions, and look at them, allowing a story to build in your mind – keeping in mind a sixth character, the central character.
- i. These five characters are not the *only* characters of the ten you might use eventually, but they'll be the *five most important*. Try to incorporate *all* the others in some manner, however, as they will be ready in your mind, to participate in the story.

2. *Talisman/The Call/Segue*:
   - a. Write down brief descriptions of 10 significant objects, places, events, animals, plants, and describe each:
     - i. Using all five senses, describe each of these elements – two objects, two places, two events, two animals, and two plants.
     - ii. Describe how they are significant to your central character – and preferably how they connect to both your central character and one if not more of the characters listed above.
   - b. Once you have written all these Talisman descriptions, turn them over, and mix them up.
   - c. Turn over four of the descriptions (you may use ALL of them eventually, but these are the *four most important*), and look at them, and the five characters you have mind, and the sixth character – the central character.

3. The Story
   - a. Now that you have five characters and four talisman descriptions, use each of these characters to weave five separate stories that feature your central character as the one who links them all. Feel free to use all the other characters and talismanic objects in concert with these most important, focal ones.
   - b. Use the talisman to provide the segue between each of the stories.
   - c. Feel free to use any of the other characters or talisman within the world of these five stories.

d. Pay attention to the interweave between the stories – can you connect the characters not just to your central character, but also to each other?
   e. How do the talisman transform the scenes – what unknown country in your character's life do they take you to?
4. The Screenplay
   a. Once you've written the five stories – then treat each as separate sequences of a brief screenplay.
   b. See if the interwoven connections tell their own stories about the characters, and how they are connected not only to your central character, but each other.
   c. If you were to create an entirely different film on one of the other characters, which of the characters would it be and why?
   d. What new mystery has this series of sequences revealed to you about your central character, how might that help you in your major current screenplay?

By exploring the nature of the uncanny connection between your characters and experimenting with a "call" or talisman, you are unlocking the hidden nature of characterization, which is tied to the secrets all characters have. Each character in your dramas have their own world of characters within, since we are built of our interactions with other human beings, who indelibly change us. In the plays of Sarah Ruhl, and the films of Karen Moncrieff, women's lives take them center stage, instead of being foregrounded behind men, and in doing so, we are allowed into a rich new realm of imagination that adds immense color and vibrance to the stage and screen. At the same time both writers focus on a kind of miniature of focus in their dramatic expressionism, creating uncanny twists and theatricality on a small and very human scale, that engages our hearts and our minds with a very precise pinch of reality.

In the next chapter, we'll look at an extension of expressionism, epic theatre, which followed in expressionism's tradition of questioning the masses, questioning society, and in the process, knocking its audiences off their feet, unbalancing them, and at the same time, forcing them to see the world as it truly is, a place where people's actions grow out of an insistent economic power struggle. The dramatists we'll explore, Bertolt Brecht and Lucy Alibar are comfortable revealing the engine under the hood of their artifice, celebrating its artificiality, and in so doing, as lucid dreamers, they unmask our own daily, quotidian mendacity.

CHAPTER 11

Epic Theatre and The Lucid Dream

Bertolt Brecht's The Threepenny Opera *and Lucy Alibar's* Beasts of the Southern Wild

As I noted in Chapter 7 on Tony Kushner and Charlie Kaufman, the lucid dreamer is one who realizes they are caught in a dream, and its oneiric quality is wrestled into a pliable state, and thereby, control of the dream's mechanics is then put into the hands of the dreamer. The lucid dreamer needs a few tricks of the trade, however, to understand when they are actually dreaming, as a dream reality is almost always accepted as real by the dreamer, unless something "breaks" in that realm to unmask the meta reality of the dream. In this chapter we'll be exploring two writers who delight in revealing the internal mechanics of the dramatic dream, Bertolt Brecht, and Lucy Alibar. Brecht, whose enormous oeuvre of theatrical writings, both in terms of his essays and his dramatic work, would seem to overpower with Alibar, whose single major film *Beasts of the Southern Wild* gets at the powerful connection between a father and daughter, couched in a uniquely socially engaged dramedy involving economics, race, class, and the environment. For both writers, key to being "lucid" in the real world is to borrow from the nature of lucidity in dream life.

1 Bertolt Brecht's *The Threepenny Opera* – Verfremdungseffekt and the Lucid Dreamer

Brecht began as a dramaturg working with Max Reinhardt's Deutsches Theater and later joined the "dramaturgical collective" of Erwin Piscator's first company even as wrote more of his own work for the theatre. Brecht expanded upon Piscator's socially engaged, and director-oriented Epic Theatre techniques, eventually crystalizing this into his ideas of a playwright's Dialectical Theatre. Fascinated by early experimental playwrights Frank Wedekind and Georg Buchner, Brecht became known for plays which openly encourage the audience to drop out of the interior reality of the play and connect with the external technique that creates those fictions. Relying upon what he called the *Verfremdungseffekt* or distancing effect, Brecht sought techniques that would snap an audience out of the hypnotic empathy that Aristotelian theatre sought to bring about in its spectators. This distancing is not unlike the kind of "ostranenie" or "defamiliarization" or "making strange" theorized by Russian formalists such as Viktor Shklovsky in his essay "Art as Technique" which sought to jolt readers out of the inertia of a habituated life and make ordinary life "strange" so that those readers can see the world anew.

Brecht's techniques to achieve *Verfremdungseffekt* include subverting an historical event as a model for a contemporary issue, thus many of his plays are built on history, but skew that history to get at a state of dialectical theatre, that is, theatre that shows the inherent contradictions in the world, ironically revealing them through shock and cruel humor. To keep the audience on its toes, he would drop placards into the middle of a scene, project language and images to disrupt it, and have the actors break into uncomfortable songs with purposely unpleasant and appalling lyrics. To remind the audience that they were watching actors, not the characters themselves, Brecht would have actors simultaneously comment on the characters through gesture and attitude even as they were performing them. Brecht coined the term "gestus" to get at this inherent acting artifice. Actors could then break the fourth wall, speak directly to the audience, and create a running critique of their characters, noting the contradictions in their characters even as they played them.

Because one of the goals of Brecht's theatre was to expose the social and political factors that influence what seems to be "natural" human behavior, Brecht would find ways to "break" stage reality by exposing the mechanics of the theatre itself, this included having the characters break into songs that had a dissonance rather than synchronicity between melody and lyrics. A good example of this is "The Ballad of Mack the Knife" from Bertolt Brecht's and Kurt Weill's *The Threepenny Opera* – while the melody is lilting and lovely, the lyrics are brutal, ugly, and shocking:

> See the shark has teeth like razors,
> All can read his open face
> And Macheath has got a knife but
> Not in such an obvious place.[1]

Weill and Brecht were attempting, by the mix of the jaunty melody and the cruel, violent lyrics, to throw the listener off their footing, jolt them away, and force them to rethink their own ideas about Macheath, who may seem to be a romantic highwayman, but is, in fact, a cutthroat thief, rapist, and pedophile.

---

1 Bertolt Brecht, John Willett, *The Threepenny Opera* (London: Bloomsbury, 2015), 3.

In *Threepenny Opera*, this dichotomy/dialectic sets up the reality of the play, not only is our hero, Macheath, truly a vile villain, but he is also a crook beset with other felons who reveal themselves to be even worse than he is. What is most powerful in the play is use of parody, a kind of criminalized comedy that makes fun of Macheath's low nature and at the same time celebrates his ability to wittily outmaneuver the other villains of the play. Macheath's great crime in the play is that he has dared to marry Polly, the daughter of Jonathan Jeremiah Peachum, the crooked mastermind of the most massive syndicate of phony beggars in London. Peachum sets Macheath onto a path of self-destruction, which will end in Macheath's hanging, but instead results in Macheath's vindication with the bizarre deux ex-machina of the Queen's pardon. Not only will Macheath no longer be hanged, but he is given a castle and a barony instead! In the key moment of the play, when Macheath is about to be hanged, the hidden motive behind the play is revealed – Macheath in his passionate defense declares himself no worse than a businessman, because he notes, "What's picking a lock compared to buying shares? What's breaking into a bank compared to founding one? What's murdering a man compared to employing one?" In this way, an evil character whom we would normally consider an antagonist is given a twist – the typical businessman is more of a crook than the ordinary criminal.

For our purposes, Brecht's Verfremdungseffekt technique ties into the nature of dreamwork for dramatic writing through its close association with lucid dreaming – dreaming that is aware it is dreaming.

Another great theater theorist and practitioner who derived much of his fundamental ideas on subversion of oppression from Bertolt Brecht, was Brazilian Theater of the Oppressed director and playwright Augusto Boal. In Boal's essay, "Aristotle's Coercive System of Tragedy" he lays out what he believes is the traditional bourgeois theatre's technique for neutralizing the agency of audiences and his own method for subverting this deadening effect. Fundamental to this was shaking up the audience from simply spectating the action of the play to taking *action* to change the oppressive regimes depicted in the drama – the audience moves from being spectators to "spect-actors."

Exercise 1: Bertolt Brecht, Verfremdungseffekt Playwriting Exercise

- *Step One – Revealing Aristotle's Coercive Effect – Hidden Motives:* The goal of this first step is to unmask how people manipulate other people to get what they want, without that person knowing they're being manipulated. So, working with your dream cache, focusing now on the *Antagonist* of your drama, you're going to key your audience into what that character wants, by established a central *Hidden Motive*. Your antagonist is the hero of this drama, and their Hidden Motive fuels the action of the entire play. And that antagonist has no compunctions about revealing their base desires. This isn't so surprising, as it's something that Shakespeare's villains do all the time; think of Iago in *Othello*, Richard III in his eponymous play, and Claudius in *Hamlet*, all are uncommonly direct in sharing their evil goal with the audience. The delight we have with these characters is in their naked ambition – we all have these inner antagonists; we all have these dark and negative thoughts.

- Brecht is devilishly clever in unmasking our hidden, selfish, ugly selves, and unmasking these hateful sides to our humanity. The German theatre was much in love with Shakespeare's work, with major romantic era playwrights like Goethe and Schiller being powerful devotees. Epic Theatre borrows from Shakespeare's episodic technique by including many subplots, many locations, many times, and borrowing its storylines from history. And Shakespeare was fond of revealing the theatre itself in his plays within plays, and numerous asides and soliloquies – all a kind of lucid dream technique that is quite of a piece with Epic Theatre's metatheatrical and metadramatic panache. Quite often the non-linear, non-traditional techniques like Epic Theatre that enthrall 20th and 21st century theorists like Brecht and Boal hearken to much earlier styles that were themselves rebelling against tradition. In this case, Shakespeare's episodic theatre provided a powerful antidote to the neoclassicism of the Renaissance, even as it was firmly entrenched in some of its classical traditions – repurposing bloody Senecan tragicomedy for its own uses. Brecht's epic theatre or dialectical theatre doesn't stray far from that oddly Elizabethan tradition.

- The antagonist's *hidden motive*, however, should also be tied to the playwright's deeper motives for writing the play – revealing the heart of a villain should tie directly into the playwright's desire to reform society, unmasking all those who would go otherwise unseen about their cruel, Machiavellian machinations. In Epic technique, our goal is the wake the audience up, shake them, and cajole them into action. The good guys don't always win, and the bad guy doesn't always lose – in fact, it is sometimes difficult to tell them apart, and so we might find ourselves cheering on the character that unmasks our own prejudices.

Step Two – Unmask the Antagonist – The Four Ws – The Rhythm of Epic Dramatic Units:

- In your planning of this Epic Theatre exercise, you'll be clarifying your character's *hidden motive* by foregrounding it through the four W's – What, Who, Where, and When
    - WHAT: The Antagonists' *Hidden Motive*
    - WHERE: Your character's special place
    - WHO: Four Characters: Antagonist, Protagonist, Friend, Foil
    - WHEN: At the emotional climax of the second act

Structure of the Epic Theatre Dramatic Units

1. Introduction – Character talks directly to Audience about their Hidden Motive. Keep in mind the sense of character caricature, consider writing your characters in a parodic style – which allows for the breaking of a fourth wall.
    a. Parody is the tool of political drama, and it doesn't mean your characters are not "real," but rather have a self-conscious sense of who they are within societal norms and flaunt that.
    b. You are playing with outsized aspects of the characters that you want to highlight that get at a "gestus" of the character or that character's emblematic feature.
    c. The nature of parody allows for a kind of "mockumentary" style that is key to this initial speech – the character has a sense of their own ridiculousness, and still punches it out into the world.
2. A Placard drops onto the stage (or lights up above the stage) It describes the where and Hidden Motive of the next scene (perhaps the time and location and that situation).
    a. It can be a real 3-D object, or it can be a projection, slide or video, and/or can be performed as a kind of dance or physical semaphore.
    b. It should be disruptive, subversive and have a purposely "canned" quality, even bordering on a "pop" or "camp" sensibility.
    c. It has a parodic, ironic, or comic quality that highlights its artifice.
3. Scene with conflict – with a general focus on Central character and the Antagonist but including the Friend and the Foil.
4. Song about the Hidden Motive by the Antagonist. See the ideas about Brechtian song below.
5. A Placard drops onto the stage describing the Second Scene who, where, when, and hidden motive.
6. Second Scene with Conflict, but with a focus ONLY on the Central character and the Antagonist.
7. Final Monologue/Song Sung by Central Character about the What.
8. Notes on Brechtian song-writing:
    - Brecht's songs were not dependent on empathy.

- Look and learn, not look and empathize.
- Remind the audience that this is a theatre.
- No illusions, society is alterable.
- Call out the characters and their choices.
- Consider the wider political implications.
- Nudge us to think, don't offer easy answers.
- Awaken consciousness – but not directly – force us to think.
- No preaching, shock away the emotional involvement.
- Think about the horizontal (plot) and vertical (character) dimensions of the play – and compose a song to deepen the vertical aspects.
- Brechtian lyrics are more condensed than *Oklahoma's* "Oh, what a beautiful morning, Oh what a beautiful day" – but still feels like every day speech.
    - Songs reveal heightened emotions & desires. Think: *I want, I want, I want.*
    - Be playful and childlike with your song; keep it simple.
    - Repeat an inner voice over and over – allow it to create its own tune.
    - Consider taking an existing public domain tune; add your own lyrics
    - Song lyrics are not as concentrated as poems – give them space & simplicity.
- Song Structure – Basically most songs have a simple structure. The intro, a verse or two with a chorus, a bridge, followed by another verse and chorus, and then out.
    - The intro. This can be strictly instrumental, a part of the chorus, or something completely off the wall – just talk like Johnny Cash did.
    - The verse. This is the main element of most songs – though not necessarily the most important part. This is the exposition, describing the scene, or the person, or an emotion. Very often there are two or three verses in a row that have the same musical structure, the same rhyme and poetic meter, but different words. The second verse builds on the picture painted in the first verse, etc. Most songs have a recognizable verse structure, though unless you read lyrics on websites, you may not always hear the actual words being said.
    - The chorus. This is where it all comes together – all the verses have been leading up to the chorus and is usually the part of

the song people sing along with. Think "All You Need Is Love" by the Beatles. Can you remember the verse lyrics? Maybe. Can you remember the chorus? It's easy! "All you need is love!" However, as important as a chorus can be to a song, it's not necessarily a given.

– The bridge. This is the part of the song that shifts – it can suddenly change tempo, or volume, or instrumentation – it's all fair game.

And that's the exercise – the *Verfremdungseffekt* technique is built upon Brecht's notion that "Art is not a mirror held up to reality but a hammer with which to shape it." The simple fact that the job of the artist is not to subdue the audience into a kind of pleasant trance, but rather to wake that audience to the injustices present in society. As you work through the above exercise, remember that there is a rhythm to the structure, but if you allow it to be too predictable, then the audience will be lulled, once again, into a stupor. The trick is to keep trying new ways to "unmask the obvious" and force your audience to engage their brains, rather than just their hearts. Key to this is the *hidden motive* – which is not necessarily a pleasant reality for the audience, but rather something about humanity, which is ugly, perverse, repulsive, and deeply unpleasant – and therefore, fascinating! Brecht also noted, "Sometimes it's more important to be human, than to have good taste." If being polite and being tasteful means more people will die, perhaps your art should be impolite, distasteful, and shocking, so that more people will live.

2   Lucy Alibar – *Beasts of the Southern Wild* – The Lucidity of a Child

In Lucy Alibar's *Beasts of the Southern Wild* (2012), the character of Hushpuppy, played brilliantly by then five-year-old Quvenzhané Wallis, must make sense of the chaotic world of the Bathtub ("Isle de Charles Doucet"), a Louisiana bayou community that is facing a major storm. In the film, the camera is simply spellbound by this tiny, brilliant performer. As much as Alibar's script embraces a powerful, magical, and deeply environmental message, it is Wallis's performance which is key to how one gets at the message of this drama. She lives with her ailing father, Wink (Dwight Henry), and goes to school with Miss Bathsheba, who is teaching her about the mythical prehistoric beasts the Aurochs who are about to be released from the melting ice caps. The film is a fable about climate change, and how poor communities must struggle to survive it – but at its heart is a story about a little girl Hushpuppy and her troubled relationship with her ailing father. Hushpuppy's somewhat mystical child logic guides the structure of the film – happily throwing off tragedy and comedy in bursts of the alienation affect – distancing moments that would otherwise be tragic or horrific without Hushpuppy's matter of fact, yet utterly magical thinking.

It should be noted that the film has received intense and thoughtful criticism from major theorists, including bell hooks, Nyong'o, Brown, and Christina Sharpe concerning how race, gender, economics, and environmental justice are explored in the film, and how a white, libertarian sensibility pervades Hushpuppy's response to the challenges of her world. The magical thinking that drives much of the power of the multicultural tribe living in the Bathtub seems to justify their willingness to do without the care of a government that seems, in the film, to be the enemy of the free, wild, and anarchic culture of the bayou. With that said and bearing in mind these important critics' unhappy response to the film, I feel that the non-linear narratives techniques based upon on the film's autobiographical origins in Alibar's own life have intrinsic merit, however naïve and utopian. Nevertheless, to fully understand Alibar and Zeitlin's film one must engage with this criticism if only to get at dissonance of the film's meaning with eyes wide open.

I would argue that the dream lucidity of the film comes from the casting of Quvenzhané Wallis as Hushpuppy. It's her performance that enlivens Alibar's writing and Zeitlin's direction, and creates the essence of the film, which is the uncanny, cogent, luminous yet comedic clarity of a child. An essential moment of the film, for example, is that of Hushpuppy bringing the warm body of small bird to her ear and listening to its tiny heartbeat, divining a message from that miniature drum. Another essential moment occurs at the end of the film when the Hushpuppy and the Aurochs finally meet. The Aurochs are the manifestation of the illness that is killing Wink, and when the head Auroch pauses and bends knee before a solemn, indomitable Hushpuppy, it is a moment that is both majestic and parodic. The Aurochs are enlarged, freakishly magnified baby potbelly pigs with obvious costume horns and are part of a strange mythos of the Bathtub, taught to the children by the village's eccentric schoolteacher/shaman, Miss Bathsheeba. The unreality of the film, the fact that it is both a kind of hyperrealist bayou junk kingdom and a parody of the same, is key to how the film works. In the exercise below, we'll explore this childlike parody/lucid dream technique, with the hope that your inner child will awaken, and your childhood dreams, nightmares, and fantasies will usher forth to enchant you, as you play with the weird logic of your own infant mind.

Exercise 2: Lucy Alibar – Beasts of the Southern Wild – Freeing your Lucid Child Dream

You will be mining the materials of your personal dream cache for your childhood dreams, as well as the dream caches of the major characters of the drama you are writing. As you work through the exercise, don't be afraid to find the comedy of the situation, even as dramatic narrative grows into a kind of crazy, *Our Gang*-style comedy of droll disasters.

Step One – Reviving the Dreamworld of Tiny You – Building a Childhood Dream Cache

The Alienation Effect is built on something that reminds you that you are watching a drama, a constructed theatrical or filmic action that you, as a thinking audience member can change. Epic technique can be used shake up an audience to think for any number of reasons: racism and hatred, climate change, violence against women, PTSD in returning veterans, the struggles of differently-abled individuals. It works by reminding us that the drama we are watching is a work of fiction, an efficacious lie – and it calls attention to its fictional quality. There is also an outsized childhood fairytale or myth involved. How you will do this is by reimaging a conflict scene as if the central character was a child of five, and that child's imagination transforms the situation into mythic dimensions. First you must gather details:

- Write down all the details of a childhood dream – where were you, who else was in the dream, what did you see, touch, taste, hear, and physically feel? See if you can excavate more than one dream (or nightmare) you had as a child; some of these dreams may have grown out of specific *incidents* you experienced as child – so consider those incidents as well.
- What magic abilities did you have in the dream?
- What was precious to you as a child?
- What was your favorite toy?
- Imagine your favorite foods as a child?
- Favorite songs? TV shows?
- Worst fear?
- What pets did you have?

Gather all of these into a dream cache that is specific to this exercise; decorate that dream cache with child-like symbols, images, language – maybe also use cartoon stickers that appeal to the kid inside you. Using construction paper, write each down on a slip and deposit into the dream cache. This might be your own personal childhood dream cache, or it may be the childhood dream cache of your central character.

Step Two – Constructing the Kid-sized Dramatic Scene – Exploring the Dream Cache

Now you'll gather the elements you've just found, and you'll build your dream scene based upon some of the fundamental tropes that we've already learned about in our opening workshop. Will this be a dramatic dream where things start in the banal, quotidian world of your everyday childhood, but become increasing strange? Will this be a quest dream that you might have had when you were child, setting off to tame dragons or find a pot of gold? Or is this a lyric dream, a nightmare, growing out of the fear you had of certain terrors of the night? Or is this lyric dream an erotic one, filled with your earliest imaginings of romantic, childhood love? Whatever it is, be aware that as you pull things out of your dream cache, you can add to your story/plot line whatever seems to work. You might have to take everything out of the bag and look at it, to imagine what you can do with it – or, as I might recommend highly, pull things out one at a time and make them work – as odd, difficult, or challenging as it might be.

Your Childhood Dream Scene involves:
- A central myth or story that you loved from childhood.
- A central character who has a desperate desire (that falls within a child's view of the cosmos), and some kind of superpower(s).
- Another character who has their own desperate desire that runs counter that of your central characters (this character may also have superpowers)
- A difficult, child-like, physical activity that both characters are involved with.
- A character who is kind of soothsayer or shaman with parent-like mentoring qualities.
- A monster that has emotional meaning for your central character – it may be a good or bad monster, enemy or friend, or shifting variations.
- A shifting landscape growing out of whatever you pull from your dream cache – this landscape must transform at least three times if not more.
- Magical transformation of some or all of the characters.
- Objects of childhood – toys, costumes, food, etc.

Step Three – Writing the Kid-sized Dramatic Scene – Building from the Myth

You'll write the scene, trying to keep the characters from directly asking for what they want. Keep the characters in the scene focused on and discussing the *physical activity* – everything else will percolate out if you keep the characters focused on what they're doing physically. This physical activity has some ties into the *mythical* and *magical* world being engaged by the child. It will help if what the characters are doing physically has a high level of urgency in the real world, a limited amount of time, and involves one hundred percent of the characters attention. Bear in mind that the more childlike the activity, the more the natural kid energy the scene will have. The activity might have an unreasonable, fanciful quality to it – it probably will be a *game* that is played by several characters. The myth or fairytale weighs heavily on this physical activity – the physical activity grows into a mythical experience for the children. Consider building the scene around these structural moments:

- Ceremonial Start of physical activity – Have it begin with a childish ritual, a pinky swearing or some other clubhouse oath.
- Activity begins with no problems at first – the sense we have is that everything is fine – the mythical world is in line with the real world.
- Allow some of the larger issues involved to percolate outward as the children administer the activity. Aspects of the myth aren't working.
- There is an internal complication – the game-like physical activity becomes more difficult, more challenging. The magical aspects of the myth are somehow involved.
- The problem is solved, the physical activity goes back to normal, but magic lingers.
- There is an external complication – something in the environment indoors or outdoors affects the ability of the characters to get the activity done. A monster is involved.
- That second problem is solved, the physical activity goes back to normal.
- There is a character problem – the larger issue surrounding the activity – what the central character desperately wants or needs, affects the doing of the activity. This character problem is an outgrowth of the myth or fairytale role inhabited by childlike characters.
- That third problem is almost solved, but then ...
- There is a sudden escalation of problems – internally, externally, and within the characters themselves.
- This problem is unsolvable, resulting in a comically disastrous emotional climax – the real world and the mythical world intertwine.
- This final set of simultaneous problems results in a problematic resolution that doesn't solve the situation but raises important questions about the Myth.
- The scene ends on these questions – not answers, but major questions raising the consciousness of all involved – in a childlike, simple, honest and mythical, magical way.

As we dig deeper into the realm of the lucid dreamer and the technique known as Epic Theatre, and we borrow these styles from Bertolt Brecht and Lucy Alibar, we get at the larger dreamwrighting project of surprising ourselves and our audiences and revealing the world in new and strange ways. I'm often struck by the fact that even though this work is decidedly driven by ideas of theatre and art for social change, that quite often the best way to engage and enact political ideas in theater and film are really best done by less obvious and didactic techniques. Quite often the subliminal ideas that were suggested by Antonin Artaud and his Theatre of Cruelty provide a much more tangible tactic for provoking audiences into seeing the world in new ways.

Our next two writers, playwriting Luigi Pirandello and screenwriter Eleanor Perry (adapting John Cheever) are distinctly post-modern writers, which means that they build on the notions of a world that needs to be wildly reformed, but do so with a kind of reeling, dizzying slippage that relies on the unreliable, the unstable, the shifting realities of a world where all our fondest and most stable institutions are revealed to be built on massive lies. Nothing, including language, can be trusted, and those that allow themselves to trust in these capricious realities will find themselves disappearing into worlds where their deepest beliefs are revealed to be horrific lies.

CHAPTER 12

Postmodernist Worlds of Slippage

Pirandello's It Is So! (If You Think So) *and Eleanor Perry's* The Swimmer

The two writers and the dramas we'll examine in this chapter, Luigi Pirandello's *It Is So! (If you Think so)* and Eleanor Perry's *The Swimmer*, fall into the realm of postmodernist technique and in order to discuss what that means, we'll need to come up with our own definition of postmodernism – since we'll be experimenting the dream essence of postmodernist technique. Before we do that, however, we will discuss these two writers in terms of their oeuvres.

Pirandello was a major Italian playwright and fiction writer, who received the Nobel Prize in Literature specifically because of his innovations as a dramatist. He was prolific, writing forty plays, seven novels, innumerable short stories (fifteen volumes), and seven volumes of poetry. Much of his writing was in Sicilian, and his keen psychological insights had an almost uncanny ability to unsettle his readers, as if he was wielding a kind of magical wand that broke all the rules of reality into which his readers tumble. Pirandello was fascinated by the nature of art and often broke the barrier between reality and illusion. His tragic comedies were seen to be antecedents for absurdism, and his work bears more in common with Beckett, Pinter, and Ionesco (who we will be discussing next) than with any writers who came before him. His work presages the avant-garde writing of 1960s off-off-Broadway and seems experimental even now.

Eleanor Perry, like Pirandello, had a fascination with the broken parts of the human psyche, and received a master's degree in psychiatric social work before she was a screenwriter. This background in abnormal personalities shows in several of her films, many of which she made with her then husband, Frank Perry, many of which deal with mental issues. Perry was one of the few women screenwriters in her time, and faced serious challenges because of her gender, which she wrote about in her semi-autobiographical novel, *Blue Pages*, which deals with her screenwriting career and her marriage to Frank Perry. One of her first major successes on film, *David and Lisa*, grew directly out of her training in clinical psychiatry and deals with a young man, struggling with severe neuroses (including a fear of being touched), and a young woman equally ill with a split personality. The film earned Academy Award nominations for both Perry and her husband, and led to their later successes in film, which included *Last*

Summer, Diary of a Mad Housewife, The Deadly Trap, and the film *The Swimmer* which was based on a John Cheever short story of the same name.

Postmodernist technique is a far-reaching, almost impossibly broad subject, but for the purposes of dramatic technique, we'll focus on how it has manifested within playwriting and screenwriting. Postmodernism as a project was, like so many other "isms," a reaction to what came before. If modernism really begins with Richard Wagner's Gesamtkunstwerk or the idea of a "master artwork" then postmodernist drama rebels against its notion that everything residing in the dramatic text is in harmony with everything else on the stage or within the film. It reacts against the notion that the theatrical or filmic event is one, unified experience with costumes, lighting, music, sound, scenic design, acting, directing, and language all serving the same vision. Instead, and really beginning with the plays of Bertolt Brecht, the drama should represent a world up against itself, with all its parts representing competing if somewhat complementing texts and the resulting cacophony is closer to what the world is like.

Postmodernism presupposes a natural slippage of meaning, not unlike the notion of deconstruction, which according to the great French thinker, Jacques Derrida, argues that with the very language that is used for the creation of a literary work, a kind of decay has erupted, which always already infects the artwork with conflicting, equally accurate/inaccurate depictions of what that art means. Postmodernism questions all and any authority and eliminates the dividing lines between high and low art, between genre, between class and economics, revealing all the troubling fault lines that reveal the unfair power structure dominated by white male hegemony.

Postmodernism argues against traditional notions of race, gender, class, economics, and faith and insists upon a far more democratic embrace of multicultural sensibility. Instead of the unified artwork, it asks for pastiche, collage, medley, hodge-podge, and random collective sensibility. With thinkers such as Jacques Lacan, Umberto Eco, Jacque Derrida, Michel Foucault, Jean Baudrillard, Gilles Deleuze, Pierre-Félix Guattari, Fredric Jameson, Emmanuel Lévinas, Jean-François Lyotard, Richard Rorty, and Slavoj Žižek, postmodernism stands against totalizing, unified theories of anything. Highly relativistic, it posits a totally skeptical subjectivism, and is suspicious of claims of reason, deeply sensitive to hidden ideologies that seek only to gather and maintain power.

Instead, postmodernist dramatic technique reminds you it is artificial, it winks at you self-consciously, reminding you it is art, it is theatre, it is film – and doesn't allow you to enjoy a kind of sleepwalking experience and empathy with the world it creates. If this sounds a lot like Brecht's epic theatre, that is because it has at base, a Marxist sensibility of dialectical materialism throbbing beneath it. It's always reminding you that there is slippage in your thinking, that you are undone by your certainty, and that the only thing that might save you is a powerful, ironic cynicism and an eye open toward inequalities based on race, gender, economics, and societal norms. The ideal piece of art is a pastiche, an homage, a pasting together of myriad elements, echoing the ever-repeating reflection of multiple images, styles, techniques, conflating and erasing the lines between past and present, high art and low art, and the direct descendent of the pop/camp, mass culture.

1   Luigi Pirandello's *It is so! (If You Think So)*: The Conundrum of Conflicting Realities

Pirandello was a playwright far ahead of his times; his postmodernist sensibilities drew from a deeply skeptical sense of reality. To his mind, we always already live in a world that only makes sense if reality only exists in the eyes of the beholder. If there is another beholder there is another reality – and whose reality is the real one is always at the heart of Pirandello's drama. In his play *It is So! (If you Think So)* Pirandello forces his audience to decide between two characters, Signora Frola and her son-in-law, Signor Ponza, as to whether one or both are insane. Signor Ponza insists that his current wife, Giulia, is his second wife, after the death of his first wife, Lina. However, Signora Frola insists that this alleged second wife is actually his first wife, Lina, who went mad, and spent time in the asylum, and only agreed to come home if she was remarried to Signor Ponza as his second wife. Giulia. This debate has led to an investigation by Commendatore Agazzi, the provincial councillor, and in the play, the truth of the situation cannot be adequately explained and perhaps, at least according to the Commendatore's brother-in-law, Lamberto Laudisi, it may never be known.

Pirandello was the master of ambiguity, and in his most famous play, *Six Characters in Search of an Author*, the lines between what is fiction and what is reality are so blurred as to become impossible to divide. To add to this confusion, one must contemplate the instability of Pirandello's own connection with reality as he was a devoted Italian fascist, and he donated his Nobel Prize to Dictator Benito Mussolini's Fascist government to be melted down for Mussolini's Abyssinia Campaign. Yet Pirandello's fascism was tied to his native Sicilian roots, and at times he abandoned it when he felt it went against his grain, ripping up his fascist membership card to pieces in front of the startled secretary-general of the Fascist Party in 1927 because of his declared artistic apolitical nature.

In the exercise below, we'll explore Pirandello's specific postmodern technique which is a kind of anti-surrealism. His style is tied a kind of storytelling where there is a debate over the nature of reality itself. For Pirandello, reality is only discernible through art, and to his mind what is most real is built upon that which is most totally fictitious. This concept is not unlike that of Oscar Wilde's notion that as he articulated in *The Decay of Lying*, "Art makes us love Nature more than we loved her before." Therefore, in the spirit of exploring Pirandello's essence, our characters will be self-conscious performers, knowing they are themselves always wearing a mask presented to society; a mask which gives them pleasure to wear, and which gives us pleasure to watch them wear. In the exercise the story has already happened, what is being enacted is a bit of shell game, the action of the scene that you'll write is a version of reality, but it bears in mind that reality itself is unknowable.

> A man will die, a writer, the instrument of creation: but what he has created will never die! And to be able to live forever you don't need to have extraordinary gifts or be able to do miracles. Who was Sancho Panza? Who was Prospero? But they will live forever because – living seeds – they had the luck to find a fruitful soil, an imagination which knew how to grow them and feed them, so that they will live forever.
>
> From *Six Characters in Search of an Author*, LUIGI PIRANDELLO 1921

Exercise 1: Luigi Pirandello: It is so! (If You Think So) – Competing Realities

Two characters, in conflict from your play, describe the same situation from two entirely different points of view. The rules are:
- There will be two different versions of the events, and in the telling of those events, the stories will change, evolve, and improvise off each other.
- The scene will be a collective creation and both storytellers will somehow attempt to undo what the other has done, with the intent of trapping the other storyteller in their own creation.
- They will each have their own personalities which are too much for them, and they'll fight this by creating a fictional self, which they will abandon at times finding it too difficult to fight off their real self.
- There *is* ultimately a *true* reality, but between the two storytellers, we'll only see flickers of it, taunting us, flirting with us, and that hint of reality engages both stories. And yet you, the writer, *must* know the actual reality – and

what *really* happened (and you may never reveal it directly – take that to your grave!).
- The Storytellers create a show for each other, a kind of text that each will criticize in order to attempt to change it.

A Third Character is an interrogator – who *must* get at the bottom of the situation, *now*. They are describing the situation to get something they want and need *now*. There are three Movements to this storytelling: each storytelling follows the energy of musical notation, each part told by a different storyteller:

1. Piano, Part One & Two
2. Adagio, Part One & Two
3. Forte Allegro, Part One & Two

One Bell Chime before each; and the play ends with a final three chimes.

There must be an end to each story, but no real solution for either – and both characters must be entirely wrong about what happened. There must be a third actual story – shared by the Interrogator – *that which actually happened* – and neither has it right. And both are stunned by the truth, and their reality, and the reality of the drama you've created will shift – and suggest a new direction for your plot, characters, and resolution. If you have developed the exercise with the right amount of ambiguity – even the final telling of the story, with the Interrogator's version laid out in precise detail – there cannot be a true version, only a version that approaches the realm of truth.

2   Eleanor Perry – *The Swimmer* – Multiverse Pools of Desire

Moving from Pirandello to Eleanor Perry's *The Swimmer*, it is suggested that you first read John Cheever's original short story, which came out in *The New Yorker* in 1964. Cheever's powerful and incandescent writing unpacks the harsh realities of Westchester County WASP culture. It follows the misadventures of Ned Merrill, an aging Golden Boy, as he swims his way from pool to pool making his way across the affluent New York suburban county of Westchester, discovering, as he does, the decaying culture of privilege that has fed his ego through his life. The story is both surreal and uncanny, as Ned's world diminishes from pool to pool. In the film, in Eleanor Perry's able hands, it is the women of Ned's world who suddenly unmask him, as each of them reveals Ned for who he truly is, a brute, a rapist, a smug inhabitant of polluted male caste of cruel, unthinking, and deluded individuals. He was played by a handsome fifty-five-year-old Burt Lancaster, bronzed, burnished, almost uncannily youthful with gleaming muscularity that seems just this side of God-like. Scantily clad in a tight bikini bathing suit most 20-year-olds would find too revealing, Lancaster exudes confidence, virility, and vigor that becomes increasingly bristling even as his world collapses around him.

Ned starts his journey off at the pool of the Westerhazy's who are nursing hangovers after a particularly wild party. Ned realizes that the backyard pools form a kind of river that he can follow back home, even as the Westerhazy couple wonder why he's making the journey, considering how his life has recently fallen apart, something that Ned doesn't seem to remember. Ned continues his journey jumping into pools and exiting them, but also finding himself drawn to the lovers, friends, and colleagues who mark important signposts in a life that is decaying before him. Ned revisits with 20-year-old Julie, who once babysat his children for him, and now confesses an attraction to him; for a time, the two travel together and even share a glass of champagne, before Ned's aggressive sexuality becomes too much for Julie and she escapes from him. He befriends a small boy, attempts to teach him to swim (in an empty pool), but leaves the boy in a precarious situation (on the diving board).

Ned runs into an actress, Shirley Abbott, with whom he had an affair, and their encounter is one of the more brittle, brutal moments of the film, as she attacks him for relegating her to the role of the "other woman," never attempting to solidify their relationship, even though he promised many times. This is one of many moments in the film, where Eleanor Perry digs in deeply into male privilege, revealing how little men understand women's lives, and how cruel and thoughtless they are not only to their wives, but to all the women they draw into their dominion. Ned's encounters grow increasingly petty; he gets into fights with those around the various pools he encounters; his icy blue eyes flashing and his original bucolic undertaking of swimming upstream a river of pools becoming an increasingly hostile ordeal. Groups of people he once knew become progressively more disagreeable, and the disaster his life has become grows clearer and clearer, until at last he climbs out of his own pool only to discover that his home is derelict, the tennis courts covered in weeds, the front door locked, and the windows boarded up. He is left in a downpour, the air temperature having dropped, freezing, in his tiny wet bathing suit, as the Indian summer has drifted into a rainy, frigid fall with no warning. Ned is limping, bitter cold, his now clearly aging face etched with the harsh lines of a Greek mask confronting a tragic fate. The film ends with Ned in this pitiable state, finally confronted with the reality of his life, as he collapses hanging on the front door of his home, drenched in rain, a muscled Rodin statue at the Gates of Hell.

Eleanor Perry's screenplay is lean, simple, building on the surreal nature of Ned's journey from pool to pool, lily pad to lily pad, with moments that seem to flow into a dizzying, blurred dreamlike fantasy, only to confront a clear, harsh reality that is almost too much to bear. Ned's face, once youthful and determined as he races with a young horse, becomes lined and painful, as he fields rejection after rejection, and as his present financial disaster becomes excruciatingly clear. The structure then is not unlike the expressionistic stations of the cross that we've seen in some of the previous dramatic work, but in this exercise, we'll be focusing on a specific type of location – one that has a ritualized meaning and function – and we'll move from one to another through time and space. Key to Perry's postmodernist technique is her peeling back the veneer of polite society, revealing the cruelly victimized women who are given a kind of agency in the unmasking of the debased white male gaze.

Exercise 2: Eleanor Perry – The Swimmer – Juxtaposed Heterotopias of Life in Reverse

Consider the structure of *The Swimmer* – below is a table of the various pools and scenes that Ned Merrill swims in and out of as he makes his way across Westchester County. Note the progression from pool to pool, scene to scene that the structure is both moving forward in time, but also backwards through a life. Michel Foucault, the postmodern theorist who was primarily interested in exposing how power moves through culture and society, coined the term heterotopia to refer to spaces that are somehow "outside the norm" of daily life, and which have "more layers of meaning or relationships to other places than immediately meet the eye." In this case, we are examining locations which have a quality of being a heterotopia, where certain behaviors are permitted which are not generally permitted in more formal environments, such as an office or a public space.

Step One – Channeling Heterotopias – Dream Cache Interpretation
First take a moment to go back to the screenplay of Eleanor Perry's *The Swimmer*, think about how each of these locations different from each other – and yet retain a similar quality that draws them all together. Note what the screenwriter has attempted to do with each pool and its cast of characters in terms of the plot structure of the screenplay. I've suggested a few useful screenplay structural terms (inciting incident, plot point, pinch, etc.), to help give you a sense of how Perry fits nonlinear storytelling into filmed performance structure, using the page numbers of the shooting script:
– Opening Credits – Page 1
– The Westerhazys – Page 1 (Inciting Incident: Declaration of Intent)
– The Grahams – Page 10 (end of scene moves to Mrs. Hammar's)

- The Lears (pick up Juliet) – Page 14 Plot Point 1 (Juliet not in Story)
- The Country Lane – Page 17
- The Bunkers – Page 19
- The Pasterns Riding Ring – Page 24 Pinch I
- The Lindleys – Page 28 (Not in the Film)
- The Hallorans – Page 30 – Midpoint
- The Gilmartins (Kevin) Page 35 (Kevin not in Short Story)
- Mrs. Hammar's – Page 40 (Moved to earlier in the film after 3)
- The Biswangers – Page 41 Pinch II
- Shirley Abbott – Page 47 Plot Point II
- The Thruway – Page 57
- Recreation Center Pool The Merrills – Page 57
- The Clydes – Page 63 (Not in the Film)
- *The Merrills – Page 64 (Final Resolution)*

Bearing *The Swimmer's* structure in mind, we now start in a similar manner, taking our structure from the various scenic heterotopias we'll create in order to unmask our protagonist.

1. Borrow some settings from the dream cache of the central character involved in your drama; or from cache you've created for your screenplay as a whole.
2. Allow your imagination to be divided into a series of similar heterotopias like the pools in the film, each one a variation on a theme. These places have a freeing sensibility – a location where one's hair may be let down for both good and dark reasons. People in these spaces have the freedom to behave in ways that are normally unacceptable or odd in more formal locations. The rules have been relaxed, the characters can breathe and be themselves – or because of a dangerous situation, must take on roles they normally never would, but now must in order to save lives. Think about places and events like bars, parties, family events, cruises, vacations, or to be dark, wars, gang fights, a shooter situation, a natural disaster such as an earthquake or tornado, etc.
3. Allow your breath to adjust to these different places each with specific qualities, physical and psychological – each is different, but share an overall similarity – in the case of *The Swimmer* these locations are all pools, but their shape, affluence, emotional quality, physicality – all different. Is it hot or cold – does it exist at the same time or a different time than the original scene – or we moving back or forth in time? Does it feel warm and pleasant, cold and ominous, nostalgic, transformative, triumphant, warm and comforting? Create at least five to six different heterotopias – each different from the next.

Step Two – Peopling Heterotopias – Dream Cache Interpretation

1. Now attach characters to each location – Some grow out of the location, the way that characters grow out of the locations in a dream. Some will come from your current drama, and others might grow out of your characters' dream cache. They become a part of the location, almost like plants – how does your central character respond – what is their own transformation/journey?

2. Bear in mind that the characters will shift and develop as each location, transforming to fit the location, yet retaining qualities that may remain the same throughout – these different characters may be played by the same group of actors, disguised to fit within each specific heterotopia. Consider also, that some of the characters might remain with your central character who moves from one heterotopia to the next, even as your central character may transform or not, along the way.

Step Three – The Maze of Heterotopias – Clarifying the Journey

1. The first step or the final step may be designing your heterotopic journey – and this might be something that either develops as your write the heterotopias, moving from one to the next and allowing a writerly improvisation to occur. Or you might plan out the heterotopias, give each a certain quality and comparing those qualities against the overall journey you want your central character to make. Is it a downward journey as in *The Swimmer* or it is an upward journey? After all, this could be a comedy! Or it is a static journey emphasizing the fact that your central character is in a kind of limbo, caught between worlds.

2. How are the heterotopias connected – through a region? Through time? Are they linked based on specific characters tied to your central character's life, career, quest? If this is a quest, what was the goal? The major obstacle to that goal? Who is the antagonist, and what is *their* goal? Is there an overarching geometric or symbolic shape to the journey – consider the lotus, the tree of life, the wheel of life, or even a kind of mythical beast such as a serpent swallowing its tale, or a fish swimming upstream. Or is the structure of these heterotopias tied to a larger political or social vision?

3   Entering the Absurd – Final Clarity of the Insane Vision – Collapse of Drama into Performance

As we end this chapter, we're moving into the final section of this book which is built on absurdist technique. The fascinating aspect of dream logic is that it is built on a deeply absurd structure, one where associative freedom is far more important than linear coherence. As we move into the last few chapters of the book we'll be digging deeply into the realm of the absurdist dramatists, who represent the postmodern vision in ways that continue to create massive slippage of technique, truth, and reality as only drama can depict it. We'll be looking at Eugène Ionesco, Samuel Becket, and pairing them with, perhaps a surprising choice, Quentin Tarantino. These are three writers who mostly live within what Bert O. States calls the "dramatic" trope of dreams, where a truly crystalline reality is slowly and surely distorted to reveal the massive cracks in its logic, and those cracks escalate into the frenzied madness of these writers' comic vision. Having launched into this realm with Pirandello's *It is So (If You Think So)* and Eleanor Perry's cult masterpiece, *The Swimmer*, we'll remain with the absurdists continuing what some might consider strange pairings in theatre and film including Edward Albee and Agnès Varda; Harold Pinter, Irene Fornes, and Jean-Luc Godard.

The absurdists are perhaps the most surreal of dramatists, preferring to abandon the rules of reality, and depend almost entirely upon the logic of dreams, since dreams do not purposefully lie – but instead tell alternate truths that we'd often prefer not to hear. Ionesco was one of several playwrights who were identified as members of "The Theatre of the Absurd" by theatre critic and journalist, Martin Esslin, in his book of that title. Other playwrights who fell into this realm, all later discussed in this volume, included Samuel Beckett, Harold Pinter, Edward Albee, and Jean Genet among many others.

These writers, according to Esslin, share some similar qualities – they challenge traditional notions of linear plot by instead building on circular structures that repeat. Instead of plot, they explore illogical patterns – instead of explicitly meaningful dialogue, language is the basis for experimentation, and rather than write fully rounded characters, instead characterization is built on bizarre broad caricature and parody. But in response to accusations of meaninglessness and purposefully confusing plots and characterization, scholar Michael Y. Bennett has coined a new term for this generation of writers – "parabolic dramatists." It's his assertation that instead of these writers being considered authors of purposefully meaningless, useless, and despondent drama in the existential nightmare of post-World Warr II Europe, that their work is instead parable-based, ethics-driven experimentation using parody and humor to effect social change. In the chapters that follow, we'll explore these theatrical writers paired with their filmic equivalents and discover that instead of absurdist traditions leading writers into a miasma of meaningless, hollow, and inconsequential ramblings, the writing techniques provide new insights into how nonlinear technique can reveal the innermost workings of the human heart and mind.

CHAPTER 13

The Absurdist Nightmare and the Dramatic Wet Dream

Ionesco's The Bald Soprano, *Samuel Beckett's* Play, *and Quentin Tarantino's* Pulp Fiction

If Pirandello blazed the trail for the European absurdist playwrights, Eugène Ionesco was its clown piper. Samuel Beckett, on the other hand, was its minimalist prophet, exploring how little a human being could live with and still go on. While both shared an affection for the vaudevillian comedy of the films of Charlie Chaplin, Harold Lloyd, and Buster Keaton, Ionesco's plays feature a kind of comedic violence, while Beckett's work calls forth the black humor of the concentration camp. Both playwrights were profoundly affected by the horrors of World War II, and their dramas reflect the profound madness of that time, the lies that allowed the mass carnage to occur, the failure of all known governments, social institutions, and religious organizations providing the fodder for the human catastrophe that was to ensue. For these playwrights, language itself provided the slippery slope to the ovens of Bełżec, Treblinka, and Auschwitz-Birkenau and for that reason, in their plays language becomes impossible, incomprehensible, incommunicable. Therefore, when exploring absurdist technique, language, or rather the shifty, irrational, nonsensical aspects of language, becomes key.

In addition to the mutability of language, in almost all Absurdist (or Parabolic as Michael Y. Bennett calls them) playwrights' work, menace and comedy play an important part, and we'll get a deeper dose of that comic menace in Harold Pinter's work later in this book. With that in mind, falling well within the tradition of the absurdist dramatists of the 1950s, is screenwriter and director Quentin Tarantino whose work will also be explored in this chapter. Tarantino fits perfectly with the absurdists; he escalated the genre-based film noir of the 1950s, 1960s, 1970s, and 1980s, and transformed them into a meta-camp parody of form. With his film *Pulp Fiction*, Tarantino transmogrified and anesthetized the violence of American cinema into a kind of madcap, frenzied meaningless comedy of manners. Tarantino's films epitomize the filmic appropriation of absurdist techniques, slipping easily into its circular patterns of miscommunication and mindlessness, while aggressively punching all the genre buttons, including the western, the action film, the romantic comedy, and the noir detective drama, keying into a bloody melee of parodic pop culture characterization and plot. We'll recognize the seeds of Tarantino's work especially in the plays of Eugène Ionesco and with the slow devolution of social mores and behavior in Ionesco's radiant and radioactive first play, *The Bald Soprano*.

1 Eugene Ionesco: The Devolving Dramatic Dream of *The Bald Soprano*

Beginning with Ionesco's *The Bald Soprano*, which we'll be examining here, and ending with his final plays, *Man With Bags* and *Journeys Among The Dead (Themes and Variations)*, dreams for Ionesco were both a source of inspiration and a means of structure. Ionesco was a Romanian playwright, who spent the better part of his career as an expatriate living in Paris and began his career writing sketches or "anti-plays," as he called them, very late in his career as a writer. In terms of technique, Ionesco considered himself a direct descendant of Alfred Jarry, the author of the proto-absurdist farce *Ubu Roi*, and Ionesco shared Jarry's notion of pataphysics, a wild satire of metaphysics that had an insistent uselessness at its core. Ionesco was also an admirer and considered himself a descendent of both the Dadaists, with their notion of chance art, and the Surrealists, who were deeply affected by dream logic and automatic, stream of consciousness writing.

In *The Bald Soprano*, he reveals the simplicity of an English lesson gone terribly wrong. At the time he was writing the play, Ionesco was studying English with the Assimil method in which students "assimilate" whole sentences in the learning process. So, notions such as "Mr. and Mrs. Smith have several children," and "Mr. and Mrs. Smith live near London" took on larger and more bizarre meaning, at least in Ionesco's imagination, as the phrases were insistently and inanely repeated over and over again in his lesson book. *The Bald Soprano* is simple – it is about two couples, Mr. and Mrs. Smith and Mr. and Mrs. Martin, who have a visit together – and beyond that, chaos ensues. At one point in the play, the town Fire Chief enters and after his mention of "the bald soprano," the play slips into bizarre non-sequiturs – and ultimately devolves into nothing but vowels. It feels very much like the type of dream trope Bert O. States calls a "dramatic dream" in which an almost hyperreal world degenerates into an increasingly bizarre experience where ordinary situations transform into something bordering chaos, spurring a dream awareness that one is not in Kansas anymore.

Exercise 1: Eugène Ionesco – The Bald Soprano – The Babble of Brilliant Bees

In this exercise you are going to take a very basic argument or discussion and allow it to progress through a kind of logical illogic into the very maddest moment you can create. Think of the fantastic moment when Mr. and Mrs. Martin in Ionesco's *The Bald Soprano* realize to their surprise that they have met before. This discussion/argument rests on the bizarre reality that they already are, in fact, husband and wife, and seem to have just now forgotten that fact. Worse, as we later discover from the maid, Mary, they are actually wrong, and only *think* they have rediscovered each other (and of course, Mary declares that she is really Sherlock Holmes)! You might also recall this kind of logic in the wonderful sketch comedies of Monty Python such as the Parrot Routine, where the customer insists a parrot is dead and the Pet Shop owner insists the parrot is alive – or the scene in which one character pays another to have an argument and then they have an argument over whether they are actually having an argument.

Step One – The Insulting Reality of Truth and Enigma
– Establish a scene with two characters who are quite ordinary, banal, and safe, and place them in a setting that is equally banal, safe, and ordinary. Make sure the specific physical details are described – whether it is a home, an office, a shop, wherever, the sense of that hyperreal crystalline reality should be fully realized.
– The characters want something from each other, desperately, but it quite an ordinary thing – nothing surprising, as simple as the purchase of meat at a butcher shop or acquiring insurance from an insurance agent. And yet, that simple desire grows into something monstrous.
– The characters must have a physical activity they are doing – tied to what it is they want from each other – but also a bit at a tangent with that need.

Step Two – I Thought You Came here for an Argument? Rhythm of Thrash and Relax
– Let an existential argument build out of that physical activity – again, the larger need is present, but the argument or discussion will be the focus – and bear in mind it is not a huge argument, but an insistently small, petty one which would seem to have a rather simple solution.
– Allow the argument to grow more childish – with each of the characters becoming more insistent and allow their language to begin to become equally childish and petulant.

- Let them recover, find their heads, grow more sensible, and pretend that the argument never happened – allow them to pass the day – and perhaps enjoy the moment of comradery.
- Then, let the argument resurface briefly. A little burble of trouble.
- Let them tamp it back down, insisting upon politeness and bonhomie.
- Let the argument pop back up, a bit more petulantly.
- Let them again bury it in pleasantries, politesse, joking.
- Let the argument explode suddenly, the characters become suddenly quite maddened by it!
- Just as suddenly, have them revert back to pleasantries, though the quips and joking have a somewhat more deadly edge.

Step Three – Psycho killer, qu'est-ce que c'est? – Good vs. Evil: No One Wins

- Then the argument reappears in an explosion with the two characters suddenly wielding weapons, clashing almost as superheroes and villains.
- And again, allow the argument to be forced back down.
- It rears up, boom!
- And back down to almost nothing – as the actors take over from the characters, break the fourth wall and apologize for the problem, and ...
- Allow the scene to end either in another explosion, an annihilating version of the argument with murder and mayhem – and/or allow the scene to end on a non-sequitur. End of exercise!

It's important to note, amid all this arguing, that Ionesco eschewed an overt political focus in favor of a subliminal one. This makes sense in that dreams seem to do the same thing – the politics of our lives are revealed in the anxieties, inconsistencies, violence, and horror that lay within the dream journey. For Ionesco the politics that flow beneath are more subtle, though clearly represent a sensibility that was shaped by the forces of both the Nazism he experienced during World War II and the Communism he later survived while in Romania. Ionesco famously hated, however, the political nature of Brecht's writing and exchanged a heated dialogue with Kenneth Tynan on this subject in a section of his writings on the theatre, *Notes and Counter Notes*, titled "The London Controversy." He writes in response to Tynan's criticism:

> A playwright simply writes plays, in which he can offer only testimony, not a didactic message – a personal, affective testimony of his anguish or the anguish of others, or which is rare, of his happiness – or he can

express his feelings, comic or tragic, about life. A work of art has nothing to do about doctrine.[1]

Ionesco's early plays, *The Bald Soprano, The Lesson, Jack, or the Submission, The Chairs*, and *The Future is in Eggs*, among them, are his most radically bizarre, where both language and reality break down and the behavior grows from comically quotidian and pedestrian to becoming increasingly distorted, threatening, and discombobulated. The lingering sense of threat moves through all of Ionesco's work, and this is not surprising – Ionesco lived through the horrors of World War II in Europe, and depravations and depravity of that experience, as well as the comical ineptitude of European bureaucracy to deflect any of it away from its inhabitants, is key to his work.

The extent to which Ionesco actually used his dreams was well documented; Ionesco would write short stories based on the reality suggested in his dreams and then create plays from those short stories – a transcription of a transcription of a dream.[2] This method of moving beyond the dream, and thereby into dramaturgy, is more important than the dream itself, since it is questionable how much of the actual dream can be remembered at all. Freud used a similar concept to justify his interpretation of dreams for the purposes of psychoanalysis, and it serves well here.[3] The dream itself is unimportant; the dream thoughts and writing are what matters. "The dream, then," States offers, "is an occasion for talking about something exterior to or beneath it."[4] Interestingly, as Ionesco grew older he became obsessed with approaching an exact replication of his dreams in that he believed that "logical, rational coherence is nothing compared to the coherences of oneiric images and symbols."[5] Despite the impossibility of exact replication, for Ionesco the line between his dreams and his art became nearly invisible. Thus, Ionesco arrived at nearly the same conclusion States arrives at in his own books, that fiction itself is voluntary dreaming and dreaming is in fact involuntary fiction. And for Ionesco, it was a purer fiction.

---

1 Eugène Ionesco, "The London Controversy," *Notes and Counter Notes* (New York: Grove Press, 1964) 90.
2 Claude Donnefoy, *Conversations with Eugène Ionesco* (New York, Holt, Rinehart and Winston, 1971) 63.
3 Sigmund Freud, *The Interpretation of Dreams*, trans. Joyce Crick (Oxford: Oxford UP, 1999) 334–35.
4 States, *Dreaming and Storytelling* 141.
5 Eugène Ionesco, "Towards A Dream Theatre," *The Two Faces of Ionesco*, eds. Rosette C. Lamont and Melvin J. Friedman (Troy, NY: Whitston, 1978) 244–46.

One of the fascinating ways that Ionesco works in his dream plays is to create an alternate reality built on a strict set of rules, which though bizarre, helps provide structure and progression, so that the audience develops a sense of expectations, even within the weirdest of circumstances in his plays. I'd like to borrow from Ionesco's notion of alternate realities, only taking a slightly more comic and extreme notion of characters who are so maddeningly polite, that they might commit violence to do so!

Exercise 2: Eugène Ionesco – The Bald Soprano – Politeness is a Loaded Weapon

Step One: Choose at least two ubiquitous, pedestrian people and place them in an almost mind-numbingly ordinary and conventional space, and then choose a third exceedingly and maddeningly boring character who consistently does things to make the space intensely claustrophobic.

1. Key Behavior: Being Polite to the Point of Absurdity – In Ionesco's plays, characters will do anything and everything to be exceedingly well-mannered – even to the point of murder.
2. Characters: Create three impossibly, even unbearingly, ordinary people. Describe them in some detail, but don't write your play in your descriptions – let's discover who they are through their specific, odd behaviors.
3. Setting: Describe a very carefully conventional enclosed space – claustrophobically so – the third character makes the space more confining by bits and pieces.
4. First two characters in the space: one wants something desperately from the other. The other refuses to give the first character what she/he wants.
5. Three characters in the space. They are engaged in a respectable dinner – following all the rules of their very polite lives. Third character comes and goes, changing the space, making it more claustrophobic or dangerous.
6. They play a game that makes no sense with rules that are impossible and arbitrary. REMEMBER IT'S OKAY TO KILL SOMEONE IN THIS PLAY, AS LONG AS IT'S THE POLITE THING TO DO!
7. There are indistinct, incoherent rules of politeness – to break them is forbidden – by decree of death – see below.
   THE RULES OF POLITENESS
   (ALL CHARACTERS *MUST* BE POLITE!)
WHAT YOU *CANNOT* DO:
– One may not be impolite.
– One may not make logical sense.

- One may not talk about God.
- One may not talk about Money.
- One may not talk about Personal Relationships.
- One may not talk about Politics.
- One may not talk about Death or Dying.
- One may not talk about Love.
- One may not talk about anything not age appropriate.
- One may not cry.
- One may not laugh.
- One may not scream.
- One may not express an opinion.
- One may not talk about the past intelligently.
- One may not hurt anyone else's feelings.

WHAT YOU *CAN* DO
- One may play the game.
- One may kill another if they break the rules.
- One may brutally assault verbally or physically another.
- One may talk about one's dreams.
- One may be offended by anything.
- One may babble incessantly.
- One may recite one author, but no other author.
- One may cite scripture through one's own bizarre interpretation.
- One may translate other's ideas into a totally new language.
- One may babble incoherently about absolutely nothing – including all that you may not be allowed to discuss coherently.

Once the dinner bell has rung, you may feel like you're writing the scene, but allow the characters to write the scene for you – the rules are only really guidelines but enforce them with only with random bizarre cruelties. If murder happens, then be aware that the characters may not *stay* dead but may simply decide to pop back up and continue to play. If this feels childish – it isn't working; but if it feels *childlike* – it is. Remember that the characters only know this world and no other, but somehow, they feel like people you know in this world, only very, very polite versions of those people. When the dinner is ended, the dessert has been served, use the period of cordials to plan a final set of murders – these murders will never take place, but provide your characters with something pleasant to do, so that they may end their existence with a sense of purpose.

Now that we have reveled through the charming, yet carnivorous inanities of Ionesco's technique, let's move onto the dark splendor of Beckett's minimalism.

2 Samuel Beckett's *Play* – Pushing On/Pushing Through – I Can't Go on, I'll Go On

In Samuel Beckett's plays such as *Waiting for Godot* and *Endgame*, there is a powerful inertia driving the plays created by characters who are energetically, obsessively, and frustratingly waiting for something, anything to happen. The joke has always been that *Waiting for Godot* is a play in which nothing happens ... twice. Yet, this is a deep misinterpretation of what goes on in a Beckett play. There is, in fact, a tremendous wrestling of language as the characters make sense of their tangible, weird, yet very human reality in moment-to-moment frenzies of private frustration. In both *Endgame* and *Waiting for Godot*, the characters are broken, ailing, unwell, and dependent on each other. In fact, their frailty drives the big question – can they even go on? In *Waiting for Godot*, Vladimir and Estragon wait for their master, Godot, with little or nothing to eat, endless tedium, and the occasional visit from madmen such as Lucky or Pozzo with infrequent interruptions from a boy, a messenger for Godot, who tells them nothing and expects them to keep on waiting. In *Endgame*, the two central characters, Hamm and Clov, are living on the edge of a great no man's land, crippled by blindness and other physical impairments, with only Hamm's crippled parents, Nagg and Nell, living in a pair of garbage cans for company. Again, the question is how long can they live like this – as all are near death? Again, the challenge with this play – at its heart, how much can a human being take and still go on?

Beckett's work is deeply tied to his involvement with the French resistance in World War II and should be interpreted through that lens. How much could people take in terms of deprivation in Nazi-occupied France, in trenches of war, in the concentration camps, and still want to go on? From Beckett's own experiences in hiding from the occupying forces, the answer was a lot, in fact more than most people can imagine. Each of Beckett's plays embrace that situation in a different way, and the questions remain today, although it might be framed a bit differently in terms of race, gender, and economic hardship, but the answer is pretty much the same – human beings despite being disadvantaged, disabled, disenfranchised, and totally oppressed still aspire to a life with dignity and meaning.

In the dream exercise that follows, we will borrow from Beckett's essential techniques that he used in his play *Happy Days* in which a woman, Winnie, begins the first act buried to her waist in sand, and in the second, she is buried up to her neck – and despite that, continues in her day as if nothing has happened, continuing her daily routines remembering "happier days," with her husband Willie resting nearby.

In Beckett's *Play*, an even more bizarre script, the three characters, a man and two women, are sealed up to their necks in urns, forced to retell the story of their ménage à trois. Compelled to repeat their stories in a strange, hellish limbo, with a light darting instantaneously from one face to the next, the pace of Beckett's *Play* is relentless, cruel, demanding, and yet, at times, strangely merciful. The confines of the urns strip the characters of their ability to protest, complain, or withdraw, and instead as the light illuminates their faces, they are forced to tell their story over and over again, complete with emotional explosions, burps, rephrasings, and other peccadillos. In the process their humanity is revealed, even as they tortuously unmask their secrets, lies, and hidden motives.

Exercise 3: Samuel Beckett – The Subtraction Ballet – I Can't Go On; I'll Go On.

In this playwriting drill, the question is "how do people survive when all else has been stripped away?" As you work through the exercise, work toward the kind of pristine, crystalline, everyday reality that happens in a dream – an almost hyperreal, quotidian day with those kinds of banal tasks at hand.

Beckett Essence – Building the Subtraction - At each blackout you remove or disable your characters, but they continue, as if nothing has happened.

1. Choose Characters, give them a specific, brutal physical activity.
2. Choose a Location; give it a meaningful if bare visual specificity.
3. The essence is: "I can't go on; I'll go on."
4. One Character wants something, desperately, but *secretly*.
5. 1st Six Lines: Characters discuss any banal conversation about the physical environment, activity, anything, BUT not their desperate desire.
6. OBSCURE: Characters obscured by smoke, darkness, curtain, fog, brightness – there is an abrupt sound.
7. Light comes back up, one character is restricted physically in some manner, not completely, just partially.
8. 2nd Six Lines: Characters again continue discuss in pedestrian, ordinary terms the physical environment, activity, the want or need comes through more strongly though not directly, but characters can't discuss restriction, but just accept it.
9. OBSCURE: Characters obscured, there is an abrupt sound.
10. Light comes back up, the other character is restricted physically in some manner, not completely, just partially.

11. 3rd Six Lines: Characters continue discuss physical environment, want comes through *even more* strongly though not directly, characters can't discuss restriction, just accept it.
12. OBSCURE: characters obscured, abrupt sound.
13. Light comes back up, 1st character is restricted physically more severely, in some manner.
14. Character 1 Aria
15. OBSCURE: Characters obscured, abrupt sound.
16. Light comes back up, 2nd character is restricted physically more severely, in some manner.
17. Character 2 Aria
18. END

In Beckett's *Play*, there is a kind of new world order created – an awareness that even though the characters are essentially interred in urns, they are alive, driven by powerful motives, relentless in their desire to have their say, powerless to turn away, and because of that we are unable to stop watching. The piece is designed to be performed three times which because of the rapidity of the performance, helps the audience to understand the complexity of the ménage à trois as it is revealed repeatedly.

Moving forward, we will leave behind this stage absurdism of Beckett and Ionesco and look at its influence in the world of film and specifically in the wildly incongruous realm of Quentin Tarantino's movies. These flicks are filled with a gleeful embrace of Grand Guignol violence that is so sickening, horrifying, and brutal that it becomes very nearly comic, yet so real and mesmerizing that it is difficult to look away. If anyone has captured the sly, comedic, and menacing style of Beckett and Ionesco in film, it is this director/writer changeling, who continues wreak masterful havoc in his creation of outlandish, over-the-top characters; complex and conflicted storylines, and landscapes that violently rub up against pop art and camp sensibilities.

3   The Maw of Pop Culture: *Pulp Fiction* and the Structure of Story Threads

In Quentin Tarantino's screenplay, *Pulp Fiction*, we encounter multiple story threads that are carefully wound not into three acts, as is the tradition in film manuscripts, but four. What makes *Pulp Fiction* particularly dream-like is how these story threads are wound about each other not necessarily in a linear fashion, but in an associative manner that throws off the viewer. This is compounded by characters who behave in a realistic, normal way to rather horrific incidents that would send most people into a nervous breakdown. Some of these more horrifying moments include the story threads for Honey Bunny and Pumpkin (which bookend the entire film) robbing the diner; Vincent's and Jules' hard day's work of a hit job, Butch's throwing of his match for Marsellus Wallace, Vincent's having to babysit Mia – Marsellus' wife, the accidental death of Marvin, and the rape of Marsellus by Zed & Maynard, and the clean-up of Marvin's death by Winston Wolf. What makes *Pulp Fiction* unique is its comedic approach to movie violence epitomized by Jules' oddly biblical approach to his job of assassination. It is this bizarre sense of serenity in the face of horror that gives the film its absurdist quality – and it's become Tarantino's signature technique that pops up in many of his films, including *Reservoir Dogs, From Dusk till Dawn, Kill Bill I & II, Inglourious Basterds, Django Unchained*, and *Once Upon a Time in Hollywood*.

Quentin Tarantino's Dramaturgical Essence – the Cacophony of Scenic Sequencing

Key to Tarantino's technique is a slippery sense of scene order. Consider below the purely chronological order of the scenes in *Pulp Fiction*. If the film had been made in this way – it would have been much less interesting with the major focus on Jules and Vincent's day. Note that when put into chronological order, the story becomes flat, predictable, and doesn't reveal interiority the way that it does in the final version of the film:

4   **Pulp Fiction (Scenes in Chronological Order)**

ACT ONE
– Jules and Vincent drive to retrieve Marsellus's briefcase.
– Jules and Vincent execute the briefcase thieves.
– One thief tries to ambush Jules and Vincent; Jules and Vincent kill him instead.
– Jules is convinced he and Vincent have been blessed by a miracle.
– While leaving the scene of the briefcase incident, Vincent accidentally kills Marvin.
– Jules and Vincent go to Jimmy's and wait for The Wolf to show up.
– The Wolf comes to Jimmy's and cleans up their Marvin problem.
– Jules and Vincent go to a diner.
– Pumpkin and Honey Bunny hold up the diner.
– Jules, Pumpkin, Honey Bunny, and Vincent have a standoff.

THE ABSURDIST NIGHTMARE AND THE DRAMATIC WET DREAM

- Jules, who wants to leave killing behind, lets Pumpkin and Honey Bunny go.
- Jules and Vincent exit the diner.

ACT TWO

- Marsellus convinces Butch to take a dive in his boxing fight.
- Jules and Vincent show up at Marsellus's club with the briefcase.
- Vincent insults Butch.
- Vincent buys drugs from Lance.
- Vincent gets high.
- Vincent shows up at Mia's to take her to dinner.
- Vincent and Mia flirt, dance, and go home together.
- Mia finds Vincent's drugs and overdoses.
- Vincent drives Mia to Lance's to save her life.

ACT THREE

- Butch has a flashback to the survival tale of his father's watch in Vietnam prior to his fight.
- Esmeralda hears Butch killed his opponent in the ring, double-crossing Marsellus.
- Esmeralda picks Butch up in her cab and drives him to a motel to meet his girlfriend.
- Butch and Fabienne have sex.
- Butch wakes up in the morning and realizes Fabienne forgot his father's watch.
- Butch takes Fabienne's car back to his apartment to retrieve his watch.
- Butch gets his watch and kills Vincent, who was waiting for him.
- Butch encounters Marsellus on the street and they're both injured in a car wreck.
- Butch and Marsellus wake up in a redneck sex dungeon run by Maynard and Zedd.
- Maynard and Zedd sexually assault Marsellus while Butch escapes.
- Butch goes back and kills Maynard and critically wounds Zedd to free Marsellus.
- Marsellus tells Butch his double-cross debt has been repaid and he's free to leave L.A.
- Butch and Fabienne leave L.A on Zedd's motorcycle and drive off into the sunset.

Now let's look at the film as it was written and filmed:

ACT ONE

- *Pumpkin and Honey Bunny hold up the diner.*
- Jules and Vincent drive to retrieve Marsellus's briefcase.
- Jules and Vincent execute the briefcase thieves.

ACT TWO
- Marsellus convinces Butch to take a dive in his boxing fight.
- Jules and Vincent show up at Marsellus's club with the briefcase.
- Vincent insults Butch.
- Vincent buys drugs from Lance.
- Vincent gets high.
- Vincent shows up at Mia's to take her to dinner.
- Vincent and Mia flirt, dance, and go home together.
- Mia finds Vincent's drugs and overdoses.
- Vincent drives Mia to Lance's to save her life.

ACT THREE
- Butch has a flashback to the survival tale of his father's watch in Vietnam prior to his fight.
- Esmeralda hears Butch killed his opponent in the ring, double-crossing Marsellus.
- Esmeralda picks Butch up in her cab and drives him to a motel to meet his girlfriend Fabienne.
- Butch and Fabienne have sex.
- Butch wakes up in the morning and realizes Fabienne forgot his father's watch.
- Butch takes Fabienne's car back to his apartment to retrieve his watch.
- Butch gets his watch and kills Vincent, who was waiting for him.
- Butch encounters Marsellus on the street and they're both injured in a car wreck.
- Butch and Marsellus wake up in a redneck sex dungeon run by Maynard and Zedd.
- Maynard and Zedd sexually assault Marsellus while Butch escapes.
- Butch goes back and kills Maynard and critically wounds Zedd to free Marsellus.
- Marsellus tells Butch his double-cross debt has been repaid and he's free to leave L.A.
- Butch and Fabienne leave L.A on Zedd's motorcycle and drive off into the sunset.

ACT FOUR
- *One thief tries to ambush Jules and Vincent; Jules and Vincent kill him instead.*
- *Jules is convinced he and Vincent have been blessed by a miracle.*
- *While leaving the scene of the briefcase incident, Vincent accidentally kills Marvin.*
- *Jules and Vincent go to Jimmy's and wait for The Wolf to show up.*
- *The Wolf comes to Jimmy's and cleans up their Marvin problem.*

- *Jules and Vincent go to a diner.*
- *Jules, Pumpkin, Honey Bunny, and Vincent have a standoff.*
- *Jules, who wants to leave killing behind, lets Pumpkin and Honey Bunny go.*
- *Jules and Vincent exit the diner.*

First, what you should notice is that the film is NOT all that jiggled out of order – it is in fact only in the very first scene with Honey Bunny and Pumpkin that is different in the first act, and what has been added is a FOURTH act, in which the different stories are pulled together in a way that throws off the audience. Tarantino opens by showing us the start of the robbery and then makes us wait over an hour to find out how it resolves, which creates suspense, tension, and uncertainty in the audience. We know we're in unsettled waters here. Also, by opening with a mundane discussion that erupts into a threat of violence, Tarantino tells the audience three things:

- This is the kind of film where anything can happen.
- This film is going to show you the story of people you don't usually see.
- This film is going to keep you guessing.

Exercise 3: Quentin Tarantino – The Worst Things Last: A Discordance of Narratives

Showing the sequences out of chronological order breaks the action up into four mini-arcs instead of three, which creates better pacing. It also solves a functional problem, which is the necessity of rising action. Jules and Vincent's day is so over the top that if we watched it all happen chronologically, the rest of the film would feel flat by comparison. Plus, by breaking their day up, we forget just how absurd it is. So how does the exercise work?

Method:

1. Divide your story into a series of three to four story threads – with one story as your anchor story featuring your central character – working out the events in each thread with a separate line of colored plot cards.
2. Each story line should have at least eight to ten event cards. Arrange these cards in chronological order. You can find these story threads by creating dream cache for each of the characters in the screenplay, or by creating one large dream cache for the entire work.
3. Create the story threads by asking your characters what has happened to them that changed their lives – if you ask your characters this kind of a question, they are more than likely to show you what happened using a dream-like compulsion to tell their stories.

4. Once you have your three to four story threads – again using your main story as your anchor – then look at how you might weave these stories together – keeping their chronological stories intact – so you might want to do:
   a. Story A, Event Card 1; Story B, Event Card 1; Story C, Event Card 1; Story D, Event Card 1, and continue so on.
5. But consider, as you move through the story threads and event cards, changing things up a bit, particularly as you move through closer to the end – ala *Pulp Fiction*.
6. So, what you might have is (assuming you have about 7–8 events for each Story Thread):
   a. Story A, Event Card 4; Story B, Event Card 3; Story C, Event Card 5; Story D, Event Card 2, and so on.
7. As you do this, think about tension and release, and the rhythm of your film – are scenes more violent than others – how can could keep the pacing and tension.
8. Can you withhold a mystery for a while and go back to a moment that intrigues you? How does comedy play into it? Can you get a laugh by going back or going forward? Can you portray the violence at a remove, perhaps ironically attaching the violence to a piece of famous music, or as a kind of dance sequence, or highly stylized in slow motion so that it becomes a kind of shadow play itself.

Building your screenplay using a discordance of narratives is a challenging technique to come to after you've already written a lot of your film, but it will help shake up the whole of your storytelling, especially if you allow a bit of chance to enter into the mix – if you built the stories on a series of index cards, what would happen if you tossed all the cards in the air and built those stories using pure chance. The violence might seem over the top and gratuitous, but your goal is to make it "strange" so that the audience might view it in its full horror without the kind of habitualized response that limits emotional connection. One of the reasons Tarantino's violence is relatively palatable in his films, is that he takes it so far that it becomes an ironic comment on violence in the entertainment community.

In the next chapter, we'll deal with another structure of violence within dramatic writing, building from yet another source of non-linear structure – music, and its sometimes-ceremonial sacrificial nature. Remember that for the Ancient Greeks, drama was an offering to the God Dionysus, the god of theatre, but more importantly to wine, fertility and of the life juice. The deaths that occurred within Greek plays were part of that bloody gift. Both Edward Albee, the three-time Pulitzer prize-winning playwright, and Agnès Varda, the avant-garde French New Wave filmmaker came up in the 1960s and 70s, and in the case of both dramatists, the rhythm and musicality of their work is tied closely to an ongoing exploration of the nature of sacrifice. We'll be looking at Albee's stage plays *Who's Afraid of Virginia Woolf?* and his *Tiny Alice* in our discussion, though I encourage all dramatists of either the stage or the screen to watch the film of *Who's Afraid of Virginia Woolf*. We'll also look at Agnès Varda film *Vagabond*, which essentially serves up its protagonist, Mona Bergeron (played brilliantly by Sandrine Bonnaire) in kind of Dionysiac sacrifice to the listless nomadic existence of young people in the 1980s. As Mona wanders around the Languedoc-Roussillon wine country one winter, she becomes increasingly detached from the world, even as she engages in it – and dies of exposure by the film's end – a sacrifice made by her own inability to cope in the unblinking, anonymous world of the 1980s.

CHAPTER 14

The Breathing of a Play: Music and Ritualized Sacrifice

Edward Albee's Tiny Alice *and Agnès Varda's* Vagabond

I must confess that my relationship with Edward Albee is a personal one; he wrote the foreword to two of my books and I spent many years interviewing him on stage in front of a live audience. He was my mentor and teacher. I also had the great pleasure of watching him work with young playwrights on numerous occasions, and his process of finding the one thing that took him out of a playwright's script was a fascinating one. He had the ability to find the essence of a play, the way we're working in this text, and then find the elements in the play that seemed at odds with that essence. He would point out this inconstancy to the playwright; that way the writer might tighten his dramatic work, following that playwright's own intentions to develop it further, giving it a richer, more powerful dramatic energy. Albee, however, did not tell the playwright how to write their play; he was very uncomfortable about that notion – whether it was actors, directors, dramaturgs, etc. – no one knows better how to write their own play than the playwright himself. Albee was not a fan of new play development in general, and didn't like workshop readings, and did not like others telling playwrights how to revise their plays. He would joke, "did anyone tell Jackson Pollack how to paint his paintings? Would anyone dare to say, 'Hey Jackson, slap that spatter of paint there instead of there!' So why do we feel comfortable doing the same thing to playwrights?" Albee fought ferociously for playwrights' rights with the Dramatists Guild, and his influence there remains to this day.

Albee's own plays also had a profound effect on me, and I began my acting career by playing Jerry in Albee's *The Zoo Story*, which was first produced in 1959, downtown in NYC's Provincetown Playhouse, just off Washington Square. Albee was highly influential with a generation of playwrights, and his work reflected a deep attachment to his fellow absurdists in Europe. The news of Albee's downtown fame grew with this short, violent play that pits the wildly theatrical Jerry, the ultimate street hustler, against the complacent, passive Peter, a wealthy denizen of the Upper East Side. Every young New York playwright of the 60s generation made the pilgrimage to Greenwich Village to see Albee's electrifying new play. John Guare, author of many plays off-off Broadway, and most well-known for his plays *House of Blue Leaves* and *Six*

Degrees of Separation, remembered wanting to devour the play, to make it part of himself, because it was so powerful. When Guare went home to Queens to tell his parents about the play, they found him so captivated by the story that they initially thought he had killed someone himself. Almost every off-off Broadway writer interviewed for my book *Off-Off-Broadway Explosion* made a similar comment about the experience of seeing *Zoo Story*. This single short play created an entire school of playwriting. It was now possible to write a play with just two characters, a simple park bench, and a tough, terrifying, and unforgiving story, and somehow to become wildly successful as a playwright. At the heart of the play is the final sacrifice tendered by Jerry, the offering of his life, to save Peter's own, and to actually communicate with each other – really, truly, and honestly – despite living in a world of comfortable lies, deadened to language, meaning, and existence.

1 Edward Albee's *Tiny Alice* – An Uncanny Gothic Chamber Opera

An important aspect of Albee's technique was that he was secret composer. As a young, struggling artist in New York's Greenwich Village, Albee's lover was William Flanagan, a composer protégé of Aaron Copeland. Albee ran around with Flanagan's composer friends, such as Ned Rorem, David Diamond, and Virgil Thomson, and so was, in essence, a dramatist raised by a wolf pack of composers. In an article that he later published in his book of essays, *Stretching My Mind*, on dialogue, Albee wrote:

> Since a playwright must be able to "hear" his or her characters, what the character says and how the character says it must be precisely "notated." I use the composer's term intentionally, for a playwright must be able to hear as a composer hears, as precisely, and indicate it all, as a composer puts it down on paper. There are duration differences between a quarter note and a dotted quarter note, for example. We playwrights should hear these distinctions as precisely as a composer does, and use them as precisely.[1]

Albee's powerful connection with music is terribly important to understand his plays, but also to get at the essence of his technique. It was rare to enter Albee's Tribeca loft or his home in Montauk and not hear chamber music playing – such as the crisp, tight, flawlessly executed performance of Mozart's String Quartet No. 2 in D, K. 155 or Schumann's Piano Quintet in E flat Major,

---

1 Albee, Edward, "Dialogue," Dramatist. Sep/Oct2017, Vol. 20 Issue 1, p38–41.

Op.44. And that same impeccable, crystalline dream-like structure was key to Albee's relationship with language in his plays.

The unique musicality of Albee's language is best savored in one of his most unusual plays, *Tiny Alice*, which premiered right after his box office hit, *Who's Afraid of Virginia Woolf?* The play, a kind of grand guignol gothic horror drama, begins with one of the most carefully crafted verbal battles that Albee has ever written, between the Lawyer and the Cardinal, two remarkably sociopathic creatures, whose deeply personal enmity brings them to into a snarling, bestial, and bare-knuckle verbal sparring that tests the limits of his audience's willingness to witness it. And yet the play that follows is a strange unveiling of a deeply mysterious and very nearly innocent and beautiful lay brother, Julian, much adored by the Cardinal, who is sent as an offering to the mysterious Miss Alice. This Miss Alice, as we first meet her, is personified by a woman who we think of as the ultrawealthy – a weirdly theatrical figure who we assume will consummate an awful kind of romance with Julian, who seems to be rather asexual. In fact, Miss Alice is only a stand-in for the real Alice, who is a creature that is represented as a queer light in a miniature mansion at the stage center. This Alice is an invisible monster of Lovecraftian horror, who will consume poor Julian in a grisly moment of human sacrifice, after been shot and mortally wounded by the Lawyer. Yet at the heart of the play is Julian's sheerly euphonious arias – a stylistic signature of Albee muscular musicality as a playwright. Below is an exercise designed to help writers get at the kind of musical diapason that one might find in *Tiny Alice* or another of Albee's plays such as *Three Tall Women* or *The Goat*. Note that even the characterizations grow out of a sense of melody, harmony, and yet, dissonance.

Exercise 1: Albee's Musical Notation in Playwrighting

In this exercise you will write a scene that incorporates a bit of Albee's own obsession with musical notation – use this to hone a scene you've already written, or to create an entirely new work:

1. In the scene two characters, Characters A & B, work at a physical activity that is difficult, has a limited time frame for completion, and serious consequences if it is not done in time. Other characters, tied to Characters A & B's specific needs or desires, enter and leave the space, which has a specific emotional meaning for the characters.
2. Character A wants something desperately from Character B; Character B may not give Character A what they want, and in fact has equally strong

reasons for not doing so. The two characters may not discuss this deeper want or need directly; all they may discuss is the physical activity.
3. No two characters speak the same way – each has a precise musicality – think of each character as a musical instrument playing a specific melody or harmony (or dissonance) within a larger symphonic or chamber work.
4. The playwright must "hear" the characters precisely, using correct notation the way a composer uses duration. Consider the use of silences as well – how long can the characters work at the activity without speaking, and yet getting across needed backstory?
   a. Consider durations of:
      i. a period
      ii. a semi-colon
      iii. a comma
      iv. an ellipses
      v. an m-dash
   b. Consider emphasis of:
      i. ALL CAPS
      ii. Italicization
      iii. Bolding
   c. Consider musical pacing and phrasing
      i. Forte Loud
      ii. Piano Quiet
      iii. Pianissimo Very Quiet
      iv. Allegro Fast
      v. Presto Really Fast
      vi. Andante slow
      vii. Adagio Really slow
      viii. Dolce Gentle
5. Allow the scene to have a distinct beginning, middle, and end, and note the tension and release of the scene to correspond to the musical notation listed above.
6. The scene comes to an end with a particular sound and consider using music throughout as a backdrop against the scene – keeping in mind the notion of a melody drama or melodrama, that uses percussion, pitch, rhythm, and volume to create meaning over the backdrop of the gloomy set and yet a harsh exterior reality that is bright with possibility.

As we complete this first exercise focusing on the musical notation inherent in playwriting, another essence of Edward Albee's plays comes forward out of his dream technique, and this is directly tied to his deep and significant connection to ancient Greek drama. At the heart of almost all of Albee's work there is a sacrifice that haunts the play – whether it is the sacrifice of Brother Julian in *Tiny Alice*, the "bumble of joy" in Albee's *The American Dream*, the non-existent baby in *Who's Afraid of Virginia Woolf?* or the non-existent baby in *The Play about the Baby*. Also consider the stroke that transforms the central character in *Three Tall Women*, or even the actual sacrifice of the goat at the end of *The Goat, or Who is Sylvia*? There are many more examples, but nearly every single one of Albee's plays has this kind of sacrifice going on, and this links Albee's plays with those of the Greeks, such as the plays of Aeschylus, Sophocles, Euripides, or Aristophanes. This dream element of sacrifice in Albee's plays almost always provides the dramatic crisis moment in his works, and is the structure around which he builds his plays. The next exercise allows you to play with the essence of this ancient Greek dramatic element, the notion of the *offering* or *sacrifice*. Key to our understanding of tragedy, which translates to goat-song in Greek, was the slaughter of a goat to the God Dionysus, as this is believed to have been a key element of the ritual of Greek theatre.

Exercise 2: Edward Albee – The Melody of Sacrifice – (Who's Afraid of Virginia Woolf, The Zoo Story, Tiny Alice, The Goat, etc.)

In this exercise consider writing a new scene or use the structure of this prompt to help you revise an older script. Consider playing the chamber music cited below as you write, allowing the music to drive the rhythm of the slaughter you will be exploring. You'll be taking pauses between musical pieces to meditate and explore the silences between your characters. Write automatically, without editing, and when you go back to the work, once again slip into the musical accompaniment as you contemplate the scene you have written, connecting to its melody, harmony, and dissonance as think about the characters and plot. I will suggest specific pieces music here, by Schoenberg, as Albee was a great fan of the composer's dissonance.

a. Preparing the Lamb for Slaughter
   i. The Private Ante-chamber: Two to Three Characters – one wants something desperately – which will demand a sacrifice of some kind from the other.
      1. The Preparation of the Sacrifice (SCHOENBURG – Transfigured Night – Adagio Molto Tranquillo)
         a. Piano, Dulce
      2. The Invocation of the God (ARIA) (SCHOENBURG – Six Little Piano Pieces – Etwas Rasch)

                 a.   a. Andante
b.   The Offering to the Gods
      ii.   The public ritual – Choose a location that is public, theatrical, slightly unreal.
           1.   The Ritual Slaughter (Schoenburg – Transfigured Night – A Tempo)
               a.   Allegro Forte
           2.   The Laying Forth of the Sacrifice (Schoenburg – Six Little Piano Pieces – Sehr lansame Viertel)
               a.   Pianissimo
c.   The Sacrifice Has Change the World – Life is No Longer the Same
      iii.   The characters are transformed, retreat from the public world back to their private one.
           1.   The Ritual Retreat (Schoenberg – Five Orchestral Pieces, Op. 16 – Das obligate Rezitativ)
               a.   Adagio, Dulce

What you'll discover is how powerful the notion of sacrifice can be in the building of a play. However, Albee isn't the only dramatic writer who explores the ritualized nature of sacrifice in his work, in this next sequence of work, we'll consider the films of Agnes Varda, who came of age in the 1960s and 70s as a filmmaker, and who also structured her major works around the notion of sacrifice.

2   Agnes Varda – Oneiric Cinécriture – Writing Your Dreams in Film

Vagabond (1985) is a film by Agnes Varda, who was one of the filmmakers who defined what was known as French New Wave film. Varda's invention, Cinécriture, is an important one for those who want to bend the notion of documentary into an investigation into the uncanny. Like a lot of the other French New Wave directors, Varda was likely influenced by auteur theory, which conceives as the director/writer controlling all aspects of their craft (not unlike Richard Wagner's notion of Gesamtkunstwerk or Total work of art). Varda was known for using the camera as her "pen" and called this technique cinécriture (cinematic writing or "writing on film"). She merged the words cinema and writing to create a cohesive notion of filmmaking that brought together all its elements – cinematography, screenwriting, and direction. To Varda's mind, all should merge to create one powerful, socially engaged, embodied message growing out the corporeality of the film's protagonist.

In *Vagabond* (French: Sans toit ni loi, "without roof nor law") she structures her film into 47 episodes, each of which is taken from a different point of view. The film focuses on a young woman, Mona Bergeron, played by Sandrine Bonnaire (who became famous for the role) who after leaving her office job in Paris, wanders through French wine country in the winter, in an extended act of suicide/freedom. The film is built on a pseudo-documentary structure, with the various people being interviewed (perhaps by a police detective) about Mona. Some important moments are left out – forcing the viewer to piece things together for themselves.

Exercise 3: Agnes Varda – Without Roof or Law – The Dream Documentarian

METHOD: In this exercise you'll build a short film starting with its final resolution (in the case of the film, the dead body of Mona) and work back and forth in time, using both traditional narrative sequences, moving forward, in which we see the central character living her/his life day-to-day. Then there will be pseudo-documentary sequences looking back, based on the interviews of several different people reflecting on what actually happened, after the corpse has been found – in *Vagabond* this involves a police officer interviewing witnesses, but in your film, it could be someone else, looking back, unveiling what happened, even as we seeing the story unfold in real time:

1. Film starts: Final Result – Dead Body (objective narrative scene)
2. Documentary Scene 1 (First witness scene)
3. Moment before death/Final Result (objective narrative scene)
4. Documentary Scene 2 (Second witness scene)
5. Days before Death/Final Result/Character reveal (objective narrative scene)
6. Documentary Scene 3 (Third witness scene)
7. Weeks before Death/Final Result/Major Complication (objective narrative scene)
8. Documentary Scene 4 (Fourth witness scene)
9. Inciting Event/Reason for it all (objective narrative scene)

The film *Vagabond* moves swiftly between its lyrical tracking shots and uses elliptical editing to surprise you – slipping from what seems to be traditional narrative and moving into documentary-style. Still at the heart of this technique is a heart-breaking mystery: Why does Mona choose this hard life of the vagabond? This is something that is left unresolved in the film, and it is another key to Varda's technique – avoiding easy explanations, cliché summations, and a conclusion that resolves all loose threads and ties them into a bow. Instead, we are left to contemplate Mona's wine-soaked, damaged, cold corpse, and the horror of what our own culture has created, an empty, meaningless landscape of greed, cruelty, and desolation.

The film you create, borrowing from the style of *Vagabond*, should have the distinct effortless blend of objective filmmaking, and that of a subjective documentary – a weaving of what feels poetic, flowing, haunting, and then the sudden clamping down of the facts – as merciless and unkind as possible. What happens is that you are again moving backward in time, but explaining less as you go there – so that between the objective narrative and the documentary film, you have some gaps – which are unexplained, mysterious, and while challenging to understand – are possible to solve.

This kind of structure shakes the audience out of empathy for the character and raises questions in their mind, and forces them to engage intellectually, rather than emotionally, with the work of art – this is a filmic version of what we explored earlier as Brecht's "alienation effect" or Verfremdungseffekt. As you move back and forth in time between the objective reality and the subjective documentary investigation of that reality, experiment with where the truth may lie, teasing the audience with the fact that either objective reality, or subjective documentary, or both may be true. Resist the urge to explain everything away, and instead for the audience to work. Leave a knot for the audience to wrestle with and force them to think about what they would do in the shoes of the protagonist.

In the next chapter, this same dark realm of futility and hollowness is joyfully embraced with two powerful and lacerating tools – comedy and menace. The three writers and the dramatic works explored include Harold Pinter's *The Birthday Party*, Irene Fornes' *Conduct of Life*, and Jean-Luc Godard's *Weekend*, and culturally they could not be more different. However, all three writers cuddle up to terrifying jeopardy and peril with an invigorating blast of humor that is both stunning and refreshing. Who knew that our worst nightmares could so exhilaratingly funny, and at the same time, still so horrifyingly awful? This is the realm of the lyric, and in the dream world it is place of pure sensation, where story takes second fiddle to mood, atmosphere, and vulnerability.

CHAPTER 15

Comedy Shock: Rhythms of Menace and Joy

Harold Pinter's The Birthday Party, *Irene Fornes'* Conduct of Life, *and* Jean-Luc Godard's Weekend

The last chapter of this book deals with a rather fundamental technique – and it's tied to our relationship with our audiences – and how they react emotionally to the drama we create. If we allow our scripts to become too intense, too stressful with dramatic tension, our audiences will check out – often unintentional laughter occurs because the audience needs a break. Audience members need an emotional release valve to handle the often very challenging material in our drama. Our dreams and our dramas are filled with the rhythm of tension and release, and in the world of the Absurdists, this is particularly important in terms of how drama is structured. No longer is the thrust of a play built on the notion of the male orgasm – with an initiating stroke, a turbulent middle, and an explosive conclusion. Instead, these dramatic works are conceived within the context of an ongoing process of tension and release, menace and joy, conceived of as both the kind of horror one feels when locked in with one's killer, and yet still able to joke and trade barbs with that same Monster as they prepare their hot poker or sharpen their axe blade. The comedy of these dramas, and in particular those of Harold Pinter, grows out of an amassing horror that is only complete when the characters, both protagonist and antagonist, achieve a kind of deep vulnerability that makes it impossible for either to escape, and yet provides ample rope for them to hang themselves, or make a break for it.

1   Harold Pinter – Playwright of Tension and Release – the Comedy of Unease

In the years that followed World War II, the people of Great Britain suffered long after the war ended. London had been bombed practically into oblivion, and its economy was in ruins. It was the time of some of the Labor Party's greatest achievements, including the nationalization of major industries, its healthcare, and the welfare system. But it was also a time of great poverty, rootlessness, and crime, and it was during this time that Harold Pinter was growing up into young adulthood. Having already suffered the privations of war, now came a great threat, the calamity of destitution which claimed the lives and souls of England's working class as the country struggled to regain any sense of normality after the war. Pinter's plays, like many of his fellow European absurdist writers, were as much a critique of the failings of those public campaigns to resuscitate the British economy, as they were a realistic depiction of the hardships being undergone by its citizens. This was the time of John Osborne's *Look Back in Anger*, when a generation of young men who fought in World War II, struggling against the reality of British class structure, had struggled to get an education, find a job, and thrive. Prosperity had passed them over, even though they had fought to save their nation, and now there was a deep, rumbling chasm of economic disparity, driven by class distinctions, fueling a repressed rage that was surging against the steely English tradition of the "stiff upper lip," remaining resolute and unemotional when faced with adversity. Harold Pinter's writing takes this simmering fury to another level, submerging it, and at the same time, allowing it to twist the nature of reality itself into something dark, lethal, and threateningly comic.

Of the many plays that Pinter wrote, one of the most mysterious and menacing of his plays is *The Birthday Party*, his first play, which focuses on a young stranger, Stanley, who has moved into a small seaside boarding house owned by an elderly couple, Petey and Meg. Into this very lived-in, disheveled world enter Goldberg and McCann, two gangsters, who weirdly decide to throw Stanley a birthday party. During the birthday party, the world becomes increasingly disturbed, and Stanley grows unhinged, eventually sexually attacking a young woman, Lulu, who has come to visit. Stanley lives in fear of these two men, but we never know why – and the play ends with the two of them somehow turning Stanley into a kind of automaton. In the process, the world of the drama grows increasingly unstable, unclear, and Meg and Petey are left haunted by the mystery of what has happened to Stanley. Pinter's plays are powerfully structured upon the build and release of tension. In *The Birthday Party*, the structure of events alternates between moments of terrible anxiety and strain and just as suddenly, a kind of expansive joy and vulnerability. The closer that Stanley comes to annihilation, the greater the tension. Also *humor* and *absurdity* are played against the terror, both raising and lowering tension.

The play moves from the playful/dangerous flirting of Meg and Stanley to the cat and mouse game between Goldberg, McCann, and Stanley, and then to the final strange, ritualized transfiguration of Stanley. There is a build of pressure mounting upon Goldberg and McCann's manipulation of Stanley who plays along at times, and at other moments fight back aggressively. At no time, however, is anything made clear about what is at stake, though on some level, it becomes clear that *everything* is at stake. In addition, there are moments of bizarre, unexplained behavior, that which border on a kind of extended dream logic. Why is McCann tearing strips of newspaper at the kitchen table? And why does McCann suddenly explode with rage when Stanley touches those paper strips? What are we to make of Stanley's banging of the drum?

Questions are raised; there are inconsistencies, illogical statements are made. What is clear is that all of this translates into a theatricality based on an essence of alternating rhythms of menace and joy that work as forwarding, making us hungry for next, as David Ball instructs in his excellent small blue book of play analysis, *Backwards and Forwards*. And yet the traditional rules of drama here have been broken – instead there is a forward motion of questions that are raised, with no clear answers to solve them.

Exercise 4: Harold Pinter – Menace and Joy, Ominous Transport, and the Arc of Love

This next essence exercise is a kind of moveable feast of horror and ecstasy, in homage to and expanding upon an exercise in Jean-Claude van Itallie's wonderful *The Playwrights Workbook* and in it, the world without informs the world within, although it does so by hint and hearsay rather than through direct moments of exposition. Instead, we find ourselves thrust forward, driven by the accumulation of mysteries, and the rhythm of terror and joy. The scene incorporates at least two characters: CHARACTER A has a powerful, specific want from CHARACTER B, strong enough to lead to murder. CHARACTER B has what the first character wants, but refuses to acquiesce, also to the point of murder. Both are charming, warm, ingratiating, and deadly. There will be two major modes of behavior – Joy and Menace.

1. *The Scene*: A moving location – a car, a train, a boat, an airplane. The quality of the location is somewhat seedy, questionable, dangerous. The two characters have some familiarity with the means of transport and can see outside through a window of some sort.
2. *Joy*: Have each character discuss something she or he loves more than anything in the world – something that is tangible – something they can discuss passionately with all five senses. Write at least THREE short paragraphs building to a climactic expression of this thing.
3. *Menace*: This is a moment of serious tension between the two characters – they can discuss what's happening outside the window, an activity they are doing together or separately, a news item, something that's recently happened to them, but whatever it is, it is a threat tied to either the WANT of CHARACTER A or the REFUSAL OF THE WANT by CHARACTER B.

- *BEAT 1*: MENACE: Six Lines of Dialogue – Establish location, and the situation at hand.
- *BEAT 2*: JOY: CHARACTER A discusses something she or he loves – the FIRST paragraph of CHARACTER A'S JOY EXERCISE.
- *BEAT 3*: MENACE: Six Lines of Dialogue – Something happens outside as they are moving. CHARACTER A and CHARACTER B discuss it. The talk becomes somewhat threatening.
- *BEAT 4*: JOY: CHARACTER B discusses something she or he loves – the FIRST paragraph of CHARACTER B'S JOY EXERCISE.
- *BEAT 5*: MENACE: Six Lines of Dialogue – Something ELSE happens outside as they are moving, that is more threatening. CHARACTER A and CHARACTER B discuss it. The talk becomes even more tense.
- *BEAT 6*: JOY: CHARACTER A discusses something she or he loves – the SECOND paragraph of CHARACTER A'S JOY EXERCISE.
- *BEAT 7*: MENACE: Six Lines of Dialogue – Something happens inside their vehicle as they are moving. CHARACTER A and CHARACTER B discuss it. The talk becomes even more threatening.
- *BEAT 8*: JOY: CHARACTER B discusses something she or he loves – the SECOND paragraph of CHARACTER B'S JOY EXERCISE.
- *BEAT 9*: MENACE: Six Lines of Dialogue – Something ELSE happens inside their vehicle as they are moving. CHARACTER A and CHARACTER B discuss it. The talk becomes even more tense and now the situation is becoming dangerous.
- *BEAT 10*: JOY: CHARACTER A discusses something she or he loves – the THIRD and FINAL paragraph of CHARACTER A'S JOY EXERCISE.
- *BEAT 11*: MENACE: Six Lines of Dialogue – Something ELSE happens inside their vehicle as they are moving. CHARACTER A and CHARACTER B discuss it. The talk becomes extremely threatening and now the situation is very dangerous.
- *BEAT 12*: JOY: CHARACTER B discusses something she or he loves – the THIRD paragraph of CHARACTER B'S JOY EXERCISE.
- *BEAT 13*: MENACE: Six Lines of Dialogue – An act of violence. It is deadly. CHARACTER A and CHARACTER B discuss it. The scene ends. We do not know if someone is going to die or when. They are not dead yet. But the scene ends, and then we think we know. Or perhaps not.

2   María Irene Fornés: The Torturer and the Tortured – Conducting Cruel Comedy

One of America's finest and most influential teachers of playwriting, María Irene Fornés was very much a product of the Off-off-Broadway scene, as the principal playwright of Judson Poets' Theatre as well as the Theatre of the Absurd. Though first a visual artist and a painter, Fornés saw the original French production of Samuel Beckett's *Waiting for Godot*, directed by Roger Blin in the late 1950s. Transformed by this experience, Fornés became a playwright, initially beginning her career writing outlandish musicals for the Judson Poets' Theatre, directed by lay minister Al Carmines. Most of these shows, such as her plays *The Successful Life of Three* or *Promenade* took a distinctly skewered view of modern life, and mixed both violence and comedy with uniquely distanced dialogue, so that the characters and the world they inhabit are seen as if comically commenting on their own foibles and murderous tendencies. While clearly influenced by Beckett in her minimalist approach to character and plot, Fornés borrows ostranenie, "making strange" from Brecht and the Russian futurists, so that her writing forces its audiences to question their assumptions.

One crucial aspect of Fornés's technique grows out of her heritage as a Cuban exile – uniquely accomplished in the realm of conflicting political beliefs and realities, Fornés attacks the issue of government-sanctioned torture and violence in her play *The Conduct of Life* in a peculiarly understated comedic fashion. Because Fornés wrote in English as a second language, her dialogue always has a kind of distanced, formal quality, an inherent dissonance, that brings attention to itself in a kind of dialogic ostranenie. Fornés's oddly formal quality of language adds an uncanny quality to the satiric, parodized nature of torture in *The Conduct of Life*.

In the play, the central character of Orlando is an ambitious low-level military attaché whose function as an interrogator and torturer in an unspecified Latin American country causes him to become dangerously desensitized to the level of cruelty and brutality he is expected to maintain as part of his job. Orlando's growing brutishness extends to his wife, Leticia, and eventually to the twelve-year-old girl he kidnaps and keeps in his basement to sexually abuse and torture. Observed by his fellow soldier and friend, Aleja, but not stopped or questioned, Orlando becomes increasingly violent and brutal, even as the comedy within it grows more odd and complex. The language of the play is built on a serious of disjointed monologues which Olimpia, the stubborn and willful housekeeper who comically guides her mistress, Leticia, and exhorts her to control Orlando's growing animalistic desires, even as Nena, the girl kept in the basement, is sexually assaulted repeatedly.

Because the structure of this intensely dense one-act is built upon 19 short scene bursts, the exercise I've created below is tied directly to Fornés's own interest in creativity and creative bursts – rather than traditional structure. Still, you'll have a good sense of an energy build as the comedy of the exercise grows out the increasingly bizarre reaction to the violence that occurs.

Exercise 6: Irene Fornés's Conduct of Life – 10 Staccato Scenes of Comedic Cruelty

In this exercise you will create a central pathetic figure of villain, who is surrounded by wholly incompetent, self-involved people who don't seem to be able to change the villain's activities in the least, even though they attempt to do so. Each of their attempts to stop the violence result in an escalation that grows comically worse. The trick here is to bear in mind that we'll be using the structure of a Dramatic dream to create the world of this dramedy. A Dramatic dream is one where the normal world becomes increasingly more bizarre in small drips and drabs, until it resembles a kind of inescapable hellscape that we most associate with absurdist technique.

Method: You need to dig into your personal dream cache for this exercise, and I suggest that you add a prompt to add dream elements that will help you create your central antagonist.
- This prompt is: Create seven characters who are driven by one of the seven deadly sins: pride, greed, wrath, envy, lust, gluttony, and sloth.
- For each character you create tab in their name, personality, a brief physical description, and a specific obsessive need or want tied to the sin that they represent.
- Add each of these characters to your dream cache, and then once they are all there, draw them randomly from your dream cache.
- The first of these characters to appear will be your central antagonist.
- Also draw out of your dream cache at least two to three additional characters (and these may also be antagonists!), a few locations (at least three), and a few objects, plants, or animals.

STEP 1: Given Irene Fornés's own predilection to avoid traditional plot and story structure in her plays, you'll create the structure of your play by drawing from your dream cache a total of ten elements of any kind.
1. At this point, you should add at least five to ten different kinds of music elements (these would include specific songs, types of music, specific instrument music, etc.), to your dream cache. The more you add, the deeper the dream cache can serve. Each of these elements will become,

through association, the scene title for each of the ten scenes you will write. Each scene should be as short as you can get.
2. You'll need ten scenes, and the dream cache element will somehow affect how that scene plays out – whether it refers to an object within the scene, a structural suggestion, a location, or the suggestion of the dramatic conflict within the scene.

STEP 2: Bearing in mind that Fornés was a painter before she was a playwright, you will create a story photo or painting for each of these scenes growing out of dream elements.
1. The pictures can include the people, objects, locations, flora, and fauna of each scene – and suggests the conflict going on in the scene.
2. Create this story board of ten pictures/paintings before you start writing the scenes.

STEP 3: Creating the drama – write ten scenes, in no particular order, based upon the 10 dream elements you have pulled from your cache, and flowing around the 10 pictures you have created.
1. Bear in mind that key to the essence of this exercise, following the brutality of Fornés's *The Conduct of Life*, is to work with an antagonist who brings some kind of violence to their presence on the stage. That violence may be depicted directly or indirectly on the stage.
2. Consider also playing *music* that grows out of the dream cache as you are writing, as this will feed your trance state as you're writing and slipping into the zone. Draw the music suggestions from your dream cache, and play them, if you have the music, as you write.
3. Consider too the element of ironic comedy in this, and don't back away from scenes that are funny – even in their violence. Key to Fornés's work was her unremitting sense of comedy – and the humor you discover may be key to how the scenes as a whole pull together to ironically comment on the darkness you've discovered in human nature.

STEP 4: Now go back to the scenes and consider the order.
1. Bear in mind that they may or may not track in a linear sense, but they give a real throb of dramatic action, and the flow of the order of scenes may grow out of a transformation of character rather than traditional linear causality.
2. Another way to create the order to is simply allow the scenes you have written to flow into each other from association; one scene may lead to the next because one scene may make you think of another scene, and so the flow begins.
3. Finally, consider the emotional flow of music – allow the order to grow out of an organic stream of musical logic tied to opening and closing of

phrases, the resolution of dissonance, the rhymical phrasing of scenes growing from downbeats, upbeats, and closure.

4. And the flow may grow out of all the above, without canceling the possibility of causal, linear moments even as things progress in a less traditional manner.

STEP 5: Conclude the sequence of scenes.

1. After writing these ten scenes, putting them into an orderly flow, consider the journey you have been on. Keep in mind that you may have written a rather funny, if violent comedy.

2. You don't have to tie up loose ends, and in fact, those loose ends may suggest that this piece has some continuance – either in a new work of drama, a character's future story, or a mystery that will remain in the characters past.

3. But importantly, you conclude in a way that feels right in terms of the characters' ongoing transformations and growth – even if that means that the play ends in death and tragedy and a final joke. There may be an afterlife, after all.

Exploring the terror and comedy of Harold Pinter and Irene Fornés get at the powerful ability of dramatists to tie into a very dream-like form of ironic commentary that our brains do naturally. Puns, bad jokes, dad humor all has a place in the process of alienation that grows out of the specific use of comedic menace that exists in both playwrights' work. We'll end this chapter looking at the extreme and murderous comedy of Jean-Luc Godard's *Weekend* – which twists our sense of humor into a kind of mobius strip of emotion, turning in on itself even as we grow out of ourselves in surprise with where the journey has taken us.

3 Jean-Luc Godard's Weekend: The Horrible, Wonderful, Murderous Success of Corinne and Roland

If Harold Pinter's technique of balancing terror and ecstasy is key to understanding his particular brand of drama and Irene Fornés could use the comedic depiction of violence to twist our notions of right and wrong, then filmmaker Jean-Luc Godard's violent, satirical film comedy, *Weekend* cheerfully works from a growing sense of gleeful horror as corpses pile up, while the mystery of a family inheritance and the calculated murder that drives much of the plot falls helplessly apart in a kind of nonsensical celebration of cannibalism!

In Jean-Luc Godard's *Weekend* Corinne (Mireille Darc) and Roland (Jean Yanne), a bourgeois Parisian couple, plot together to murder their way into a family inheritance (including murdering each other once the money has been gotten). These two corrupt figures leave on a Saturday morning to pick up Corinne's father from a clinic where he is dying, but they are hamstrung by a series of bizarre incidents in the French countryside where they encounter a strange mix of wealthy parasites like themselves, murderous vagabonds, twisted revolutionaries, creepily bourgeois vacationers, and deeply sleazy politicians. One particularly memorable sequence involves an auto pile up that becomes increasingly bloody, even as the very nature of cinema is itself questioned. In the end, these cynical assassins, Corinne and Roland are themselves the victims of even less morally stable revolutionaries and gangsters. Godard attempts to horrify his audience and yet there is a distancing effect throughout, so that the audience is strangely numbed to the more murderous elements of the film. At the heart of *Weekend* is a kind of smiling, joyful, even merry comedy of horror that expands upon the comic menace of Harold Pinter and transforms it into a gleeful, chirpy, and oddly sunny mix of absolute terror and jaunty and deeply disturbing anarchy. The movie is a parody of the "road" film, in which two characters set off on a road trip to secure a "treasure" of sorts – and Corinne and Roland's utterly venal, mercenary, totally egotistical lack of self-awareness leads them into a fate far worse and pathetic than, let's say, the eponymous central characters in Ridley Scott's *Thelma and Louise*. The exercise below is about making that terrifying leap into a new brand of highly carnivorous film comedy – one that threatens the nature of moviemaking itself.

Exercise 6: Jean-Luc Godard's Weekend – Vignettes of Horror and Hilarity

This exercise takes the previous Pinter exercise a bit further – so that the entire world of the drama begins to shift and change along with the characters, culminating in a wholly transformed landscape, one that is no longer recognizable to the characters, and becomes particularly threatening, and yet retains some resemblance to the real world before the apocalypse that transforms it all.

Method: In this exercise you'll write a series of film sequences that will follow the journey of two characters – and what they see outside [EXT SCENES] their car will vary with the personal revelations is happening inside [INT SCENES] the car – the scene will vary between HORROR or moments of tension and brutality which are interspersed with HILARITY, moments when the characters encounter the utterly bizarre.

Eventually the transforming world without enters the world within – to the detriment and perhaps annihilation of our heroes. Note that this entire film sequence will take place during a *liminal period* in both the character's lives – like Godard's *Weekend*, a kind of no man's zone of time, outside the normal workaday world, like a weekend, or a getaway, or a family vacation, or even holiday. Because of that liminal period, aspects of the world are already a bit askew, as people take advantage of this break from their regular lives. The transformation of the world into this strange, twisted holiday world will then transform back at the end of the sequence, but with a few stray aspects that will be forever transformed.

1. Two characters: CHARACTERS A & B have a powerful, specific want, strong enough to lead to murder. There is an aspect of criminality to what they need to do. They must attend to this need together; once they get what it is they prize, they may or may not kill each other. We feel the intensity of this need, as well as the edge of violence between them. And yet they are polished, charming, and oddly carefree about this project.

2. CHARACTERS A & B are also about to enjoy a vacation of some sort from their lives. This vacation is tied to a holiday period in the real world when people are not behaving quite as normal. The holiday has been corrupted in some way – so that it has the feel of something dangerous about it. All around these characters people are preparing for this odd period of holiday, and when this holiday is over, we'll see them preparing once again for every day, workaday life.

3. CHARACTERS A & B are driven to do what they must do to get what they want, even to the point of murder. We sense that they are both a threat to each other. Both are warm, ingratiating, and deadly. While two characters are clearly at odds with each other, yet they must work together, for now, and they even have fun together, and may even be quite romantic and tender. Yet there is something deadly wrong in their relationship – both are aware of it, and the sense that they might stab each other in the back at any given moment gives their connection a sparkling, sexy edge.

4. JOKER Characters & Locations: Your central Characters A & B will encounter a series of JOKERS – characters who are so bizarre as to be hilarious, but at the same time have the quality of the Joker in the DC Universe of Batman. These are characters that are utterly lethal even as they are absolutely ridiculous. At the same time, the Joker characters are like the characters used in Augusto Boal's Joker system of dramaturgy, where the Joker is like a Joker in a deck of cards – it is an "anybody" character who can be anybody and everyone, instantly transforming as needed, yet at the same time reminding us of the inherent artifice of the theatre, and the social masks we wear. There will be three Joker actors who can all

play the same character or split into different characters – and thus the Joker characters are unstable, fluid, and always changing.
5. The scenes: We start in moving location – a car, a train, a boat, an airplane. The vehicle has a seedy, uncanny quality. The characters always encounter the locations initially from the vehicle, but then directly encounter each setting, each becoming increasing strange, and faced with a mutable Joker/Trickster character:
    a. Location 1: The Horror Home – this location is the weird family estate of your central Characters A & B – it has something terribly wrong about it – which gets progressively worse as Characters A&B begin there – a series of three incidents occur which propel them out.
        i. Incident 1: The death inheritance – the death of a matriarch or patriarch leave a fortune which precipitates the journey.
        ii. Incident 2: Characters A&B receive a bizarre quest, or a mission tied to their inheritance which they must embark on to receive their fortune.
        iii. Incident 3: There is some specific terrible obstacle directly tied to the quest which hampers the possibility of Characters A&B getting the fortune they lust for.
    b. Location 2: The Snarl – Characters A&B find themselves in a traffic jam – and this sequence, each car of the jam is a miniature station of chaos with Joker characters creating different, increasingly bizarre mini-worlds with each car – perhaps one car is filled with a violent fight between its passengers, another is tailgating, another reveals a serial killer at work, another is filled with mimes, but Characters A&B, getting out of their car, must negotiate this strange world with ever increasing blends of violence, horror, and the bizarre in order to get past the Snarl.
    c. Location: The Field of Historic Conundrums – in this sequence Characters A & B have gotten past the Snarl only to get caught in a strange field of Joker figures impersonating great figures from history, each of which has some horrific reputation, and each of which has the quality of threat. The historic figures are ragged, twisted, and somehow able to manipulate Characters A & B with their histrionics and their unique situations within the world of the field. Having abandoned their vehicle, Characters A&B must get past these figures to move to the next scene.
    d. Location: The Revolutionists and the Haunted Castle – in this sequence, Characters A&B wander into the ruins of a once rich

estate – which like many castles is haunted. It is haunted however, by the Jokers who have now banded together in a revolutionary movement, and they see to enlist Characters A & B as a part of their revolt – it is here that one or both of Characters A & B are somehow transfigured themselves. Perhaps, one of them dies or becomes incapacitated, at the hands of the Joker Revolutionist, but whatever the situation, at least one of them must move on, still on the quest, but now it's becoming increasingly clear that the quest is in ruins.

e. Location: The Graveyard. In this final sequence, Characters A or B or perhaps both if they have survived the Haunted Castle – and have to complete the quest. But the Quest itself has been transmogrified into something entirely different, and in fact, points to a terrible truth about the world of the film you have created – a terrible truth which reflects the great darkness of our own world.

This exercise, and indeed, this entire chapter has focused on the powerful use of humor and horror to make our trip to the gallows very entertaining indeed. It is notable that playwrights who dig deep into the realm of social engagement quite often use both comedy and confusion to tease out a liminal zone where every-day, habitualized life patterns can be broken. In a world of systemic racism, homophobia, islamophobia, antisemitism, and misogyny the dealbreaker for the dreamwright is our comfortable acquiescence to all the above. It is up to us to use our craft to somehow dislodge our audiences from their security zone, and through sudden jabs of violence, cruel punches of comedy, and in a deep ironic welter of conflict and confusion, give them the tools and opportunity to question life as it is, contemplate life as it might be with social justice in the world.

Conclusion

The Work of a Dreamwright – Transcending the Possible

With this conclusion, we end this grand scheme of dreamwork for dramatic writing and the study of what I call *dreamwrighting*. I define the term "dreamwright" as any playwright who uses the associative, non-matrixed logic of dreams, rather than the linear logic of traditional dramaturgy to create drama – whether or not the playwright has written something recognizable as an actual dream play. Sometimes a little bit of magic and theatricality go a long way. I fundamentally believe that every dramatist, regardless of whether they feel more comfortable with traditional, linear, kitchen sink realism always has a touch of theatricality up their sleeves. And I particularly loathe when dramatists decide to polarize into two different camps – linear and nonlinear, realistic vs. non-realistic, traditional vs. non-traditional. I don't believe that making art is police work. We are talking about styles, after all, and I think most writers use the style that is organic to the subject and the story. I don't believe most writers fall into specific camps – but rather we all, at various moments, depending upon the dramatic work we decide to create, fall onto a continuum of styles that provide useful maps to guide our work. When I think of the work of Edward Albee, for example, I know for a fact that he prided himself on his use of many different styles, and as a scholar, I know for a fact that his work ranged from an elevated, lyric naturalism to his own form of vaudevillian parody, to, at times, complete abstraction. Even when we think of more traditional American playwrights, such as Tennessee Williams or Arthur Miller, who certainly used realism and naturalism as basis for much of their dramaturgy, both used non-linear, non-traditional, expressionistic technique in nearly all their plays, and this is especially true of Eugène O'Neill who was as much of an experimentalist as was Thornton Wilder.

Of course, even as we conclude this book, I must point out that this kind of dramatic wrighting, wresting an unsettling story from human behavior, built on the notion of the dream play, has existed in some form in drama since the time of the Greeks. As I have noted, one may see this nonrealistic technique in the Greeks' use of the Chorus – a small tribe of dramatic characters that somehow appear out of nowhere, flowing forth as representatives of the community, dissolving into the choir of arguing voices within the mind of the protagonist, and then finally coalescing into a gathering of priestly figures participating in ritual prayer.

Furthermore, in the famous medieval mystery play *Everyman* the protagonist takes a dream journey to his own death, even as his personal attributes become anthropomorphically changed into fair-weather friends unwilling to follow him into the grave. As I've pointed out in the chapter on José Rivera's work, in *Life is a Dream,* Calderon de la Barca famously has Segismundo murderously confused whether he is living in actual reality or the nightmare world his father has conjured for him, and because of this he is alternately a royal heir or a royal monster. Fairies and beasts in *Midsummer Night's Dream* prey upon Shakespeare's cross-wired lovers, and in Heinrich Kleist's *The Prince of Homburg,* the titular character's confusion of reality and the oneiric is crowned with a laurel wreath.

Strindberg's *A Dream Play* is perhaps the most famous of these fantastical plays, exploring the unreality of the dream itself through a kind of Hindu nightmare. Likewise, Tristan Tzara devolved the form into a series of cavernous nonsequiturs with *The Gas Heart,* whereas the surrealist Guillaume Apollonaire used adventurous abandonment to extend the form in *The Breasts of Tiresias.* For his part, Stanislaw Ignacy Witkiewicz's "non-Euclidean" dramaturgy evolved the dream play into what could be termed its "pure form," moving toward an abstract expressionism within the dramatic form. Ionesco admits the deep influence of both the surrealists and Dadaists in his own work. And of course, there are many other writers who experimented in nonrealistic, dreamwrighting predating the writers who we have discussed here, including Antonin Artaud, Alfred Jarry, Roger Vitrac, Gertrude Stein, Thornton Wilder, Elmer Rice, etc.

What matters in this work is that it helps free you from convention and allows your creative juices to flow – fighting back the demons of cliché, writer's block, and self-doubt. Your dreams and more importantly, entering into a waking dream state, provide an endless source of theatricality, magic, and dramatic innovation – there you may find form and content for nearly every genre and at the same time you are drawing upon a source that is uniquely you. As I did at the start of the book, I encourage you to record your dreams on a regular basis and build a daily regimen of dream harvesting – you'll find your work transform and with it, you will grow as a writer and a human being.

1   The Dream Cache

At the heart of this book, and the centering device that we have used from the beginning of our work together, as well as throughout the process in many of the exercises I have created here, is the use of a *dream cache,* a receptable for all the creative bits and pieces of the dream elements that enter into your mind over the course of your day – and/or material from your actual dreams. I remind you that you do *not* have to become an expert in recording your dreams. Much more important to the notion of the dream cache is the idea that random thoughts and ideas, tiny ripples of creative recognition as you move through life, are worthy of your attention. Bearing in mind that our creative processes are working whether we are laboring at our work in front of our notebooks or computers or walking our dog around a park, it is important that we have this receptacle available to us – and for those of us who have never been able to maintain a formal journal (yours truly included), this technique is a really useful and rather effortless way to keep adding to the tools of our trade.

Forget about the formal journal if that's not organic to how your work. My dream cache exists at times on my cell phone, where I scribble a thought or two in my Notes App, and it exists by my bedside, where I drop a few images, experiences, and thoughts to be randomly accessed when I hit certain moments of blockage. I encourage you to come back to your dream cache frequently, as I do, without any intention of writing anything, just to wonder at why I found something interesting at a particular moment – or why something evoked a powerful emotion in me.

One last note – if you use any of the exercises in this book and create a new work of drama, please contact me, and let me know (crespyd@gmail.com). I am very interested in the work of dreamwrights and how they explore their dreams to write drama. It is probably not the norm for authors of practical texts like this one to make that kind of request, but in the interest of continued experimentation I encourage you to do so – happy dreamwrighting!

Bibliography

Arriaga, Guillermo. *21 Grams: A Screenplay*. London, UK: Faber & Faber, 2004.

Akutagawa, Ryunosuke. *Rashomon and Seventeen Other Stories*. Jay Rubin, trans. London, UK: Penguin Classics, 2009.

Albee, Edward. *The Collected Plays of Edward Albee. Volume 1*. New York: Overlook Press, 2004.

Albee, Edward. *The Play About the Baby*. New York: Dramatist's Play Service, 2002.

Albee, Edward. *Three Tall Women*. New York: Plume, 1995.

Albee, Edward. *Who's Afraid of Virgina Woolf*. New York: Signet Book, 1988.

Albee, Edward. *Who's Sylvia? Or The Goat*. New York: Overlook Press, 2003.

Alibar, Lucy. *Beasts of the Southern Wild*. 2012; Los Angeles:Fox Searchlight Pictures. DVD.

Allen, Woody. *Annie Hall*. 1977; New York: A Jack Rollins and Charles H. Joffe Production. 2012. DVD.

Aristotle: *Poetics*, Sachs Joe, trans. Bemidji, MN: Focus, 2006.

Artaud, Antonin. *The Theatre and Its Double*. Grove Press. 1958

Bakhtin, Mikhail. *Problems of Dostoevsky's Poetics*. Minneapolis, MN: University Of Minnesota Press, 1984.

Ball, David, *Backwards and Forwards*. Carbondale, IL: Southern Illinois University Press, 1983.

Baraka, Imamu Amiri. *The Autobiography of LeRoi Jones* New York: Freundlich Books, 1984.

Beckett, Samuel *Collected Shorter Plays*. New York: Grove Press, 1984.

Beckett, Samuel. *Endgame and Act Without Words*. New York: Grove Press, 1970.

Benedikt, Michael. *Theatre Experiment: An Anthology Of American Plays*. New York: Doubleday, 1968.

Bennett, Michael Y. *Reassessing the Theatre of the Absurd: Camus, Beckett, Ionesco, Genet, and Pinter*. London, UK: Palgrave Macmillan, 2011.

Bergman, Ingmar. *Wild Strawberries*. 1957; Sweden: AB Svensk Filmindustri. 2002. DVD

Berkowitz, Gerald M. *American Drama of The Twentieth Century*. New York: Longman, 1992.

Berkowitz, Gerald M. *New Broadways: Theatre Across America 1950-1980*. Totowa, NJ: Rowman and Littlefield, 1982.

Betsko, Kathleen and Rachel Koenig. *Interviews with Contemporary Women Playwrights*. New York: Beech Tree Books, 1987.

Bigsby, C W E, comp. *Edward Albee: A Collection of Critical Essays*. Englewood Cliffs, N.J.: Prentice-Hall, 1975.

Blumenthal, Eileen. *Directors in Perspective: Joseph Chaikin*. Cambridge: Cambridge University Press, 1984.

Bly, Robert. *Iron John: A Book about Men*. Cambridge, MA: Da Capo Press, 2015.

Boal, Augusto. *Legislative Theatre*. Routledge. 1998

Boal, Augusto. *Theatre of the Oppressed*. Urizen Books, . 1979

Braid, Donald. "'Did It Happen or did it not?': Dream Stories, Worldview, and Narrative Knowing," *Text and Performance Quarterly*. October 1998: 329.

Braid, Donald. *Scottish Traveller Tales: Lives Shaped through Stories*. Oxford, MS: University Press of Mississippi, 2002.

Brater, Enoch, and Ruby Cohn. *Around The Absurd: Essays on Modern and Postmodern Drama*. Ann Arbor: The University of Michigan Press, 1990.

Brecht, Bertolt. *The Threepenny Opera*. Eric Bentley ed. and trans. New York: Grove Press, 1994.

Brecht, Bertolt and Kurt Weill. John Willett ed. and trans. *Brecht on Theatre; The Development Of An Aesthetic*. New York: Hill and Wang, 1964.

Breton, Andre. *Manifestoes of Surrealism*. Richard Seaver, tr. Ann Arbor, MI: University of Michigan Press, 1969.

Brockett, Oscar G. & Robert Findlay. *Century Of Innovation: A History of European and American Theatre and Drama Since The Late Nineteenth Century*. Boston: Allyn & Bacon, 1990.

Bryant-Jackson, Paul K. and Lois More Overbeck, eds. *Intersecting Boundaries: The Theatre of Adrienne Kennedy*. Minneapolis, MN: University of Minnesota Press, 1992.

Burgoyne, Suzanne. *Creativity in Theatre: Theory and Action in Theatre/Drama Education*. Berlin, Germany: Springer, 2018.

Campbell, Joseph. *The Hero with a Thousand Faces*. Novato, CA: New World Library, 2008.

Camus, Marcel. *Black Orpheus*. 1959; Brazil: Lopert Pictures. 2016. DVD.

Castagno, Paul. *New Playwriting Strategies: A Language Based Approach to Playwriting*. New York: Routledge, 2001.

Chapman, Gerald. *Teaching Young Playwrights*. London: Heinemann. 1992.

Cheever, John. *The Stories of John Cheever*. New York: Vintage, 2000.

Chekhov, Anton. *The Complete Plays*. Laurence Senelick, trans. New York: W. W. Norton & Company, 2007.

Cole, Toby. *Playwrights On Playwriting*. Cooper Square Press. 2001

Congdon, Constance. *Tales of the Lost Formicans* in *In Plays from Actors Theatre of Louisville*. Broadway Play Publishing, 1989

Congdon, Constance. *Tales Of the Lost Formicans*. New York: Theatre Communications Group, 1995.

Crespy, David A. and Lincoln Konkle, eds. *Edward Albee as Theatrical and Dramatic Innovator*. Leiden, Netherlands: Brill, 2019.

Crespy, David A. *Off-off-Broadway Explosion*. New York: Back Stage Books, 2003.

Crespy, David A. *Lanford Wilson: Early Stories, Sketches, and Poems*. Columbia, MO: University of Missouri Press, 2017.

Crespy, David A. *Richard Barr: The Playwright's Producer*. Carbondale, IL: SIU Press, 2013.

Csíkszentmihályi, Mihály. *Flow: The Psychology of Optimal Experience*. New York: Harper, 2008.
Curb, Rosemary Keefe. *The Idea of the American Dream in Afro-American Plays of the Nineteen-Sixties*. Dissertation. University of Arkansas, 1977.
Dali, Salvador. *The Andalusian Dog*. 1929; Paris: Les Grands Films Classiques.
Dash, Julie. *Daughters of the Dust*. 1991; Kino International. 2000. DVD.
Davy, Kate. *Richard Foreman and the Ontological-Hysteric Theatre*. Ann Arbor, MI: UMI Research Press, 1981.
De La Barca, Pedro Calderon. *Life is a Dream*. New York: Theatre Communications Group, 1999.
De Moraes, Vinicius. *Orfeu da Conceição*. São Paulo, Brazil: Companhia de Bolso, 2013.
Drury, Jackie Sibblies. *Fairview*. New York: Theatre Communications Group, 2019.
Dukore, Bernard. *Dramatic theory and criticism: Greeks to Grotowski*. Holt, Rinehart and Winston. 1974
Duras, Marguerite. *Hiroshima Mon Amor*. 1959; Paris: Cocinor.
Egri, Lagos. *The Art of Dramatic Writing*. Simon & Schuster. 1977
Esper, William and DaTues Dimarco. *The Actor's Art and Craft: William Esper Teaches the Meisner Technique*. New York: Anchor, 2008.
Esslin, Martin. *The Theatre of the Absurd*. New York: Vintage, 2001.
Euripides. *Three Plays of Euripides: Alcestis, Medea, The Bacchae*. Paul Roche, Trans. New York: W. W. Norton, 1974.
Farrell, Gordon. *Power of Playwrights Vision*. Portsmouth, NH: Heinemann, 2001.
Field, Syd. Screenplay: *The Foundations of Screenwriting*. New York: New York: Delta, 2005.
Fornes, Maria Irene. *Promenade and Other Plays*. New York: Performing Arts Journal Publications, 1987.
Freud, Sigmund, *Interpretation of Dreams: The Complete and Definitive Text*. New York: Basic Books, 2010.
Fullagar, Clive J.; Kelloway, E. Kevin (2009). "Flow at work: an experience sampling approach". *Journal of* Occupational *and Organizational Psychology* 82 (3): 595–615.
Garfield, Patricia. *Creative Dreaming: Plan and Control Your Dreams to Develop Creativity, Overcome Fears, Solve Problems, and Create a Better Self*. New York: Atria, 1995.
Garrison, Gary. *Playwrights Survival Guide*. Heinemann. 1999
Genet, Jean. *The Balcony*. Frechtman, Bernard, trans. New York: Grove Press, 1966.
Godard, Jean-Luc. *Weekend*. 1967; Paris: Athos Films. 2012. DVD.
Hobson, J. Allan. *Dreaming: A Very Short Introduction*. Oxford, UK: Oxford University Press, 2011.
Hornby, Richard. *Drama, Metadrama, And Perception*. London: Associated University Presses, 1986.
Hudes, Quiara. *Water by the Spoonful*. New York: Theatre Communications Group, 2012.
Ionesco, Eugene. *The Bald Soprano and Other Plays*. New York: Grove Press, 1982.

Jenkins, Len. *Dark Ride and Other Plays*. Los Angeles: Sun & Moon Press, 1993.
Jung, C. G. *Dreams*. Princeton, NJ: Princeton University Press, 2010.
Kahn, David and Donna Breed. *Scriptwork*. Southern Illinois Univ Press. 1995
Kaufman, Charlie, et al. *Eternal Sunshine of the Spotless Mind: The Shooting Script*. New York: Newmarket Press, 2004.
Kennedy, Adrienne. *Adrienne Kennedy In One-Act*. University of Minnesota Press. 1988
Kennedy, Adrienne. *The Adrienne Kennedy Reader*. Minneapolis, MN: Univ of Minnesota Press, 2001.
Kirby, Michael. *The New Theatre: Performance Documentation*. New York: New York University Press, 1974.
Kushner, Tony. *Angels in America: Part 1: Millennium Approaches*. Theatre Communications Group, 1993.
Lawson, John Howard. *Theory and Technique of Playwriting*. New York: Hill and Wang, 1960
Lynch, David. *Mulholland Drive*. 2001; Los Angeles: Universal Pictures. 2015. DVD.
Maeterlinck, Maurice. The *Plays of Maurice Maeterlinck*. Madrid, Spain: HardPress Publishing, 2013.
Mardrus, J.C., and E.P Mathers, eds. *The Book of the Thousand and one Nights*. Oxfordshire, England, UK: Routledge, 1986.
Marranca, Bonnie. *Ecologies of Theater: Essays at the Century Turning*. Johns Hopkins University Press, 1996.
McDonagh, Martin. *The Beauty Queen of Leenane*. New York: Random House, 1998.
McDonagh, Martin. *The Pillowman*. New York: Farrar, Straus and Giroux, 2004.
McKee, Robert. *Story: Substance, Structure, Style and the Principles of Screenwriting*. Methuen, 2005.
Meisner, Sanford and Dennis Longwell. *Sanford Meisner on Acting*. New York: Vintage, 1987.
Moncrieff, Karen. *The Dead Girl*. 2006; Alchemy/Millennium, 2007. DVD.
Nolan, Christopher. *Memento*. 2000; Universal City, California: Summit Entertainment. 2018. DVD.
Overmeyer, Eric . *Collected Plays*. Hanover, NH: Smith & Kraus, 1993.
Overmeyer, Eric. *Collected Plays*. Smith & Kraus. 1993
Parks, Suzan-Lori. *The America Play*. New York: Dramatists Play Service, 1995.
Parks, Suzan-Lori. *Top Dog Underdog*. New York: Theatre Communications Group. 2002
Parks, Suzan-Lori. *Venus*. New York: Theatre Communications Group. 1997
Pinter, Harold. *Harold Pinter Plays 1 (Contemporary Classics)* London, UK: Faber & Faber, 1996.
Perry, Eleanor. *The Swimmer*. 1968; London: Horizon Pictures.
Pirandello, Luigi. *Naked Masks: Five Plays by Luigi Pirandello*. Eric Bentley, ed. New York: Plume, 1957.

Potter, Sally. *Orlando*. 1992: Los Angeles, Sony Pictures. 2010. DVD.
Progoff, Ira. *At a Journal Workshop: Writing to Access the Power of the Unconscious and Evoke Creative Ability*. New York: TarcherPerigee, 1992.
Rivera, José. *Cloud Tectonics*. New York: Broadway Play Publishing, 2017.
Robbe-Grillet, Alain. *Last Year at Marienbad*. 1961; Paris: Cocinor. 2019. DVD.
Rossiter, Drake. "David Cronenberg takes on dreams, Freud in compelling 'Method'," December 12, 2011, *San Francisco Examiner* Online Edition. http://www.sfexaminer.com/entertainment/movies/2011/12/david-cronenberg-takes-dreams-freud-compelling-method#ixzz22nPq2Yl1.
Ruhl, Sarah. *Eurydice*. New York: Samuel French, 2008.
Sardou, Victorien. *A Scrap of Paper: A Comedy in Three Acts*. London: Forgotten Books, 2018.
Sartre, Jean-Paul. *Saint Genet*. New York: Mentor, 1964.
Satyamurti, Carole. *Mahabharata: A Modern Retelling*. New York: W. W. Norton & Company, 2016.
Scribe, Eugène. *A Glass of Water (Great Translations for Actors)*. Cornthwaite, Robert, Trans. Hanover, NH: Smith & Kraus, 1995.
Shakespeare, William. *The Oxford Shakespeare: The Complete Works*. Wells, Stanley, Ed., et al. Oxford, UK: Oxford University Press, 2005.
Shargel, Raphael. *Ingmar Bergman: Interviews*. Jackson, ME: University Press of Mississippi, 2007.
Shklovsky, Victor "Art as Technique," in *Russian Formalist Criticism; Four Essays*, trans. Lee T. Lemon and Marion J. Reis, 3–25. Lincoln, NE: University of Nebraska Press, 1965.
Smiley, Sam. *Playwriting: The Structure of Action*. Englewood Cliffs: Prentice-Hall, 1971.
Sophocles. *The Oedipus Plays of Sophocles: Oedipus the King; Oedipus at Colonus; Antigone*. Paul Roche, trans. New York: Plume, 1996.
States, Bert. *Dreaming and Storytelling*. Ithaca, NY: Cornell University Press, 1993.
States, Bert. *Seeing In the Dark*. New Haven, CT: Yale University Press, 1997.
States, Bert. *The Rhetoric of Dreams*. Ithaca, NY: Cornell University Press, 1988.
Stein, Gertrude. *Literary Cubism - Geography & Plays*. St. Petersburg, FL: Traveling Press, 2011.
Strindberg, August. Harry Carlson. trans. *Strindberg: Five Plays*. University of California Press, 1983.
Tarantino, Quentin. *Pulp Fiction*. 1994; Los Angeles: Miramax Films. 2011. DVD.
Tolkien, J.R.R. *The Lord Of The Rings Deluxe Edition*, New York: William Morrow, 2013.
Tzara, Tristan. *Seven Dada Manifestos and Lampisteries*. Wright, Barbara, trans. London, UK: Alma Classics, 2013.
Valency, Maurice. *The Breaking String: The Plays of Anton Chekhov*. New York: Oxford University Press, 1966.

Van Gennep, Arnold. *The Rites of Passage*. Chicago, IL: University of Chicago Press, 2019.
Van Itallie, Jean Claude. *The Playwright's Workbook*. New York: Applause, 1997.
Van Itallie, Jean Claude, *America Hurrah and Other Plays*. New York: Grove Press, 2001.
Varda, Agnès. *Vagabond*. 1985; Paris, MK2 Diffusion. 2008. DVD.
Vogel, Paula. *The Mammary Plays*. New York: Theatre Communications Group, 1998.
Vogler, Christopher. *The Writers Journey: Mythic Structure for Writers, 3rd Edition*. Studio City, CA: Michael Wiese Productions, 2007.
Welles. Orson. *Citizen Kane: 75th Anniversary edition*. Studio Distribution Series. 2016. DVD.
Wellman, Mac . *The Bad Infinity: Eight Plays* . New York: Performing Arts Journal Publications. 1994
Wilder, Thornton. *The Collected Short Plays of Thornton Wilder*. New York: Theatre Communications Group, 1998.
Wilder, Thornton. *Three Plays: Our Town. The Skin of Our Teeth. and The Matchmaker*. New York: Perennial, 2003.
Wilhelm, Richard, tr. *The I Ching, or, Book of Changes*. Princeton, NJ: Princeton University Press, 1967.
Willett, John. *Brecht on Theatre*. New York: Hill and Wang. 1966
Wilson, Lanford. *Book of Days*. New York: Grove Press, 2000.
Wilson, Lanford. *Lanford Wilson: 21 Short Plays*. Hanover, NH: Smith & Kraus, 1993
Wilson, Lanford. *Lanford Wilson: Collected Works, Vol. 2: 1970–1983*, Hanover, NH: Smith & Kraus, 1999.
Wilson, Lanford. *Lanford Wilson: Collected Works, Vol. 3: The Talley Trilogy*. Hanover, NH: Smith & Kraus, 1999.
Wright, Michael. *Playwriting Masterclass*, Second Edition. Focus Publishing, 2010.

Index

Absurdism   50
Albee, Edward   10, 43, 50, 143, 160, 202,
    218, 219, 220, 221, 221n1, 222, 223, 224,
    225, 240
    Tiny Alice   50, 219, 220, 222, 224
Alexander Technique   20
Alibar, Lucy   49, 180, 181, 187, 188, 189, 191
    Beasts of the Southern Wild   49, 181,
    187, 189
Aristotle   69, 76, 163, 183
    Poetics   69
Arp, Hans   30
Arriaga, Guillermo   47, 118, 119, 120, 138, 139,
    139n1, 140, 141
    21 Grams   47, 118, 119, 120, 138, 139, 139n1
    Amores Perros   47, 139
Artaud, Antonin   91, 91n2, 91n3, 91n4,
    91n15, 192, 241
    Theatre of Cruelty   91, 91n2, 192

Bakhtin, Mikhail   81, 82
Baktin, Mikhail
    carnivalesque   81, 82, 83, 84
Barca, Calderón de la   152, 241
    La vida es sueño, (Life is a Dream)   152
Beckett, Samuel   50, 193, 202, 204, 210, 211,
    212, 213, 232
    Play   50
Bennett, Michael Y.   202, 204
    parabolic dramatists   202
Bergman, Ingmar   7
Boal, Augusto   183, 184, 237
Braid, Donald   6, 6n7, 115
    *The Black Laird and the
    Cattleman*   115
Brecht, Bertolt   6, 6n3, 49, 103, 136, 180, 181,
    182, 182n1, 183, 184, 185, 187, 191, 194, 207,
    227, 232
    gestus   182, 185
    The Threepenny Opera   49, 181, 182,
    182n1
    Verfremdungseffekt   181, 182, 183, 187, 227
Breton, André   161
    Surrealist Manifesto   161
Buchner, Georg   181

Campbell, Joseph   134
    Hero's Journey   134
Camus, Marcel   45, 69, 81, 84
    Black Orpheus   45, 69, 81, 82
Carmines, Al   162, 232
Castagno, Paul   40
    New Playwriting Strategies   40
    the call   40
chance art   28
Character Dreams   41
Cheever, John   49, 192, 194, 197
Chekhov, Anton   26, 47, 142, 143, 144, 145,
    145n2, 145n3, 146, 147, 148, 148n8, 149,
    149n12, 149n14, 150, 151
    The Cherry Orchard   47, 142, 143, 144, 145,
    145n3, 146, 147, 147n6, 148, 148n8, 149,
    149n12, 150
Cronenberg, David   7
Csíkszentmihályi, Mihály   14
    Flow   17
Curb, Rosemary   88, 89, 89n3

Dada   30
Dash, Julie   45, 46, 86, 87, 93, 94, 98
    Daughters of the Dust   45, 87, 93, 94, 98
daydreaming   3
de Moraes, Vincius
    Orfeu da Conceigao   81
de Moraes, Vinicius   81
Derrida   194
Derrida, Jacques   194
    deconstruction   194
Diamond, Elin   88, 88n1, 88n2, 221
dream cache   2, 3, 11, 12, 14, 22, 23, 25, 28, 30,
    31, 32, 33, 34, 35, 36, 38, 39, 41, 43, 57, 64,
    66, 77, 78, 83, 84, 92, 101, 104, 111, 112, 114,
    117, 119, 140, 164, 165, 168, 171, 173, 178, 183,
    189, 190, 200, 201, 217, 233, 234, 241, 242
Dream Journeys   40
Dream Monologue   41
Dream Scenes   41
Dream Tropes   29
    Dramatic Dreams   29
    Epic Dreams   29
    Lyric Dreams   29

Dreamer's heart, the   107, 108, 111, 113, 115, 118
Dreamwork   2
dreamwrights   42
Duras, Marguerite   47, 48, 142, 143, 156, 157, 159
    Hiroshima Mon Amour   47, 142, 143, 156, 157, 159

emotional preparation   3
Esselin, Martin
    "The Theatre of the Absurd"   202
Esslin, Martin   202
Euripides   50, 224
    The Bacchae   50
expressionism   9, 44, 48, 53, 63, 68, 107, 170, 174, 177, 178, 180, 241

Faulkner, William   166
Film Noir   66, 106, 107, 166, 167
Fornes, Irene   43, 51, 153, 202, 227, 228
    Conduct of Life   51, 227, 228, 232, 233, 234
Freud, Sigmund   2, 208*n*3
    The Interpretation of Dreams   161, 208*n*3
Fuchs, Elinor   90, 90*n*11

Garfield, Patricia   11
Genet, Jean   43, 46, 98, 99, 100, 102, 202
    The Balcony   46
Godard, Jean-Luc   51, 202, 227, 228, 235, 236, 237
    Weekend   51, 227, 228, 235, 236, 237
Goffman, Erving   100
Goffman, Irving
    The Presentation of Self in Everyday Life   100
Golden Age of Spanish Drama   152

Harry Potter   27
heterotopia   199, 201
Hobson, Allan   1

Iñárritu, Alejandro González   47
Ionesco, Eugène   6, 43, 50, 193, 202, 204, 205, 206, 207, 208, 208*n*1, 208*n*2, 208*n*5, 209, 210, 213, 241
    Journeys Amongst the Dead   50
    Man with Bags   50

The Bald Soprano   50, 204, 205, 206, 208, 209

Joyce, James   166, 208*n*3
Jung, Carl   1, 2, 58

Kaiser, Georg   174
    From Morn to Midnight   174
Kaufman, Charlie   47, 118, 119, 120, 136, 141, 181
    Eternal Sunshine of the Spotless Mind   47, 118, 119, 120, 136
Kennedy, Adrienne   6, 43, 45, 46, 59, 86, 87, 88, 88*n*1, 89, 89*n*3, 89*n*6, 90, 90*n*11, 91, 92, 93, 97, 98
    Funnyhouse of A Negro   45
Kurosawa, Akira   117
Kurosawa, Akiro
    Rashomon   117
Kushner, Tony   47, 59, 118, 119, 120, 126, 127, 136, 141, 181
    Angels in America   47, 118, 119, 120, 126, 128, 129, 131, 136

Lynch, David   48, 159, 160, 161, 165, 166, 167, 169
    Mulholland Drive   48, 160, 166, 167

Maeterlinck, Maurice   144, 145*n*1, 149, 149*n*14
    "The Tragical in Daily Life"   144
    Pelleas and Melisande   144
    The Bluebird   144
Magic abilities/disabilities   42
Magic Overheard Voices   36
Magic Plot Cards   47, 119, 124
Magic Realism   47, 151, 152
Mahabharata   51
Márquez, Gabriel García   151, 152, 153
McDonagh, Martin   46, 106, 107, 108, 109, 110, 118
    The Pillowman   46, 107, 109, 110, 112, 118
Meisner, Sanford   3
Moncrieff, Karen   48, 170, 177, 178, 180
    The Dead Girl   48, 170, 177, 178

Nolan, Christopher   46, 106, 107, 108, 113, 118, 136, 176
    Memento   46, 107, 108, 113, 114, 118, 176

INDEX

Oedipus the King   45, 69, 121
One Thousand and One Nights. See Scheherazade

Perry, Eleanor   49, 192, 193, 197, 198, 199, 202
phenomenological attitude   1
Pick Up/Persephone   61, 62
Pinter, Harold   43, 51, 193, 202, 204, 227, 228, 229, 230, 235, 236
   The Birthday Party   51, 227, 228, 229
   The Homecoming   27
Pinter, Harold   27
Pirandello, Luigi   49, 192, 193, 195, 196, 197, 202, 204
   It Is So! (If you Think so)   49, 193
Plato   145
Postmodernism   194
Potter, Sally   46, 98, 99, 102, 103
   Orlando   46, 98, 99, 102, 103, 105, 232
Progroff, Ira   12, 137
   At A Journal Workshop   12

Rechtschaffen, Allan   90
Rivera, José   47, 142, 143, 151, 152, 153, 155, 241
   Cloud Tectonics   47, 142, 143, 151, 152, 153, 155
   Marisol   152
   Sueño   152
   The Motorcycle Diaries   152
Romanticism   44, 47, 142, 143, 144, 156, 159
Ruhl, Sarah   48, 170, 171, 172, 173, 174, 180
   Eurydice   45, 48, 81, 83, 170, 172, 173, 174

Sardou, Victorien   27
Sartre, Jean-Paul   99
   Saint Genet   99
Scheherazade   110, 111, 116
Scribe, Eugène   27
Shakepeare, William   49
Shklovsky, Viktor   6, 6n4, 182
   "Art as Technique"   6, 6n4, 182
   defamiliarization   182
   ostranenie   92, 103, 182, 232
Single-mindedness   38
Smith, Joseph   47, 126, 130, 136, 205
   The Book of Mormon   47
Sophocles   45, 69, 76, 224
   Oedipus Rex   69, 70, 71, 76, 107

States, Bert O.   5, 5n1, 5n1, 5n2, 6, 6n5, 12, 29, 39, 46, 89, 89n4, 89n5, 90, 90n10, 90n8, 90n9, 91, 92, 202, 205, 208, 208n4
   Harrison Ford Syndrome   39
   involuntary fiction   12
Stein, Gertrude   160, 162, 163, 241
   Do Let Us Go Away   162
   In Circles. See Carmines, Al
   Please Do Not Suffer   162
   What Happened   162
Strindberg, August   45, 52, 53, 54, 54n1, 55, 56, 63, 64, 68, 90, 91, 241
   Dream Play   53
   The Dream Play   53
Styan, J. L.   147, 147n7
Surrealism   48, 160, 161
Symbolism   9, 44, 142, 143, 146, 159

Tarantino, Quentin   50, 202, 204, 205, 213, 214, 217, 218
   Pulp Fiction   50, 204, 213, 214, 218
The Ask   12
The Baader-Meinhof phenomenon   174
The Chair Play   37
The Lord of the Rings   27
The Myth of Kore/Persephone   61
Time Mutations   40
Toller, Ernst   174
   Man and the Masses   174
Tynan, Kenneth   207
Tzara, Tristan   28

van Gennep, Arnold   83, 94
   Les Rites de Passage   94
van Itallie, Jean Claude   34, 59, 230
   The Serpent   34, 59, 61
   The Playwright's Workbook   59
Varda, Agnes   50, 202, 218, 219, 220, 225, 226
   Cinécriture   225
   Vagabond   50, 219, 220, 225, 226, 227
Vogel, Paula   45, 69, 74, 75, 76, 77, 79, 81, 171
   How I Learned to Drive   45, 69, 74, 75, 76, 77, 78

Wedekind, Frank   181
Weill, Kurt   49, 182
Welles, Orson   45, 46, 52, 53, 63, 68
   Citizen Kane   53
   the subjective camera   64

Wilde, Oscar   160, 196
   The Decay of Lying   196
Wilder, Thornton   48, 74, 159, 160, 161, 162, 163, 164, 165, 169, 170, 171, 240, 241
   Our Town   48, 161, 162, 165
   Pullman Car Hiawatha   48, 160, 161, 162, 164, 165

Wilson, Lanford   43, 45, 69, 73, 74, 79, 80, 81, 143, 160
   Book of Days   45, 69, 79, 80
Woolf, Virginia   46, 98, 102, 166, 219, 222, 224
Wright, Michael   43
   Playwriting in Process   43
wrighting   2